D1545303

MACHIAVELLI AND

THE HISTORY OF PRUDENCE

Lying Down Together: Law, Metaphor, and Theology
Milner S. Ball

Politics and Ambiguity
William E. Connolly

Machiavelli and the History of Prudence
Eugene Garver

The Rhetoric of Economics
Donald N. McCloskey

Therapeutic Discourse and Socratic Dialogue: A Cultural Critique
Tullio Maranhão

The Rhetoric of the Human Sciences: Language and Argument in Scholarship and Public Affairs
John S. Nelson, Allan Megill, and Donald N. McCloskey, eds.

The Unspeakable: Discourse, Dialogue, and Rhetoric in the Postmodern World
Stephen A. Tyler

Heracles' Bow: Essays on the Rhetoric and the Poetics of the Law
James Boyd White

Machiavelli and
the History of Prudence

EUGENE GARVER

THE UNIVERSITY OF WISCONSIN PRESS

Published 1987

The University of Wisconsin Press
114 North Murray Street
Madison, Wisconsin 53715

The University of Wisconsin Press, Ltd.
1 Gower Street
London WC1E 6HA, England

First printing

Printed in the United States of America

For LC CIP information see the colophon

ISBN 0-299-11080-X

To Jane

ὁ μὲν οὖν δεσπότης οὐ λέγεται κατ᾽ ἐπιστήμην ἀλλὰ τῷ τοιόσδ᾽ εἶναι, ὁμοίως δὲ καὶ ὁ δοῦλος καὶ ὁ ἐλεύθερος.

The term *master* does not refer to someone in virtue of his knowledge but because of the sort of person he is, and similarly for the slave and the free man.

— Aristotle, *Politics* 1.2.1255b21–24

CONTENTS

To the Reader xi

Acknowledgments xiii

Introduction 3

Chapter 1 *The Prince:* A Neglected Rhetorical Classic 26

Chapter 2 Discursive Virtuosity and Practical Virtù 46

Chapter 3 The Politics of Rhetorical Invention 63

Chapter 4 Paradigms and Princes 92

Chapter 5 The *Discourses on Livy:* Virtù Universalized 117

Chapter 6 Civic Virtue and the New Rhetorical Virtues 141

Conclusion 164

Notes 171

Bibliography 225

Index 235

TO THE READER

If *phronesis* had become an English word the way *praxis* has, this book would be better titled *Machiavelli and the History of Phronesis*. Since I have to translate *phronesis*, I prefer the more traditional rendering, "prudence," to the preferred but more technical modern translation, "practical wisdom"; "prudence" contains connotations of virtue — that is, of a praiseworthy ability connected to character — while "practical wisdom" or "practical reason" suggests a more detached skill whose operation can be identified apart from the characters who use it and the purposes they use it for. The history of *phronesis*, even the one act of that history that concerns Machiavelli, consists largely in the oscillation between those two meanings and translations.

Because of the exemplary functions of the texts I will refer to throughout the book — Plato's dialogues contain the Socratic paradoxes about prudence that generate and articulate its problems; Aristotle's *Nicomachean Ethics*, *Politics*, and *Rhetoric* provide a structure of terms and arguments; and Machiavelli's argumentative tactics upset and transform the relatively stable meanings and conditions that Aristotle can attribute to prudence — little should turn on textual and editorial matters. While my argument does depend on close textual analysis, what is currently called a thick reading, I have rarely been concerned with dissecting particular paragraphs or syntactic puzzles, but have instead concentrated on the more tactical and strategic sides of argument. Except for Aristotle's *Politics*, the works featured in this book have few textual problems, and even their textual history and the history of their reception is relatively uncomplicated. I have consequently for the most part relied on the most readily available editions and translations of the works cited, though the translation of the epigraph is my own. For the Greek texts of Plato and Aristotle, I have used the Oxford Classical Text editions; for the translations of Plato, Aristotle, Cicero, and Quintilian, I have quoted the Loeb Classical Library editions listed in the Bibliography. For quotations from Machiavelli I have used, for *The Prince*, Mark Musa's bilingual edition (New York: St. Martin's, 1964), and for the *Discourses* and occasional other works of Machiavelli, the translations in Max Lerner's Modern Library volume, *The Prince and the Discourses* (New York, 1940), and in *Machiavelli: The Chief Works and Others*, translated by Allan Gilbert (Durham, N.C.: Duke University Press, 1965). The outstanding problem in translating Machiavelli is the meaning and function of *virtù* and *fortuna*, and I have left those terms untranslated. (In the notes I indicate some of the many treatments of the meaning of *virtù* and its relation to *prudenzia*.) There are a few points in the argument when something does turn on a translation from either Machiavelli or Aristotle, and I have indicated those points, but in general, chapter numbers for Machiavelli and Aristotle, and Stephanus numbers for Plato, should allow any reader to check the references I employ.

In addition to my use of those primary texts, the book contains a number of sometimes extended notes evoking reference to contemporary argument, both about Machiavelli and Renaissance rhetoric and about associated contemporary substantive problems. For readers acquainted with the arguments I refer to, those discussions should help place my narrative in the context of contemporary debates. Readers who have no interest in current literary criticism, or the relation between history and "metahistory," or the debates in the philosophy of science over incommensurability, will not be the worse for ignoring those discussions. Since I believe that the project of constructing a history of prudence should be of wide interest, I have used these notes to try to make some connections between my project and some more familiar ones.

I should also note that with respect to the universal contemporary problem of gender-bound pronouns, my stylistic problems — if that is what they are — are compounded by my frequent use, in both *oratio obliqua* and *oratio recta*, of authors who, at a minimum, had no sensibility on these matters. I fear that I may occasionally have followed my *exempla* excessively.

ACKNOWLEDGMENTS

This book is about the interconnections between autonomy and community, self-determination and influence. When I reflect on the futility of trying to divide the merits and defects of my work between parts for which I should take credit, or blame, and aspects for which I should acknowledge assistance, I am struck by the variety of kinds of help I have had. I have been blessed with the help of a number of people who were first teachers, then colleagues at the University of Chicago, then friends—Wayne Booth, Joseph Schwab, David Smigelskis, Charles Wegener, and the late Warner Wick. They deserve credit and thanks for judicious and useful comment and advice. I am also deeply in their debt for encouragement that sustained my work over several years in circumstances quite uncongenial to the sort of sustained inquiry I have attempted; their help on this count is all the more meritorious because those circumstances were fortunately remote from their own experience.

Some of the early writing that later became this book was begun with the assistance of a leave from California State College, San Bernardino, and a Fellowship for College Teachers from the National Endowment for the Humanities. Different pieces of the work were given as lectures at meetings of the International Society for the History of Rhetoric, and at Bennington College, and the University of Southern California, and the University of Chicago. Early versions of some of my material appeared as "Machiavelli's *The Prince*: A Neglected Rhetorical Classic," in *Philosophy and Rhetoric* 13 (1980) published by The Pennsylvania State University Press; "Machiavelli and the Politics of Rhetorical Invention," in *Clio* 14 (1986); and "Paradigms and Princes," *Philosophy of the Social Sciences*, 17 (1987); and an abbreviated version of the Introduction was published in *Social Epistemology* 1 (1987). Peter Schroeder and William Sacksteder for years served as willing and constructive readers, especially in the less manageable days before word processors; referees and copy editors at the University of Wisconsin Press had to struggle with the product of a word processor, a product which is not in all respects easier to deal with than its technological ancestors. Nancy Struever and Victoria Kahn were strangers whom I came to know through this work; I found a possibly fallacious but still encouraging confirmation in the convergence of my line of argument with theirs, which are motivated by quite different traditions and interests. Even more, their conversation and correspondence has been an invaluable source of pleasure and energy.

Acknowledgments

Late in what seemed an endless career as a graduate student, I began to realize the magnitude of my debt to Charles Wegener, and the lack of express recognition of how much I have learned from him. More than a dozen years ago I vowed to offer one sort of thanks in the form of dedicating my first book to him. But that was before I met my wife, Jane Bennett, who is endowed with virtues of care, tolerance, and patience that I lack. This book would not be as good as I hope it is without her support. Charles, you'll have to wait.

MACHIAVELLI AND

THE HISTORY OF PRUDENCE

INTRODUCTION

Machiavelli occupies a position in the history of prudence or practical reason roughly analogous to that of Descartes in the history of theoretical reason and reflection on natural science. Descartes teaches his reader that only those ideas can be trusted as true which one has arrived at for oneself, independent of authority and tradition, and offers a method for achieving such autonomy and building secure foundations for knowledge. Machiavelli teaches his reader that only those defenses are secure and trustworthy which depend on one's own strength and *virtù*, and offers a method for achieving that kind of independence and building secure foundations for political rule. Just as people have in the last few years found it useful to imagine alternatives to Descartes's quest for certainty, his distinction between knowledge and traditional authority, and his encouragement of autonomous reason, Machiavelli offers a similar opportunity towards understanding the modern practical predicament, so that we can imagine alternatives to his quest for security, his complicated interrelations between virtù and the traditional virtues, and his encouragement of his own brand of the autonomy of practical reason.

Both Descartes and Machiavelli were successful enough to make their predecessors worth forgetting; only recently have people taken seriously the possibility that there might be pre-Cartesian, and non-Cartesian, conceptions of knowledge, and pre-Machiavellian, and non-Machiavellian, conceptions of ethics and politics, worth examination. But there are important differences between the history of theory and that of practice — not least because the history of practice is not independent of the development of theory — and those differences generate a series of themes that must figure in any discussion of Machiavelli's place in the history of prudence. Descartes is supposed to be the beginning of a story of progress from ignorance to knowledge whose success and costs have only recently been questioned; while Machiavelli's position at the start of a history may be analogous, the subsequent career of ethics and politics has always inspired ambivalence.[1] Where Descartes's proclamation of the autonomy of theoretical reason liberated it from the traditional restraints of established custom and belief, Machiavelli's autonomy of practical reason seemed to remove the restraints that tradition had placed on immoral, selfish, corrupt behavior. While the autonomy of theoretical reason at least initially seems an advance from barbarism to enlightenment without hidden or undesirable side effects, the autonomy of practical reason, in Machiavelli's sense, has always been felt to be a mixed blessing. In terms that will be central to the construction of a history of practical reason, Descartes's rejection of rhetoric appears evidently liberating, while to the extent that Machiavelli frees himself from the constraints embodied in traditional rhetorical appeals to the conventional wisdom and morality of his audience, he seems to purchase freedom at the price of the loss of all moral constraint. We will later need to ask whether Machiavelli, or prudence more generally, contains any restraints that can substitute for the codes and sanctions of tradition.[2] The narratives in which Descartes and Machiavelli appear differ because knowledge and self-consciousness are taken to be unmixed goods in the march of theoretical reason, while it is debatable what difference knowledge makes to practice, and whether that difference is a benefit.

Machiavelli and Descartes occupy analogous positions in the histories of practice and theory because each represents a turning to autonomy, but the histories of practical and theoretical autonomy differ because of their different conceptions of the relation of autonomy and history. History is for Descartes the realm of unstable facts, best avoided in favor of the more accessible and dependable facts of natural science, while for Machiavelli it is the material out of which the new prince can learn to be autonomous. Although Machiavelli does not think unwritten tradition and written histories any more reliable than Descartes does, he must appeal to both because his conception of a foundation, or of security, is different, and because he has resources, located precisely in the rhetorical methods Descartes rejects, for making something autonomous out of history. Some varieties of political theory — Locke's is an obvious example — *can* ground the foundation of the state in something outside of history, but this is not Machiavelli's procedure. Therefore the relations between history and freedom will be more complex for Machiavelli (they are quite simple for Descartes) and will require separate and extended treatment, a treatment that must center on Machiavelli's use of rhetorical methods to construct practical autonomy. Both Descartes and Machiavelli offer one of their principal texts — Descartes, the *Discourse on Method* and Machiavelli, *The Prince* — as models to be imitated, and both recognize the paradox inherent in gaining autonomy through imitation. In both cases, imitation is the way in which a seminal text intervenes in history and initiates a new narrative sequence or a reversal in an existing one, and so their different ways of responding to this paradox will provide a pair of internal explanations for the differences in the subsequent histories of theory and practice. The results of Cartesian and Machiavellian imitations must differ, since Machiavelli will not be able to follow Descartes in the expectation that anyone following his method will arrive at the same result, and consequently can say that disagreement is the sign that at least one party has not based his judgment on reason alone: "Whenever two men come to opposite decisions about the same matter, one of them at least must certainly be in the wrong, and apparently there is not even one of them who knows; for if the reasoning of one was sound and clear he would be able so to lay it before the other as finally to succeed in convincing *his* understanding also" (*Rules for the Direction of the Mind*, p. 11). The material on which Descartes bases his method—the single datum of the act of doubting—is so etiolated that fidelity to the method produces results that are reliably the same. The differences between the histories of theoretical and practical reason appear immediately when one attempts to draw the analogy at this point: what would be the result of all Italian princes' following Machiavelli's advice? To raise that question is to point out that Machiavelli's teachings could lead to more virtù but not necessarily less strife. Machiavellian practical reason contains the harmony automatic in Descartes only in the unified Italy of the last chapter of *The Prince*, or in the Roman republic of the *Discourses on Livy*—two rather special conditions in which the sort of material to which the rhetorical politician must appeal, the opinions and values of subjects and citizens, is for once not an obstacle to a harmonious result. The autonomy of theoretical reason, far from being a threat to the unanimity of scientists, is its only guarantee, while the autonomy of practical reason undermines consensus and seems to lead to war, not peace. Put another way, Cartesian science as a whole is a simple universalization of the activities of individual scientists, while Machiavellian politics cannot be a world of Machiavellian individual actors without some attention to the way such individuals could be integrated into a community. Although a history of prudence traces the career of a character called practical reason, practical reason is in turn embodied in several characters that can have different relations to each other, so that the history of practical reason, as opposed to a history of an idea of practical reason, is a story with some complexity. That history requires consideration of the relations between continuity and flexibility, autonomy, community, and history, and between imitation or, more generally, education and intellectual methods. While the history of practical reason is a history of the practical uses of intelligence, it will often take the dramatic form of the story of the practical functions of intelligent agents taking specific roles. Machiavelli occupies a central place in such a history as he carves out a specific place for reasoning, for discourse, and for people adept at thinking and speaking.[3]

Prudence as a Perennial Problem

Machiavelli, then, can offer a useful point for exploring prudence not only because of his position as a turning point in history, a key step in the development of our current assumptions about ethics and politics, but also because he allows us initially to approach practical reason and practical autonomy with ambivalence rather than enthusiasm. Whatever shape a history of prudence takes, it should not imitate the triumphant victory of reason over superstition so common in histories of scientific thought. An examination of prudence, what it is and how it develops, should leave open whether what we uncover as prudence should be considered a good thing.

One of the reasons why the enterprise to which this book is a contribution, a history of prudence, is not one that has been undertaken is that it is not obvious that prudence has a history at all. Indeed, the fact that Aristotle's term *phronesis* is rendered in contemporary English alternatively as "practical reason" and as "prudence" is sufficient reason to wonder if prudence has a history, not because it might, on the contrary, be an eternal idea outside of temporal development altogether, but because it is not a phenomenon with sufficient identity either to have or not to have a history. While some of the difficulties in recognizing prudence are peculiarly modern, Socrates' defense in the *Apology* can be taken as a paradigm of the deeper problems that generate doubts about the identity of prudence. When Socrates defends himself against the charges of worshipping new gods, making the weaker case appear the stronger and teaching the youth to do the same, he gives an alternative account of his career and reputation, stressing his identity throughout his life, saying that he is always the same (*Apology* 33a); his integrity of character allowed, even forced, him to resist bending to changing political or intellectual fashions. On the other hand, just what that identity consisted in, just who Socrates *was*, remains a puzzle. Socrates cannot be identified by any of the usual means: he has no special job or private property, and sends his wife and children out of the courtroom lest the verdict be tainted; he shows his political flexibility by angering both democrats and oligarchs. Socrates' constancy and integrity, and indeed his continued existence over time, cannot be located by the usual resources: Is his identity to be dated from his birth, the pronouncement of the oracle, or some event in between that led to the oracle's attribution? Does his career end with his death?[4]

Aristotle reports that Socrates' innovation was to bring philosophy down from the skies and into the cities of men; my short account of the *Apology* suggests that Socrates does more than introduce that new subject matter for reasoning, by showing in addition that this new subject matter requires a new way of thinking, that practical reason is a way of thinking with standards of its own, not necessarily the same as those of knowing about the heavens. The problem of good practical conduct, as opposed, especially, to good artistic performance and good theoretical understanding, is to see how constancy of character can be consistent with the adaptability to circumstances it sometimes seems to require. The problem of practical reason — and I hope to show that this is Machiavelli's problem as much as Socrates' — is the meaning of autonomy, integrity, and character in a faculty whose primary strength is responsiveness to circumstances: such prudence is not easily distinguished from cleverness.[5]

Socrates' rhetorical opponents had to face the same problem in their own way, by confronting the question, How can an orator base his presentation on what his audience already believes, yet persuade them to do what *he* wants, not what they already want? In the terms crucial for Machiavelli's development of the problem: how does a ruler govern when the source of his power is in the people? How can he control the people without weakening them, and how place his security in their hands without becoming dependent? (As I will show in the next chapter, Machiavelli's tyrants are precisely those rulers who can continue to reign only by weakening their subjects.) As the argument proceeds, I will show that this is not just a rhetorical problem that Machiavelli faces, by the analogy between the relation of ruler and ruled to the relation of speaker and audience, but a fundamental ethical problem of how to maintain one's integrity in the face of shifting fortuitous circumstances in which different characters and talents are called for, like Plato's philosophic dogs, who greet friends and are fierce towards enemies. In both rhetoric and practical efficacy, success seems to be bought at the price of losing one's self. (To anticipate a *topos* that I will develop in detail below, at the extreme the prince whose character is always in tune with the times, and whose acts are consequently always successful, would have no character at all.) It is in this sense that the successful speaker and actor become like their objects, persuading oligarchs by sounding like oligarchs, and persuading democrats by saying the opposite. (Socrates, by contrast, seems to have a character which is never in tune with the times.) In the *Protagoras*, Hippocrates wants to learn from the Sophists without becoming one; analogously, how can the new prince learn from Machiavelli without becoming like him, and how can Machiavelli teach the prince without becoming a flatterer?[6] Therefore one of the perennial problems of prudence is figuring out how to distinguish itself from sophistic by separating a virtuous adaptability to circumstances from sophistic accommodation.

(There is a connected political problem, one that I discuss only in the last two chapters. Half of the problem of the *Apology* is Socrates' identity in adaptability; the other half, of more immediate interest to his accusers, is a problem of universality: can there be a community of people who live like Socrates? Parallel to the ethical problem of how an individual can succeed without bowing to circumstances is the political problem of the place of practical intelligence in a community: how can a specialist, whether lawyer, soldier, or priest, serve the people without enslaving them? Above I noted that Descartes's scientific reason was universalizable in an unproblematic sense: if everyone follows his method, then everyone will agree. Whether a community of followers of Machiavelli is possible is just as questionable as whether Socrates' life of inquiry and poverty can be the basis for a community. For Descartes's new thinker to have no character beyond that specified by the method is a virtue, but it is a virtue no follower of Machiavelli or aspirant to prudence can afford.)

Given the obscurity and lack of immediate connotation that prudence or practical reason carries to modern ears, Machiavelli provides a more useful starting point than either Aristotle, Socrates, or the Sophists for a contemporary investigation of prudence, not only because of his historical position as a turning point in the development of practical reason, but also because he exhibits a rich conception of prudence in a situation of great practical indetermination parallel to the extreme intellectual indetermination we face in trying to understand prudence (and the relation of theory and practice is one of the more problematic aspects of any investigation of prudence). His reflective considerations of how to operate in a world of such indetermination offer a model for how we can get any secure understanding of practical reason and prudence in a world where our grasp of such things is as questionable as it is.[7]

The parallel between Machiavelli's discursive problems and the practical problems facing his audience shows that Machiavelli can define prudence appropriately, and, especially, set it off from the mere cleverness with which Machiavellianism is often identified, only if he can formulate a way in which the new prince can achieve stability, a stability that is recognizably different from merely temporary success. Prudent action is definable if and only if its objective—action valued for its own sake in Aristotle, stability in Machiavelli—is definable, has some measure other than the temporal length of success. If Machiavelli's notorious concept of virtù can be defined only as what has led to success, then no one could understand it until it was too late to be of practical use (and the theoretical equivalent of that practical ineffectuality is that virtù becomes nothing but a name for whatever leads to success); if stability is the simple antithesis of instability or usurpation, then stability is not a practicable goal in Machiavelli's world: Machiavelli has to make stability into the ability to confront the permanent possibility of instability, rather than an escape from it.[8] *The* problem of prudence for Machiavelli is precisely to make it into something more than cleverness and opportunism: he seems, and the actors of his time seem, to be forced to choose between the ideology of revealed ethics (religion is not always and everywhere an institution whose precepts exclude prudence, but it does in Machiavelli's eyes) and the corrupt alternative of seeking only private advantage. In both those cases, action is merely instrumental to predetermined ends, only differing in whether those ends are publicly sanctioned; one of the marks of prudence is that at least some actions are their own end.

Machiavelli is not engaged, as I am, in a project of trying to define prudence; instead, without explicitly specifying the nature of the activity he is teaching, he tries to teach it, directly in *The Prince*, and indirectly by presenting resources for understanding it, and by other discursive actions I shall examine, in the *Discourses on Livy*. Not only does he teach prudence, or, to be a bit more careful at this stage, not only does he create texts that take the form of acts of teaching, but he also exhibits the prudent activities he wants to instill, by making writing and reading into prudent acts. Machiavelli constrains the act of teaching in such a way that prudence will be its product: since no great action in the past can be pointed to as an unambiguous case of prudence, Machiavelli's own argument has to become the model of prudence, and prudence thus is defined as what Machiavelli's argumentative activity leads to.[9]

Of course I do not mean that prudence will be the necessary result of reading *The Prince* or the *Discourses on Livy*; Machiavelli can constrain his own act of teaching so that it leads to prudence, but he cannot determine how his texts are read without destroying the possibility of prudence: the only effects of reading that can be guaranteed are effects that Machiavelli would not want to aim at because they are infringements on the kind of autonomy that he wants to promote. So his strategic problem in writing will be a practical and deliberative one of figuring out what share of the job of promoting prudence is in his power; and solving that problem will be an act of prudence worth imitating. (In case my talk about reading and writing being acts of prudence sounds too metaphorical, this division of power between author and readers can serve as a first literal example. I will return to consider the connections between prudent reading and writing and other, nonverbal acts of prudence later in great detail.) Consequently our problem of understanding prudence through Machiavelli will force us to attend to his texts not simply as the proclamation of good news about new practical truths but as acts of public communication.

If all these difficulties in understanding prudence through reading Machiavelli were not enough, I have to point to further difficulty. Defining prudence has a special problem, one not encountered in trying to define other things, even other virtues or political talents. At any time when people spoke more securely about prudence, its most notable feature was its responsiveness to changing circumstances; shifts in the range of circumstances to which prudence should be relevant should force changes in the very meaning of prudence itself: the kinds of abilities required to be able to think and act in ways that are responsive to circumstances must change when circumstances change. That responsiveness generates two problems. First, we have to be alive to the possibility that prudence today is undefinable, and impossible, because such flexibility is impossible; even worse, that responsiveness might be possible today but not be a virtue, not a feature of character, but perhaps a skill or an application of scientific knowledge instead.[10] Still, the appropriateness of shifting conceptions of prudence to shifting circumstances cannot mean that prudence must change with *every* change in circumstances, or it would become a completely passive mode of responding to circumstances. (Once again, to anticipate one of the limits against which Machiavelli's argument crashes, that extreme interpretation of responsive ability sounds like what Machiavelli has in mind in chapter 25 of *The Prince*, where he says that someone who, *per impossibile*, could change his way of acting with every change in fortune would never lose. If every shift in the favors of fortune changed a person's character, he would no longer have any character; his acts would be successful by ceasing to be acts and becoming responses. (This sort of passivity must not be identified with its near neighbor, an amoral sort of opportunism towards ends and cleverness towards instrumentality often attributed to Machiavelli.) Nevertheless, prudence must change with a change in the *range* of circumstances to which it should be responsive. Therefore, what Aristotle means by prudence must be different from what Machiavelli means, and both must differ from whatever prudence can mean in the eighteenth century or today. It would be both question-begging and hyperbolic to claim that defining prudence is itself a prudential problem, but the difficulties here, of active flexibility in the light of changing circumstances, are at least parallel to the difficulties in prudent action itself. At a minimum, we will have to ask to what extent whatever Machiavelli can show about prudence has any relevance to our own difficulties in understanding prudence.

Machiavellian Prudence

The problem of prudence is always a problem of flexibility and continuity. If prudence has a history, then we have to be able to show how *Machiavelli's* problem of prudence differs from other possibilities. There are two major respects in which it is a specific variation on the theme of continuity and adaptability. First, the practical context is one of apparent instability, in which it is hard to find any place for stability, where partisans of unreflective traditional stability only make things worse for themselves and where only opportunism is likely to be successful. (Whatever one thinks is the practical intention of Aristotle's *Nicomachean Ethics*, it surely is not motivated by a judgment that contemporary unreflective morality is ineffective.) On the intellectual side, second, although there is no transvaluation of values, and in that sense we do not choose ends rather than means — we do not say, some people think *x* is a good but *x* actually is bad — there are questions about both the compatibility of ultimate values and also about the relevance of ultimate values to practical success. While any prudential use of knowledge in action must, as I shall show, involve rhetoric to some degree, the kinds of practical and intellectual problems Machiavelli faces force rhetoric into a prominence it does not always have. Machiavelli's problem is at once to find practical stability without an ineffectual rigidity and to establish an intellectual flexibility that does not become amorality. Virtù is not Aristotelian phronesis or any other Aristotelian virtue, and the stability Machiavelli seeks is not the continuity characteristic of activities undertaken for their own sake, a continuity attributable by Aristotle to actions not limited in space and time (which does not mean that they are eternal acts outside of time but that they are not defined, as Aristotle puts it, by a "whence" and a "whither"). The concept of virtù brings these aspects of the development of prudence to a head and makes Machiavellian texts especially useful for learning about prudence more generally.

Aristotle locates prudence in *Ethics* 6 by contrast to science and to artistic understanding, two kinds of rationality which can be taught; that pair of contrasts is the constructive version of a pair of polemics he must conduct throughout the *Ethics* and the rest of his practical writings, as he argues against both Plato and the Sophists. He must resist Plato's substituting wisdom for prudence, with its consequent reduction of practice to a theory that will permit us to act rightly in ways that rise above the temptations of the moment and the vicissitudes of fortune; in terms that will become important in our analysis, Plato thereby seeks to replace a state of character with an intellectual virtue.[11] At the same time Aristotle argues against the Sophists' reduction of prudence to cleverness, of an ethical state of character to a technique, a reduction which Machiavelli himself is in constant danger of making and which presents a threat to Machiavelli far more pressing than the equivalent to the Platonic danger of making stability a condition outside of activity. Aristotle's procedure in isolating prudence by contrasting it to art and science, plus the more acute difficulties in conceiving prudence at all today, suggests that a more formal treatment of prudence is called for, one that will help in stating more precisely Machiavelli's problem of prudence, as opposed to that problem's more general form. I propose therefore briefly to set out prudence as an inferential relation between rules and cases, precepts and examples. Rhetoric for Aristotle is the counterpart of dialectic and is also a part of politics; in the same spirit, my exposition of prudence — whose ties with rhetoric will be one of my themes — will initially treat it as a logical or dialectical phenomenon identified by a specific relation of rule and case, and then show the ethical and political consequences of such a relation of precept and rule.

Three Kinds of Rules

Prudence is halfway between an ethics of principles, in which those principles univocally dictate action — *Fiat justitia, ruat coelum* — and an ethics of consequences, in which the successful result is all.[12] To say that prudence is located halfway between an ethics of principles and one of consequences, though, makes it look like an uneasy, and unmethodical, compromise between principles and consequences, in which each sometimes restrains the other, a compromise according to no principle or rule or system, and prudence is consequently often lost in less fine-grained analyses: since there are many good things, and one cannot have them all, the best policy must be to forfeit some pleasure for the sake of duty, and not be an ascetic or a pharisee, but recognize that duties should be generally, although not universally, observed. It is tempting to think that there can be no overarching metatheory subsuming both principles and consequences, and so a theory, or even an account, of prudence is an inherently incoherent project.[13]

It is not difficult to articulate an ethics of principles or an ethics of consequences, although it may not be so easy consistently to live by them. But even if one can *be* prudent, it is far from clear that one could articulate principles for prudent action or give any systematic account of what prudence is. The problem for this inquiry is not whether people can make decisions and live lives that compromise between principles and consequences, but whether one can find *principles* midway between principles and consequences. While many Machiavellian projects seem easier to achieve in discourse than in other fields of action, prudence itself seems easier to accomplish than to explain: the fact that practical reason is difficult to elaborate systematically may be due to its being so closely tied to concrete experience and action, and hence easier to perform than to account for. Such prudence as the accumulation of custom and experience is unstable, though, because its unarticulated state makes it vulnerable to argument, and therefore the drive towards a method for practical reason is unavoidable. If there are prudential rules and methods, if prudence can be methodical and not just a matter of chance or experience, at a minimum such rules will be difficult to recognize because they must work in a different way from the more familiar rules employed in scientific thinking, the usual initial representation of rationality and method.

In current discussions of method, a distinction is often drawn between algorithms and heuristics, a distinction that corresponds to the difference between an ethics of principles and one of consequences: algorithms reliably, always, and certainly produce correct results if followed diligently; heuristics produce products of varying quality, and sometimes nothing at all, sometimes answers whose correctness must then be judged by some other method.[14] The value of a heuristic method lies entirely in its success — if it works, it doesn't do to ask too closely about how it works, or else one finds oneself making what Susan Sontag calls "hopeful guesses about the improving value of gimmicks" — whereas the algorithmic method itself proves the success of its results (valid inference consists in transmitting truth from premiss to conclusion: if r follows validly from p and q, and p and q are granted, then r must be true; we certainly don't then have to go and check by some other means to see whether r is in fact true). The practical analogon of an algorithmic rule is a moral principle taken as an exceptionless precept: an action is right because it follows from a good and true principle, and so the principle endows the action with rightness. In both scientific and moral algorithmic rules, the rightness of result is an inheritance from right principles.[15] In scientific contexts, when people recognize that not everything can be done by such methods, they often turn to an alternative conception of method which offers no such guarantees but which may lead to the discovery or invention of things that can, if necessary, later be verified by algorithmic methods. For heuristic procedures, whether in science or ethics, the result validates the method, rather than the other way around. Instead of inheriting their correctness, heuristic results stand or fall on their own: self-made men in opposition to those who inherit their standing.

I began by claiming that Machiavelli's place in the history of prudence was parallel to that of Descartes in a history of theoretical reason, that each represents a different kind of turning to autonomy. The new kind of reason Descartes promotes — and promotes so successfully that it has often usurped the titles of reason and method altogether — is algorithmic: given secure starting points and a reliable method, one must arrive at a result that is certain and beyond controversy. Bruns characterizes Descartes's algorithmic method by pointing out that in Descartes,

> disputation gives way to calculation. . . . Systems compromise
> every kind of autonomy, even God's. One can hardly fail to make
> the next point, which is that in Descartes's construction God, in
> creating the world, is not obliged to speak. He does not say, "Let
> there be light." Even if he did say it, no light would therefore shine.
> Systems are algorithmic rather than logocentric. . . . The God of
> Descartes, after all, is *only a term required by the system*, which is
> why his existence is so easy to prove, and so easy to forget.[16]

(For completeness' sake, if Machiavelli represents prudential methods, and Descartes algorithmic ones, the comparable representative figure for heuristics would be Ramus, whose universal logical method is a substitute for knowledge of any particular subject.)[17]

There are rules applicable in prudence, but they are neither algorithmic nor heuristic.[18] The rules and strategies of prudence offer no guarantee comparable to that promised by algorithms: I can apply them properly and appropriately to some problem and find that they lead to an unacceptable result or even a dead end. It may be a rule of prudence to follow Machiavelli's advice and rely on one's own troops rather than mercenaries, but no one, Machiavelli included, would claim that relying on one's own troops guarantees victory. In this case, though, the rule of prudence does have a categorical, algorithmic corollary: relying on someone else's troops guarantees failure, although what kind of failure cannot be specified in advance. Such interconnections among the kinds of rules are common, and it often turns out that algorithmic "fallacies" are useful rules in prudential or heuristic thinking: affirming the consequent must be one of the most common methods for discovering a cause: "He who follows the course of Numa may keep or lose his throne, according to chance and circumstances; but he who imitates the example of Romulus, and combines valor with prudence, will keep his throne anyhow, unless it be taken from him by some persistent and excessive force" (*Discourses* 1.19). The use of prudential methods comes with no guarantee that the results will be correct, because, just as rhetoric traditionally argued both sides of any question, practical reason can always produce contrary results. If it can lead to contrary results, it can guarantee neither.[19] Algorithmics eliminates controversy by severely restricting the material on which method can operate: at its extreme Descartes will limit admissible data to the single event of doubting, but even short of that, algorithmics imposes much narrower conditions on admissible data than dialectical and rhetorical methods.[20] Where Descartes characterizes algorithmic methods by saying that if two people disagree, one must not have followed the rules for directing his understanding (and the other does not understand the truth sufficiently to correct the other's error), two people can reason prudentially without their results' agreeing.[21]

Prudential methods and rules are not heuristic either; the chief reason for thinking that they might be is that people often conceive heuristics to be the only alternative to algorithms. Similarly, prudence is reduced to an ethics of consequences when that seems to be the only alternative to an ethics of principles.[22] When these are taken to be the sole alternatives, then "prudence" is not a virtue; from the point of view of principles, it is a concession to a world in which the demands of morality are not binding, and from the point of view of an ethics of consequences, prudence is a form of conservatism, of hedging one's bets, as in the strategy that Rawls claims is fundamental to rationality itself: "the guiding principle that a rational individual is always to act so that he need never blame himself no matter how things finally transpire."[23] In heuristics, the sole justification for a procedure is that it works: the result validates the method, rather than, as in algorithms, the method validating the result. Bernard Williams uses the figure of Gauguin to construct such a way of acting: "In such a situation the only thing that will justify his choice will be success itself. If he fails . . . then he did the wrong thing, not just in the sense in which that platitudinously follows, but in the sense that having done the wrong thing in those circumstances he has no basis for the thought that he was justified in acting as he did. If he succeeds, he does have a basis for that thought."[24]

For a short example of a rule of prudence which occurs in a nonpolitical context, consider the following mode of inference, based on what Hume calls the "rule of analogy" that "similar effects have similar causes": since the world is a machine, only better, and since men and only men make machines, it follows, by virtue of that rule, that the maker of the world must be like a man, only better. The rule cannot qualify as an algorithm, since it does not guarantee its results: the German Revolution was caused by a military defeat; if similar effects have similar causes, can we validly infer that the American Revolution was caused by a military defeat too? But it isn't a heuristic rule either: in the case of the argument from design, the argument is supposed to lend *support* to the conclusion and not just reveal a result we can verify on other grounds. That is the whole point of employing such a rule in theology.

Clearly, restricted versions of Hume's maxim that similar causes have similar effects can be employed successfully as algorithmic rules in carefully defined domains in the natural sciences. In the same way, Socrates' maxim from the *Apology* that the unexamined life is not worth living, although often read as a basis for an ethics of principles, needs qualifications and adaptation to circumstances, because reflection is not automatically liberating and discursive resourcefulness not automatically empowering. (Hence Socrates disavows his so-called followers in the *Apology* because they thought that the meaning of the rule was clear and that his life of inquiry was therefore easy to imitate.) When interpreted as a rule of prudence, the constancy and flexibility of Socrates become much more precarious achievements. A prudent judgment, consequently, about the relation between prudence and good action will be a subject for my last chapter.

Acting according to principles guarantees the rectitude of actions in an ethics of principles; successfully attaining some result justifies the rectitude of actions in an ethics of consequences. What, though, assures the propriety of a prudential action? If neither principles nor consequences do, what does? The answer is that nothing assures that a prudential action will be correct; the rightness and the success of a prudential action are always open to debate and to refutation by practical failure. Prudential reasoning yields conclusions that are always open to further debate because it yields conclusions that are open to further action, and for that reason prudential reasoning will always appear a weak kind of reasoning measured against standards of theoretical reason, a frustrating waste of time to hard-headed politicians and scientific-minded technocrats.[25] As a method of reasoning, prudence replicates the new meaning Machiavelli has given to security; the good use of prudential methods does not produce an invulnerable, indefeasible result, but positions the reasoner for further argument. Both algorithmic and heuristic thinking see moral and political decisions as far simpler than the prudential reasoner does; whether that is a healthy simplification or an oversimplification, and whether the simplifications of ideology, or opportunism, do not come from employing hidden premises or hidden means of applying their rules, including hidden specifications of who does the practical reasoning, are always matters for judgment.[26]

In contrast to prudence, the two other kinds of method have a great deal in common, which is why they can be employed in such smooth alternation in the natural sciences. (Their smooth alternation in practical reason has a deeper dimension, to be explored below.) For both algorithmic and heuristic methods, for both an ethics of principles and one of consequences, there is a gap between apprehending a rule and applying it, and the consequent possibility of an infinite regress, filled up by some unmethodical skill or talent, of rules for applying rules. The rules are there; they might be appropriate or not, might be well used or abused, but neither of those factors affects the rules themselves. Seeing what a rule means and seeing what it applies to are distinct, and so the rules themselves remain untouched by debates about their application. Hence categorical rules have to be algorithmic; an injunction against murder admits of no exceptions, no debate, and for such a rule to be always valid, there must be ways of pushing off any challenges by making them questions of application and not of the rule itself. Since heuristic rules are most useful when we are most ignorant of the subject, they make a virtue of such necessity, and hence they too require a gap between understanding a rule and knowing what it applies to. In neither algorithmics nor heuristics is there any judgment: in the algorithmic case because the whole point of method is to eliminate the need for judgment (in Bacon's words, to do much to level men's wits) by guaranteeing results mechanically; in the heuristic case because, although judgment is needed, it is external to the method itself and becomes something irrational and hence called by uninformative names like intuition, talent, or guesswork. If all practical rules are like the prohibition against murder, then there is no room for prudence; if all of morality could be summed up in Kant's perfect duties, there would be no need for prudence.

For both algorithmic and heuristic thinking, because of the gap between a rule and its application, there is a distinction between understanding those rules and knowing about some field; at their most imperialistic, each method can claim to obviate any need for detailed knowledge. In both theoretical and practical reason, people sometimes make the distance between rules and their applications into a source of strength: logic examines validity, not soundness, and justice is blind to everything but guilt and innocence, especially blind to who did something to whom and under what circumstances and with what motive, and the laws of logic and justice would be corrupted by any loosening of the boundaries between form and matter, rule and application. On the other hand, the successful practitioners of heuristics rely less on a system of general rules than on a well-stocked arsenal of particular techniques; although particular, they are techniques that are themselves detached both from a general theoretical framework and from knowledge of any particular subject, precisely because heuristics are of value when such frameworks and such inventories of facts are inadequate. Hence both Plato and Aristotle ridicule the Sophists, who think that they can employ their political talents in any city, without knowing the particular circumstances of that city.[27] So, where algorithmics is frustrated by the permanent incompleteness of the prudential thinker, who relies on rhetorical reasoning and never-ending debate, algorithmic thinking appears from the prudential point of view as one-sided and abstract, because an algorithm is precisely a single line of reasoning that by itself is supposed to settle an issue.

One final contrast for the three methods. Each has a manifold to which it is especially appropriate. Some situations call for methods that separate their own operation from the judgment inevitably called for in applying the method, while other situations demand that method and judgment not be separated. (To anticipate, initially making the value of each kind of rule relative to a manifold makes all the more critical, and questionable, Machiavelli's argumentative tactic, especially as he moves from *The Prince* to the *Discourses*, of beginning with prudence having a restricted domain and moving to a world in which there are no legitimate alternatives to prudence.) Heuristics is a mode of action especially appropriate to situations in which the risks are small and the potential for gain so great that one need not worry about the odds: heuristics begs to be used in situations that are the objective correlative of the emotional attitude "What have I got to lose?" In particular, scientific problems often are such low-risk or no-cost situations, in which one can try out a line of invention and simply start again with a different line if the first one fails. Science often makes heuristics affordable by making a radical separation between discovery and proof, between generating ideas and testing them, because only then does discovery proceed by "thought experiments" without risks for the "real world," as strong a separation of discourse and action as possible.

Similarly, an ethics of consequences is appropriate where winning is all, as in Hume's extramoral world of extreme scarcity that justifies all competitive methods, including the opportunism, the winning at any cost, often called Machiavellian. Faced with a radically indeterminate world, one should not be restrained from trying anything that might bring success. The state of nature is often a situation that calls for an ethics of consequences, because nothing but the consequences of action are available to sanction a given action; the state of nature is often defined as precisely a situation in which no considerations other than success can enter. Hence those who see international relations as a state of nature find Machiavelli reassuring.

Algorithmic methods and ethics of principles, on the other hand, lend themselves most readily to the opposite extreme situation, in which one wants to avoid error at all cost, where one is willing to sacrifice the rate of progress, perhaps give up on finding some new truths, for the sake of preventing one's thinking from being polluted with error. Where I cannot afford to be wrong, I need a method that itself cannot introduce errors, that cleanly transmits truth from premises to conclusion. Heuristics belongs in situations where I have nothing to lose; algorithms belong in circumstances where I have too much to lose, where gaining the whole world pales in comparison with losing my own soul. Once again, Hume's alternatives are apposite; why not follow a morals of principles in a world of abundance, where there could be no motives for cheating someone or knowing the better but choosing the worse. If my God is infinitely merciful and just and has told me what to do to be saved, and if heaven has no space limitations, I would be foolish not to follow His law absolutely. Kant's angels presumably live in a heaven in which doing the right thing always meets with success and in which it is always transparent just what the right thing to do is.[28]

There is another dimension of appropriateness to these kinds of methods. Heuristics belongs to radical individualists; if I'm competing against others, racing against them to be the first to succeed, I need a method that maximizes my chances of quick success, even at the price of perhaps failing, since probabilities suggest I will fail anyway.[29] In *The Prince*, the usurper has to worry about being overthrown in turn by other new princes, and successful revolutionaries often seem to be incapable of worrying about anything else. Algorithms are best suited to cooperative enterprises in which the contribution of the individual is intentionally neutralized; it's not *my* success I'm aiming at but the long-term progress of science or the human race: all truths will eventually be uncovered, but one must carefully guard against introducing error, even at the price of slowing down that progress. The traditional monarch not only has to defend his own individual rule against plotters and flatterers; he has to uphold the *nature* of hereditary rule, and so there are some methods of defense he cannot use without ceasing to be a hereditary ruler. Plato's state, which submerges the individual as such (hence Glaucon's puzzle about whether the guardians are happy), employs algorithmic methods and a ethics of principles, and so an esoteric wisdom can replace prudence: a scientifically authorized eugenics and educational testing program justifies the substitution of a noble lie for an appeal to a *consensus gentium*. (This removal of prudence has its revenge in the history of degenerating states, each of which mixes ethics of principles and consequences in unstable ways. That history, to which I shall return, is also an important reminder that prudence is not simply the middle ground between two extremes, the middle that any reasonable person should adopt just because extremes are bad.) For neither the opportunistic partisan of an ethics of consequences nor the principled politician is there anything like a *community;* heuristic thinking applies to individuals in a war of all against all, while algorithmic thinking applies in the sort of state Aristotle accuses Plato of constructing, which depends on too much unity, making a community into a family. Once Descartes shows that the results of his method "agree with" the nature of things, there is no need to show in addition that different practitioners will agree with each other. (Again, think of the prohibition against murder I mentioned before as the paradigm of an ethics of principles. Presumably, with respect to that article of morality, any community *is* a family without differences of interest or opinion, and so without a need for either rhetoric or prudence.) If egoism and altruism, selfishness and self-sacrifice, are an exhaustive set of distinctions, then the state of nature where Machiavelli's usurper lives, and the family in which Machiavelli's hereditary monarch locates himself, are the only alternatives, and prudence has no place. But if a community is an association of individuals different in kind, with potentially conflicting desires and understandings, then neither of those kinds of thinking can serve in a community.

I have chosen to offer such a formal preliminary exposition of prudence, presenting it as one sort of rule and method distinct from algorithmics and heuristics in order to avoid the potentially confusing associations that might be attendant on more traditional ways of talking about it; this formality, I maintain, makes it possible to identify instances and trace the career of this protean thing called practical reason. "Three kinds of rules" is not Machiavelli's way of talking about prudence: indeed, he says very little about prudence at all, instead enacting a conception of prudence and giving his audience the means for acquiring it. Aristotle is far more systematic than Machiavelli and does identify prudence with something like a rule, namely the *orthos logos*, but does not explicate the concept of prudence by contrast to other kinds of rules, methods, or *logoi*. (In Aristotle's terms, my treatment thus far has been dialectical rather than rhetorical. As a consequence of its dialectical character, there has been nothing *historical* about the exposition of prudence thus far.) While I think considerations of the relations of rule and case, general value and particular action, a useful framework for illuminating Machiavelli's contribution to the history of practical reason, it is worth noting before we enter into Machiavelli's texts directly just what the Aristotelian parallel is. Instead of contrasting prudence to algorithmics and heuristics, Aristotle isolates prudence by contrast first to science, *episteme*, and then to art, *techne*. Prudence is not science for Aristotle, because science demonstrates necessary consequences, where demonstration consists in the transmission of certified truth from principles to consequences, just like our algorithmic thinking, while prudence is concerned with the contingent, with things that can be otherwise and hence cannot be subject to such demonstration: "No one deliberates about things that cannot vary, nor about things not within his power to do. Hence inasmuch as scientific knowledge involves demonstration, whereas things whose fundamental principles are variable are not capable of demonstration, because everything about them is variable, and inasmuch as one cannot deliberate about things that are of necessity, it follows that Prudence is not the same as Science" (*Ethics* 6.5.1140a32–b2).

Prudence is not *techne* either, because art is a reasoned capacity for making — that is, producing — things that have existence and value of their own, while prudence has no end outside itself. The contrast between an ethics of consequences and prudence is apposite here; while in art, one can reliably infer from a product to the ability that produced it, and the value of an artistic skill is derived from the product, in prudence, reliable inference goes from character to deed — the good man is dependable in a way the artist is not — and the value of the deed flows in part from the doer (hence Aristotle's contrast between a virtuous act and the act done by the virtuous man). My sketch of three kinds of rules then is parallel to Aristotle's isolation of prudence from science and art.

Aristotle distinguishes between prudence and *techne* because prudence, since it has no end outside the action, is a function of character, while technical abilities are distinct from character; and so *technai*, unlike prudence, can be forgotten, and the idea of an intentional technical error makes sense (*Ethics* 6.5.1140b22). With respect to kinds of methods, one can say that prudential reasoning engages the individual intelligence in a way not required — and not desirable — in the other two methods. (One sign of this is in the choice and use of examples in methodical presentations, since in prudential methods the choice and use of examples is itself a matter of taste and judgment.)³⁰ Engaging the intellect means that there are risks which the other two methods in different ways can avoid, algorithmics by certainty and heuristics by detachment and cost-free experiments. Co-ordinate with such engagement of the intellect is a different relation of rule to case, form to matter, method to subject matter. Ideology and heuristics are universal methods in a way that prudence is not, the universality coming from an indifference to particulars justified by a process of abstraction. While prudence is not universal in either of these senses, the tie of prudence to character means that there is only one prudence, because its end is the good for man, while the arts are as many as their objects. It is therefore one of the tasks of the prudential reasoner to show that one's character is staked in intellectual operations, either necessarily involved whether one wants to or not, or because it is better that it be involved. One criterion, conversely, of ineffectual discourse is that it does not stake the character of the speaker.³¹

In what follows I will exhibit in detail the shifting connections between prudence and rhetorical argument — including some cautions against identifying them — but the first affinity between the two consists in their shared emphasis on particularity. Substantively, rhetoric is essential to practical reason because both are concerned with choice; in terms of the formal treatment of prudence I have been presenting, prudence and rhetoric are allies because rhetoric is a method for understanding and manipulating particulars. Just as rhetoric, with its appeals to taste and propriety, resists reduction to logical method, the enemy of prudence is always some form of a drive to generality. While Aristotle does not take social science, or even

Introduction

Platonic wisdom, as a practical threat, such wisdom is, for him, a theoretical error to which he must return repeatedly, as in his attacks in *Politics* 2 on Plato for wanting to achieve too much unity in the state. Where the chief appeal of prudence is in its appropriateness to circumstances, the chief value of competing modes of action will be in an indifference to circumstances — indifference not as a callous disregard for circumstances but as an ability to rise above ephemeral considerations and maintain the purity of good action. But the practical threat for Aristotle comes from the Sophists and their quite different drive towards generality, towards an argumentative ability that obviates the need for knowledge of particular circumstances and instead substitutes particulars of a different kind, lots of shoes instead of an art of shoemaking:

> The teaching which they gave to their pupils was rapid but unsystematic; for they conceived that they could train their pupils by imparting to them not an art but the results of an art, just as if one could claim to be about to communicate knowledge for the prevention of pain in the feet and then were not to teach the cobbler's art and the means of providing suitable foot-gear, but were to offer a selection of various kinds of shoes; for he has helped to supply his need but has not imparted an art to him. (*De sophisticis elenchis* 184a1–6)

Rhetoric, Prudence, and the Argument of This Book

The prudential relation between rule and case organizes the argument of this book. Machiavelli, and *The Prince* in particular, are neither mere examples of some general thesis about prudence, nor is prudence a simple generalization from them. As an initiation of a history of prudence, consequently, my argument will neither show how Machiavelli instantiates an eternal idea of prudence, nor try to arrive inductively at an understanding of practical reason from the case of Machiavelli. My exposition will alternate between focused readings of Machiavelli's arguments and the implications it holds for prudence and its history.

This alternation between an example and its more general interest for prudence can be called, in current language, a "thick" reading, but I think it is important that not only do Machiavelli and his texts thicken as my argument proceeds, but so does rhetoric. The first chapter takes its start from rhetoric in the most superficial sense as it exhibits *The Prince's* argumentative and stylistic surface, its presentation of examples and maxims embedded in a series of elaborately formal frames. Such a reading is rhetorical because it takes stylistic maneuverings as its data to make inferences about Machiavelli's basic problem, how to combine stability (not in this case integrity of character but permanence of political rule) and innovation (not mere flexibility but novelty)—how to make stability a function, as much as possible, of active ability. Machiavelli uses rhetorical methods to redefine virtù and stability, and thereby to combine adaptability with integrity. He appeals to rhetoric to generate and control ambiguity: ambiguity, while a linguistic phenomenon, has an evident practical function here, to make innovation and hence stable usurpation possible, by destroying the conventional semantic associations that *ruling* and its derivative terms have, the associations that seem to make hereditary monarchy uniquely legitimate and all other alternatives outside any moral framework. The substantive problem, then, turns on the opposition between the rhetorical and algorithmic meanings of *stability* and between the rhetorical and sophistical meanings of *adaptability*. Machiavelli addresses the problem of how to combine stability and adaptability by confronting the prince with a new intellectual problem, how imitation can lead to autonomy rather than dependence. The focus of the chapter will naturally be on the chapters of *The Prince* that revolve around virtù as a case and as a principle.

That concentration on the stylistic surface of *The Prince* eliminates, I hope, questions about whether Machiavelli *intended* to construct a new conception of prudence, whether he was influenced, directly or indirectly, by Aristotelian ideas, or whether he actually *meant* to distinguish rhetorical from sophistical flexibility. While the opportunity for virtuosity inherent in the topics and tropes of rhetoric prevents us from claiming that Machiavelli is in any way compelled to treat the issues he does, there is a force of responsible inquiry that motivates the complexities of the argument.

The second chapter abstracts from *The Prince* and rejects any simple elision between the discursive virtuosity Machiavelli exhibits and the practical virtù he presumably teaches. While the connections between discursive and practical abilities are essential to Machiavelli's project of initiating a fully rhetorical prudence, positing an effective extradiscursive imitation of discursive practices can make successful action appear too easy to achieve in a situation in which ease of achievement guarantees a new, aesthetic sort of ineffectuality for practice.

The distance created by these acts of abstraction between Machiavelli's texts and my argument might seem to make *The Prince* into something it is not, namely a work of philosophy. On the contrary, it seems to me that it is precisely the unphilosophical and even antiphilosophical character of Machiavelli's interests and enterprise that license this distancing, because Machiavelli's arguments and conclusions have a directness produced, not by any fidelity to intellectual standards but by practical urgency. They therefore reveal philosophical complexities often avoided by purely philosophical "solutions" to analogous problems.

The third chapter turns to the politics of rhetorical invention. While rhetoric appears, in Chapter 1, as a resource for finding strategies and devices, especially techniques for using topics of invention, Chapter 3 explores the way the different parts of rhetoric generate different kinds of politics, contrasting in particular Machiavelli's politics of rhetorical invention with a politics of another part of rhetoric, style. What were, in Chapter 1, argumentative tactics, here become the substance of politics, as Machiavelli's enterprise appears as a politics of invention opposed to traditional rulers who rule by style, by acting like princes: the devices and techniques of rhetoric begin to thicken into something that could be called an art or discipline. Here I consider Machiavelli as embodying and teaching a method of acting, and examine as well the contrast Machiavelli invites between his new politics of invention, with its attendant style, and the traditional politics of style.

Although Machiavelli is engaged in a critique of ideology, the alternative to ideology is not an unclouded and direct vision of reality, but prudential reasoning. When Machiavelli uses rhetoric to destroy the conventional semantic associations allied with traditional politics, showing how artificial and precarious they are, he does not offer as an alternative some nonconventional language and society, a natural or Edenic language and polity. The fable of the lion and the fox becomes, in my argument, a place for exploring the artfulness of the political world and some of the relations between the military and the political—two contrasting modes of thought about the practical, two different conceptions of the relation of theory and practice.

Machiavelli has a radical purpose—to overthrow traditional rulers and forms of rule—but must use "conservative" means, and appeal—and make the prince appeal—to a *consensus gentium*, an increasingly problematic authority. To do otherwise would indeed make him into a preacher of evil and the new prince into nothing but a usurper who rules by force, not authority. Machiavelli uses rhetoric to teach us how to use language while recognizing its ineliminable ambiguities; he teaches us how to find stability in such an unstable world.

When, as in the third chapter, rhetorical tactics become the substance of politics, the topic of appearance and reality becomes highly problematic. Consequently, the fourth chapter must return to the relations between rhetoric and action: when all straightforward access to extradiscursive reality is removed, what happens to politics, and to prudence? Are the new ways of acting that Machiavelli develops political and ethical in a recognizable sense, or do they substitute the rule of force and fraud for legitimate rule, and substitute the pursuit of power and personal gain for moral action? The interest in Chapter 1 in imitation and autonomy make the sections on virtù the center of attention; Chapter 3 focuses on the fable of the lion and the fox to treat the relations of appearance and reality; in similar fashion, Chapter 4 must follow Machiavelli as he moves to the last three chapters of *The Prince*, and to the allegory of treating fortune like a woman in particular.

Finally, the analysis of *The Prince* leads to a consideration, in my last two chapters, of the *Discourses on Livy*. *The Prince*, on my reading, attempts to make innovating, and in particular ruling, in the circumstances that face the new prince, into an art, and the text demonstrates the limits to that enterprise. If *The Prince* ends by finding, as a condition of success for this new mode of operating, that one needs to be able to choose one's character, then a whole new set of prudential problems arise. Machiavellian virtù and prudence are then not fully captured by any art or set of rules, and must be considered as forms of character that exist within a community. Rhetoric then becomes located between the arts that do not engage the character or intellect of the user and the virtues that are inseparable from character. The *Discourses* face the problems left by the ambiguous endings of *The Prince* by making virtù into republican virtue and asking whether Machiavelli's virtues can exist within a stable and flourishing community. The fifth chapter must raise questions of universality, of whether a Machiavellian community is possible; these questions give further depth to the conceptions of rhetoric and prudence involved, as they situate character and method within a community. The sixth chapter, finally, must examine the *Discourses* to locate the resources for civic virtue and to identify the new rhetorical virtues Machiavelli develops for exploiting those resources.

1   *THE PRINCE*

A NEGLECTED

RHETORICAL CLASSIC

Rhetoric, Aristotle tells us, is the counterpart of dialectic and a part of the practical science of politics, which for Aristotle includes both politics and ethics. We can turn attention from the formal dialectical relations of principle and case to the case of *The Prince* by showing how the political dimensions of prudence, deliberation, and choice, as opposed to their algorithmic and heuristic substitutes, emerge out of the formal demands of the relation of precept and example that, when it concerns the objects of choice, should be called rhetorical.

Throughout the history of its influence, people have found Machiavelli's *Prince* to be many things, but a work of rhetoric has rarely been one of them. Conversely, while recent work on Machiavelli seems to be begging to be made whole by an injection of rhetoric, recent scholars of Renaissance humanism in general have, without treating Machiavelli, drawn attention to the importance of the rhetorical tradition in providing the humanists with a method for effective communication.[1] Just as there is something missing in treatments of Machiavelli that ignore rhetoric, so treatments of Renaissance rhetorical practice are incomplete without a consideration of Machiavelli: throughout its history rhetoric has been conceived not only as a method of communication and education, and a method of verbal adornment and of style, but also as a method of invention and a means of characterizing cultural roles and presuppositions. A reminder that Machiavelli too was part of the Renaissance rhetorical tradition grounds verbal performance in its political functions, discursive virtuosity in practical virtù, and will eventually make problematic some of the conventional wisdom about imitation and the relation between prudence and decorum.[2]

Treatments of Renaissance rhetoric that ignore Machiavelli neglect the most challenging, most practically and intellectually demanding side of rhetoric, namely, its connection to prudence, represented in what I shall call Machiavelli's rhetorical politics. It is that aspect of rhetoric that forms the subject of this book. But since style is the most obvious and most immediately accessible dimension of rhetoric, I shall begin with the rhetorical surface of *The Prince*, its stylistic use of topics, tropes, and figures, of "structures of binary opposition and identity—parallelism, antithesis, and irony in both the macrostructure of events and the microstructure of style."[3] From such evidence I shall infer the rhetorical structure and achievement of *The Prince*, showing that Machiavelli was using not only a rhetoric of style and communication but, most importantly, a rhetoric of invention.

Still, taking *The Prince*'s stylistic surface for data creates the danger of a merely aesthetic reading, unconnected to the further rhetorical dimensions of Machiavelli's project. *The Prince* differs from other Mirrors for Magistrates, which would treat examples algorithmically, in Machiavelli's perception of the intellectual preconditions of useful advice and successful imitation, preconditions which will require a rhetorical art of invention.[4] Machiavelli rejects the possibility of algorithmic teaching and learning by expanding the scope of attention from good advice and good action to their intellectual and practical preconditions, and the acts of giving and taking advice will be the most immediate prudential actions of Machiavelli and his audience. My language of rhetoric, prudence, and the three kinds of rules treated in the Introduction may not be obviously connected to the language of either Machiavelli or his recent commentators; consequently, I think that drawing explicit connections between the framework of my Introduction and the problematic constructed by J.G.A. Pocock, perhaps Machiavelli's most distinguished and influential current commentator in English, can help to situate my enterprise of beginning a history of prudence within contemporary debate. Pocock reads *The Prince* as a treatise on political innovation and stabilization (without noting the connection between such political innovation and the methods of rhetorical invention Machiavelli employs), pointing out that while universal truths were the subject of science, timeless custom the subject of law, and divine intervention the subject of revealed religion, the great intellectual problem of practice, of ethics and politics, in sixteenth-century Italy was to develop a way of understanding fluctuating particular events and institutions without reducing them to the subjects of science, custom, or grace.[5] Machiavelli, I shall show, uses and adapts traditional methods of rhetorical invention to find stable and novel structures for understanding, and intervening in, changing events; his prudence can be viewed either as an attempt to make universals—especially the moral values—flexible and relevant to experience, or to make experience and custom intelligible and therefore capable of adaptation and manipulation. By themselves, neither universal values nor experiential know-how and custom (the bases for algorithmic and heuristic forms of practical reason) have a place for change; and treatments of change, since such resistance will not make it disappear, then have to be surreptitious and irrational.

Inventing stable structures for organizing changing particulars is not only Machiavelli's problem; it is the prince's problem too. That is, it is not only a literary problem but also a practical one. The prince must invent in fact, in actual event and institutions, the stable structures for changing events which Machiavelli invents in his argument.[6] The parallel problems of invention for Machiavelli and the new prince are bound together by the act of teaching: if inventing stable structures is both what Machiavelli does and what he must teach the prince to do, then the very idea of teaching, of giving advice to a prince, must be transformed. To do nothing more than present a series of precepts to be followed and examples to be imitated would be to encourage a passive sort of learning, perhaps adequate for acting in a world ruled by timeless custom, but ill-adapted to the world of changing particulars Machiavelli describes: the more straightforward relations of rule and case found in nonprudential reasoning *can* be practical in appropriate circumstances, but must be ineffectual in the situation that Machiavelli finds himself in. *The Prince* and *The Discourses* are both filled with examples of princes' going wrong by imitating examples; these must alert the prince to the paradoxical nature of the task of learning, through imitation, to become an innovator, and as this chapter proceeds, I will point to different functions this barring of simple imitation has in advancing the argument.[7]

Rather than simply present a series of precepts and examples for the prince to follow, Machiavelli presents an argument in what Bacon calls the probative mode of presenting knowledge, in which knowledge "is delivered and intimated . . . in the same method wherein it was invented."[8] Machiavelli organizes *The Prince* as a narrative imitation of his own activity of inventing a solution to the problem of how to understand and act successfully in a world of change and particularity. The prince becomes an innovator by following Machiavelli's innovative argument, and so that argument itself, rather than the particular examples presented, becomes the principal object of imitation. That argument, explicated in detail in the rest of this chapter, is the only means available to give positive meaning to what I have been calling the more complicated and reflective prudential relations of rule and case. It is easy to say how examples could be the subject of teaching, and equally easy to say how rules could be, but it is far from simple to show how the relation between rule and case could be, and it is the details of Machiavelli's own argument, as an object for imitation, that offer such an understanding. I suggested in the Introduction that the difficulties in articulating prudence often lead to the unstable oscillation between algorithmic and heuristic methods for reasoning practically; that problem appears here as the difficulty in seeing how neither precept nor example, but the relation between them, becomes the object of understanding and imitation. Machiavelli's problem, that is, is to achieve what Sidney sets forth in his *Apology*, and "not only to make a Cyrus, which had been but a particular excellency, as Nature might have done, but to bestow a Cyrus upon the world, to make many Cyruses if they will learn aright, why, and how that maker make him," or, as Rosalie Colie puts it, to employ "rhetorical education, always a model-following enterprise, [and] increasingly stress *structures* as well as styles to be imitated in the humane letters."[9] Sidney's, and Machiavelli's, method for producing many Cyruses has one further affinity with the prudential enterprise I developed above as the contrast of three kinds of rules: recall Aristotle's exposition, in *Poetics* 9, of the way poetry is more serious and more philosophical than history because it grasps more of the universal, thus mediating between philosophy and history, much as prudential rules mediate between universal algorithmics and particular rules of thumb. The rest of this chapter will proceed by giving a reading of *The Prince* as the presentation of an act of invention with Bacon's probative method as its manner of presentation.

Machiavelli begins by classifying states according to a method of division by pairs of contraries; the contraries organize *The Prince* and serve as topics of invention.[10] A state is either a republic or a principality; Machiavelli excludes republics from consideration and then classifies principalities according to how they are acquired. The subject of *The Prince* is how to preserve (*governare e mantenere*) principalities (ch. 2), and the relation between acquisition and preservation — innovation and stability — is the central topic out of which Machiavelli derives his solution for the general problem of stability in a world of particulars. Classifying principalities according to how they are acquired makes the task of the first eleven chapters one of relating the ways of acquiring a state to the ways of preserving it. Consideration of the first two kinds of principalities — hereditary and mixed monarchies — is sufficient to state a problem — not the general prudential problem of how to understand and manage particulars, but a specific problem for thought and action. Hereditary monarchies pose no problem of acquisition and are easy to hold. Inversely, mixed monarchies are difficult to acquire and even more difficult to hold.[11] This is the initial statement of the problem: acquisition and stability seem to be incompatible because the contrast between the first pair of states seems to imply that no regime can be both new and stable.

Machiavelli responds to that difficulty in chapter 3 by contrasting, not a pair of types, but a pair of examples — France and Turkey — and using them to distinguish two kinds of acquired states: those previously ruled by a prince and barons and those ruled by a prince and his servants. The first is, as expected, easy to acquire and difficult to hold, while the second is difficult to acquire and easy to hold. In chapters 4 and 5 he maximizes that distinction into the difference between those states previously ruled by a prince and those that were free: the easier a state is to acquire, the more difficult it is to keep. The argument has advanced beyond the initial difficulty by dissolving the strict relation between ease and difficulty of acquiring and keeping; here is an exhaustive set of four cases of preserving states, distinguished by the four possible combinations of ease and difficulty of acquiring and keeping. In hereditary monarchies there is no action of acquiring, and they are easy to keep; mixed monarchies are as easy to lose as they were to acquire; in states accustomed to rule by another prince, the more difficult they are to acquire the easier they are to keep; in states accustomed to freedom, there are the greatest difficulties of preservation. Consequently we now have a different problem for stable innovation: once all four combinations of difficulty and ease of acquisition and preservation have been laid out, acquiring and keeping appear to be two distinct actions, totally independent of each other. The Prince is supposed to be an education in how to preserve principalities, but the classification of states according to how they are acquired now seems irrelevant to preserving them. And so we have the opposite problem from the one presented in chapters 2 and 3: there, innovation and stability seemed incompatible, while here, they seem independent of each other. But if invention and stability are independent, then innovation can at best put the prince in a position where stability becomes a possibility; innovation cannot itself lead to stability.

Classifying states and exhibiting examples of success and failure have loosened the connection between acquiring and keeping a state, so that a prince who is both new and secure is at least a formal possibility. But stable innovation will remain a bare possibility unless Machiavelli can find some *practical* connection between acquisition and preservation, some stronger connection than innovation's putting a usurper in a position in which stability becomes a possibility. Machiavelli says in chapter 6: "In entirely new principalities, where there is a new prince, one will find more or less difficulty in maintaining them according to the greater or lesser ingenuity (*virtù*) of the one who acquires them . . . he who has trusted less in fortune has held onto his position best." The problem has been formulated in chapters 2–5 by using the topic of acquisition and preservation; it will be solved, in the rest of The Prince, through the topic of virtù and fortuna.

In chapter 6 Machiavelli selects the one formal combination of ease and difficulty of acquisition and preservation that a prospective new prince reading the text would be interested in — the state which is difficult to acquire and easy to maintain — and finds a reason which connects the difficulty of acquisition with the subsequent security. Ability, virtù, appears in *The Prince* first as a practical, causal connective term. If a state has been acquired with difficulty, acquiring it must have required ability, and therefore it will be easy to keep. (In the *Discourses* 1.10, he notes that, with one exception, "the Emperors that succeeded to the throne by inheritance . . . were bad, and those who became Emperors by adoption were all good . . . and when the Empire became hereditary, it came to ruin.") Stable innovation is innovation accomplished with ability.

But while we now have grounds for thinking stable innovation possible, and we have called the cause of stable innovation ability, thus far ability is nothing more than a name: "It matters little," Machiavelli says in the *Discourses* (3.21), "to any general by which of these two systems he proceeds, provided he be a man of sufficient courage and ability [*virtuoso*]" because his reputation and virtù can cancel "all the errors which a general may commit."[12] Locating a problem, putting it in its proper place, and giving it a name does not solve the problem, but simply restates it. Pocock says: "Once Machiavelli begins to speak of [virtù] as a means of the prince's rise to power, *virtù* becomes part of the act of innovation. . . . In short, what has happened is this: Machiavelli's development of the theme of innovation has caused him to employ the concept *virtù* in its purely formal sense of that by which order is imposed upon *fortuna*."[13] The challenge to Machiavelli at this point is to use the concept of ability in a "purely formal sense," stripped of all conventional connotations, without that concept thereby becoming a totally empty and unsatisfactory answer to the question of how stable innovation is possible. The formality of virtù is in fact a double formality: Machiavelli "empties" virtù of its conventional semantic, moral, and intellectual associations in order to substitute a prudential structure for understanding it, but in addition, the resultant virtù is itself a formal capacity, the ability to impose form on matter.[14] The man of virtù cannot be identified by his possession or lack of any of the traditional virtues, but if virtù is simply the ability to innovate, how can Machiavelli avoid trivializing his problem by identifying ability with success?

Throughout *The Prince*, the rhetorical formality that comes from emptying terms of their conventional meanings and associations — a necessary step towards innovation — is dangerously close to the rhetorical vice of verbal eloquence without meaning or substance. Emptying terms of nonformal meanings is, when successful, a central heuristic device; but when it fails, the stylistic surface of formally arranged terms becomes a substitute for meaning, instead of a way of constructing new meaning; discursive prowess becomes "merely verbal." In terms of prudence, Machiavelli's challenge is to explicate virtù in such a way that it becomes an alternative for an ethics of principles without degenerating into an ethics of results. He must find some constraint, and hence some intelligibility, for an ability which sometimes manifests itself in daring and sometimes in caution, sometimes in kindness and sometimes in cruelty. If Machiavelli can succeed in developing a formal meaning for *ability* and thus avoid the danger of empty formalism, Pocock will indeed be right in claiming that Machiavelli's "decision to use the word [*virtù*] in this purely formal way was his act of creative genius."

Machiavelli begins in chapter 7 to show that the distinction between ability and fortune is not a question-begging renaming of the distinction between success and failure by producing the counterexample of Cesare Borgia. Borgia's success shows that "he who does not lay his foundations beforehand may with great abilities do so afterwards, although with great trouble to the architect and danger to the building"; acquisition through fortune does not make preservation impossible, and hence, virtù and success are not synonymous. At this point, the term *ability* is no longer empty of reference — Borgia is a highly detailed example falling under the term — but it is still empty of any meaning that a prince could abstract. (What would a prince do who was trying to act according to the precept, Follow Cesare Borgia's example?)[15] Here then is a perfect case of what I claim for *The Prince* in general: an example functioning not as an instance of a truth already ascertained, but as the means for discovering data and advancing the argument.

Examples which are instantiations of truths already ascertained might initially seem more practical, since they are more closely tied to the usual forms of practical discourse, precept and imitation. The trouble is that Machiavelli has undercut the conditions in which such easy practicality can make sense, and, with it, any easy relation between example and an imitation consequent upon it. Therefore, the case of Borgia is not by itself a solution to the problem of stable innovation; it has served to advance the argument past one danger of empty formalism, and Machiavelli consequently is in a position to return to the methods of verbal formalism to keep the argument going: the initially apparent similarity and the formal contrast between virtù and villainy, considered in chapter 8 of *The Prince*, offers a way of giving virtù more systematic meaning. Acquiring a state through villainy is a *trope* of acquisition through ability. The prince accomplishes it by himself, without the aid of others, but villainy is distinct from virtù because it makes a different proportion between acquisition and preservation. Ability is distinguished from villainy because the actions used in acquiring a state are homogeneous with those used in keeping it.[16]

Machiavelli does not turn immediately to ask about that homogeneity, although it will be the ground of the proportion between acquisition and stability and the way Machiavelli will be able to give meaning to the still empty term *ability*. The drive toward formality moves Machiavelli to follow the demands of symmetry and turn his attention to another trope, producing a formally exhaustive set of possibilities before going on, because it is only through such a formal structure that he can invent new meanings for *virtù* and *security*. If someone acquires a state through ability, he will hold it easily; if someone acquires a state through fortune and the force of others, he will keep it only with difficulty. The trope of ability, villainy, is a mode of acquisition which depends on one's own power but one which makes the state difficult to hold. Therefore, there should be another trope, a case of acquisition through fortune or the power of another, but where the state is easy to keep. This is the civic principality of chapter 9. Because the civic principality is acquired through forces outside the prince, security is possible only if he reverses the relationship of dependence on that most powerful faction which made acquisition possible. Security both after villainy and in the civic principality depends on making the mode of acting in preservation the opposite to that used in acquisition.[17]

At this point in the argument, then, Machiavelli has succeeded in separating virtù from its conventional associations with preexistent duties and proper ways of action; virtù takes its place among four modes of acquisition, and is distinguished from the others by its characteristic proportion of acquisition and preservation.[18] The possibility of reversing such proportions means that not only is virtù not one "case" among others, not to be confined to situations which are difficult to acquire yet easy to maintain, but virtù is not unambiguously one principle of action among others. To the extent that virtù begins to absorb other methods, it is not one way of acting that the prince may choose to follow or not, but instead is on the way to being something any ruler must do; the only question then is whether he does it well or badly. Once again, Machiavelli's "achievement" of formality solves one difficulty at the cost of raising another. What Machiavelli does in these chapters following chapter 6 seems to make things worse. Virtù comes to consume the other possibilities, such that, starting from virtù as one case among others (chs. 1–6), Machiavelli moves from a verbal to an adverbial conception of virtù as he turns from virtù as a case to virtù as a principle, absorbing the contraries of virtù into it in chapters 7–9, so that it will, starting with chapter 12, become a power necessary in any case. Once everything becomes subject to virtù, then the existence of virtù becomes even more unstable: if it is not one method among others, then Machiavelli must find other means to account for it as a method.

Whether the rhetoric of his argument has left nothing but a virtuoso exhibition of the manipulation of empty symbols is the question Machiavelli raises in chapter 10, entitled "How the strength [*vires*] of all principalities should be determined." If virtù is not one method among others, if it is anything more than an unconnected and therefore unstable set of examples, it must be defined by a relation between itself as a mode of action and the circumstances to which it is appropriate. Consequently Machiavelli must ask about the power of the state, and not just the ruler. Whereas in chapters 2–5 the ruler was something external to the state (states were classified by what they were *before* the new prince appeared) and in chapters 6–9 the ruler was one part of the state (states were classified by the *method* of acquisition), here the ruler simply *is* the state, vis-à-vis other rulers and states. But this is not a simple synecdoche between ruler and state—*L'état, c'est moi.* Instead, the ubiquity of virtù shows the maximum power a prince can attain: the most one can hope for is not security in some atemporal sense but the ability to take the field against others, measuring and being measured in turn. We do not yet know how to articulate a method that will describe virtù and account for its power—or indeed know whether such a method is even possible—but at least we can give a political interpretation to virtù as a relation of form and matter and infer that maximal power will mean that all the potentiality of the state is actualized in the adventures of the ruler.

Security and stability are no longer conceived of as a state of rest produced by the process of innovation; stability is the ability to continue the same kind of acts by which the state was acquired. From being a sort of rest after the act of innovation, stability becomes the ability to perform continual acts of innovation. In the Introduction I pointed out that while the results of algorithmic methods are justified by the principles that led to them, and heuristic methods are justified by their successful results, nothing guarantees or in that sense justifies prudential methods or their products. The conclusion of a prudential method is always open to further debate, and so its evaluation is always a comparative judgment—not this conclusion is true and this inference valid, but this conclusion is better than some alternative. In the same way, the strength of a state and the security of its ruler admit only of comparative judgments against competing rulers and states.

There is one exception to the measure of power outlined in chapter 10: in chapter 11, the subject is ecclesiastical monarchies, which, once acquired, do not need to be defended at all ("Costoro soli hanno stati, e non gli defendano"). That such security is not available for secular states bars a hope for eternal security, a security that is something more than being able to use all the resources of the state for one's own benefit. Ecclesiastical monarchy is a case that functions not as an example to be imitated, or even wished for, but as the first in a series of impossible boundary conditions Machiavelli erects to lay out the area in which prudence can function.[19]

But that formulation — stability is continuing innovation — should be troublesome. Continuing innovation sounds like a fair definition of *instability*, and to identify stability with continuing innovation seems to imply that once one innovates and enters the world of becoming, one is never secure, one is constantly subject to the same usurpatious possibilities that one exploited oneself. What, one could well ask, is stable about continually being ready to go to war? Moreover, the identification of stability and innovation makes doubtful the utility of this book. If the discovery of the first eleven chapters is the purely formal maxim Make everything a function of oneself as much as possible, then *The Prince* cannot be of use. Epictetus, after all, used the same maxim to derive a rather different picture of how to act.

Redefining stability as a kind of innovation instead of as an escape from the world of innovation is a problem for both Machiavelli and the prince. For Machiavelli, it is the problem of redefining the idea of useful advice, eschewing the kind of moralizing Machiavelli is notorious for avoiding, while at the same time saying something more useful than the abstract opportunism of "Make the best of your situation." For the prince, inventing security is the problem of not only acting powerfully but acting to become powerful. For both, deriving stability from innovation is the only way of making good action, defined neither as action according to the right rules nor as whatever action happens to succeed, a practically useless idea. Machiavelli shows the prince how to avoid the world of continuing flux and instability by giving the identity of stability and innovation a different interpretation. Instead of reading that identity as meaning that preserving the new state is a continually unstable business, he shows how innovation is a paradigm case of acting securely. When neither the heady expansion of the possibilities of action suggested by the preface, and nominated as virtù, nor the recourse to withdrawal or the hope for a situation in which action is unnecessary, is a serious option, then the possibility for method becomes a live one.

And so Machiavelli turns to general resources for action in chapter 12. He is able to make innovation into the central kind of stability, and to distinguish continuing innovation from continuing insecurity, by turning, in this chapter, from the various particular kinds of state (classified by how they are acquired) to general methods for preserving the state.[20] The topic which advances the argument is the distinction between acting in general and acting with respect to the foundations of the prince's power. If Machiavelli can find general methods for making secure the sources of power, then equating innovation and preservation will no longer doom the prince to the world of constant flux, and no longer leave the prince with the useless advice to make everything depend on himself.[21]

Therefore, the problem of inventing stabilities and giving content to Machiavelli's advice is the problem of finding material that can be the foundation of power and of finding appropriate ways of controlling that material. Machiavelli sees two sources of power for the prince — his army and his people; a third possible source of power, laws, is discarded as epiphenomenal: "There cannot be good laws where good armies are lacking, and where there are good armies there must be good laws." For both arms and the people, the prince's problem takes the same form: he must derive power from a source outside himself and keep control over it at the same time. He could, thus, win particular victories by means of an army, only to become its slave. He could keep power most easily over a weak army; the problem is to keep control over a strong army. And similarly with the people: one can become a prince, or survive any particular crisis in maintaining oneself as prince, by means of the people, if one is willing to become their slave. The prince can keep power over them most easily if they are weak; maintaining power over a strong people is a problem. In both cases, general methods for making secure the sources of power involve confronting that dilemma.[22] (As I suggested in the Introduction, Machiavelli's problem resembles the traditional one rhetorical theory and practice had to face: how a speaker can be successful without simply telling the people what they want to hear. Socrates raises a similar difficulty in the Gorgias, when he claims that rhetoric, and the political practice based on it, is nothing but a form of flattery. Socrates, though, seeks to distinguish flattery from mutuality and cooperative pursuit of the good, while Machiavelli is interested in ruling, not in reciprocity and equality.)

The formal treatment of virtù threatens to become an empty formalism, a possibility Machiavelli has already noted in chapter 6, where virtù seemed to act on prime matter: "Examining their lives and actions, we see that from fortune they received nothing but the occasion; which in turn offered them the material they could then shape into whatever form they pleased." The search in chapters 12–23 is for kinds of material that will be more than prime matter, and armies and citizens will be sources of power exactly because they are not prime matter but have properties, and power, of their own, whereas the objective of flattering rhetoric is to eliminate the active properties of one's material.[23]

The Prince: *A Neglected Rhetorical Classic*

Like Socrates, Machiavelli frames the problem of good rhetoric as getting others to do what you think is best, and thereby strengthening them; for both, it is a bad rhetoric and a bad politics that would consist in either doing what the people want and telling them what they want to hear—the possibility Socrates dismisses as flattery, and Machiavelli, as the prince's self-destructive endeavor to be loved—or enslaving them, with the ruler doing all the deliberating and the people merely executing commands. In Plato, this is the Sophists' own delusive picture of what they are aiming at, while Machiavelli's tyrant shortsightedly suffers from the same delusion and aims at victories in ways that neglect his foundation of power in the people. But there are, of course, evident differences between Plato and Machiavelli. Socrates asserts that it is better to be treated unjustly than to act unjustly, and, while Machiavelli might agree with Socrates that acting justly is better still, he clearly would prefer doing wrong to having wrong done to him. Unlike Socrates, Machiavelli thinks that the choice between those two alternatives is the normal course of things (Socrates' withdrawal from politics having no appeal), and so the educative, corrective function of Machiavelli's princely rhetoric is tempered, and becomes, Get the people to do what you want; within that goal, it is better, when possible, to do so in ways that benefit them, since that increases the strength you can draw from them subsequently. In the long run, the best way to get people to do what you want is to get them to want to do it.

The only way to use arms to make one's power secure is to use one's own arms. In chapter 12 we find that any other form of armed force is either useless or harmful. Simple success or failure in an immediate crisis is not the criterion for effective action, for action leading to stability; on the contrary, the source of power is the criterion of success and failure. Win or lose, mercenaries decrease the prince's power of acting. Security here, then, is not defined as the result of action, and it is never eternal, complete, beyond the possibility of reversal; security is defined by the method of achieving it, and in doing one's best with the available resources. To this extent military affairs are rhetoricized, in that strength and stability cannot be defined independent of the methods that bring them about; rhetoric as a method of practical reason makes one redefine goals and ends at least partly in terms of the actions that bring them about. Chapters 12–23 are about the way one's eye must *not* always be upon immediate dangers, since auxiliary troops often save one from immediate danger, but are not to be chosen on that account. Machiavelli has set himself the task of finding stability in activity, a task that involves a redefinition of security.[24]

Machiavelli redefines security by finding general methods for securing the sources of power, and he finds those general methods by his usual stylistic device of presenting a series of dichotomous divisions. Since the foundation of the prince's power is in his army, the general methods for making himself secure must all lead to powerful and secure armed forces. The prince must know how to direct his troops, and he must have strong and secure troops to direct. And to direct his troops, the prince must be able to do two things: he must know the successes and failures recounted in history, and he must be able to perceive the strategic possibilities in any given situation. Machiavelli simply tells the prince, in chapter 14, that he must acquire these skills through study and practice and then leaves the subject without further instructions. More specific instructions would be superfluous, since *The Prince* as a whole is designed to teach how to use examples of the past and circumstances of the present as data for intelligent decisions.[25]

In addition to knowing how to organize his troops in battle, the prince must have troops to organize, and in chapters 15–21 Machiavelli is far more specific in confronting the question of how a prince can make his subjects into a stable source of power; specificity comes from the topics of epideitic rhetoric, "those things for which men, and especially princes, are praised or blamed." Praise and blame have the same place in the prince's relations to his subjects that military success and failure had in his relations with other states. Praise and success are preferable to blame and failure, but are not on that account to become the objects of choice for the prince:

> All men . . . and especially princes . . . are judged by some of these
> qualities which bring them blame or praise. And this is why some
> are considered to be generous, others stingy . . . ; some are con-
> sidered givers, others graspers, some cruel, others merciful, one
> treacherous, another faithful; one effeminate and cowardly, another
> vigorous and courageous; one friendly, another haughty; one man
> lascivious, another pure; one sincere, another cunning . . . and the
> like. And I know everyone will agree that it would be a very praise-
> worthy thing to find in a prince all of the qualities mentioned above
> that are considered good; but since it is impossible to have and ob-
> serve all of them, for human nature [*le condizione umane*] does not
> allow it, the prince must be prudent enough to know how to escape
> the infamy of those vices that would lose him the state. (Ch. 15)

In chapters 12 and 13 the object of wish was military success, but if it was chosen *simpliciter*, that goal was likely to lead the prince to ruin; liberality and mercy, similarly, are to be wished for, are desirable ways of acting, but they are not *therefore* automatically chosen. To the extent that Machiavelli is here teaching an *art* of stable innovation, the new prince's deviations from traditional morality fall under Aristotle's remark that in art, intentional error is to be preferred to unintentional, because the precepts of art can always be overridden by the demands of particular situations. (As we shall see, to the extent that the subject of Machiavelli's teaching is prudence rather than art, such overriding becomes a much more unstable phenomenon.) Instead of traditional virtues and short-term military victories dictating how one should act, the extent to which the prince can safely choose actions that aim at military success and actions that are praiseworthy is the best measure of his security. In general, although virtù is the power to act successfully, far from being defined by its success, virtù, and power, are defined by the modes of action elaborated in these chapters.

Like Aristotle, Machiavelli encounters a reflexive problem about prudence: prudence requires that one be responsive to shifting circumstances without thereby being passive to them, and the reflective articulation of the principles and materials for prudence also requires that the writer find some middle ground between too much universality — the superfluous and ineffectual proclamation of moralizing principles — and too much particularity — which leads to situation ethics or the slavish imitation of past models, a kind of prudence measured only by a success that comes too late to do any measuring. Aristotle finds a solution to this problem in the practical equivalent of natural species, *kinds* of actions, particular moral virtues, rather than either universal principles or individual acts. In the *Ethics* the moral virtues function as species and give an anchoring to other prudent acts, which might fall under prudence without falling under any practical equivalent of a natural kind, while in the *Rhetoric* he stakes out kinds of rhetoric tied to institutional settings and particular goals, particular kinds of successful persuasion. In Machiavelli, the solution consists instead in the use of rhetorical topics to formalize situations into the rhetorical equivalent of kinds, types of cases or issues, whose identity consists in the sort of argument appropriate to them. The particular emotions treated in chapters 15–21 are selected from the whole field of possible emotions because only they permit consistent argumentative treatment, consistency being supplied by the topics that organize the text. These emotions permit Machiavelli the right amount of specificity that will avoid both the moralizing he rejects in chapter 15 and the great examples whose edifying value he has questioned in the first eleven chapters.

Before displaying in more detail Machiavelli's use of rhetorical topics to construct more stable emotional ties between ruler and ruled, I think it worth digressing briefly to show why he rejects moralizing, which could be defined as thinking that because something is good, it ought to be done. It should no longer be sufficient simply to say that Machiavelli rejects moralizing because Machiavelli is Machiavellian.

Such moralizing is in a quite specific sense ideological, if ideology is defined as the use of algorithmic reason to govern practical affairs, the replacement of prudence and practical reasoning by the application of principles to cases.[26] Machiavelli attacks the rulers of his time for being ideological, for thinking that since their values are unexceptionable, all that successful action requires is embodying those values; right action is easy to perform, since all it takes is wanting to do it. His attack, in chapter 15, on algorithmic political language for ignoring the way people really are — there is "such a difference between how men live and how they ought to live that he who abandons what is done for what ought to be done learns his destruction rather than his preservation" — is an emblem of his more general strategy in *The Prince* as a whole, of attacking the traditional politics that constitutes the practical counterpart of such theory, the impotent rulers who think they inhabit the world described in those theories and convince their subjects that they live there too. He accuses contemporary rulers of misconceiving the relation between universal values and particular actions as algorithmic or ideological rather than prudential, and identifies that misconception as the cause of their impotence and corruption.[27] Machiavelli's topical connections between values and actions constitute his strategy for avoiding not only the simple-minded ideological connections that have led to impotence, but also the natural response in the privatizing of effective action and, with it, the modern separation of ethics and politics. Just as, dialectically, the perceived failure of algorithmic thinking often leads to heuristics, so, rhetorically, the perceived failure of ideological politics leads both to a corrupt politics of force and also to the carving out of private areas of reserved power where nonideological action can flourish and further weaken the state.

To return to the movement of the argument of *The Prince*, since the attitudes of his subjects are the source of the prince's power, Machiavelli spends chapters 16–21 finding ways in which those attitudes can be stabilized. He takes the topics that constitute the three traditional kinds of rhetoric, distinguished by their ends — the useful, the honorable, and the just — and uses each to locate a pair of opposite possible actions by the prince. With respect to the goods associated with money, the prince can be liberal or parsimonious; with respect to the honorable, a prince can be compassionate or cruel, lovable or frightening; with respect to his own promises, he can be faithful or not. Each of those alternatives can sometimes be useful and sometimes not; therefore each calls for prudence on the part of the prince; prudence consists in using examples and precepts to find stability in this, as in any other, field of variability. Prudence guides the prince by directing him to those connections of ruler and subject that are within his control, and chapter 17 ends: "Men love at their own pleasure, but fear at the pleasure of the prince; a wise prince should build his foundation on what is his own, not on what belongs to others."

The Prince: *A Neglected Rhetorical Classic*

Once more, Machiavelli is faced with the problem of how to give useful advice, how to say something specific about the world of constant change, making success depend on prudence instead of defining prudence — after the fact — as whatever leads to success. As in other moments of difficulty in the argument, the rhetorical topics of discovery become central here. Each of the topics represented by a pair of actions in chapters 16, 17, and 18 can be generalized into more concise, definite precepts, and so he begins chapter 19: "But now that I have talked about the most important of the qualities mentioned above, I would like to discuss the others briefly in this general way [*queste generalità*]." The ends of the three kinds of rhetoric — the useful, the honorable, and the just — are generalized into the three commonplaces that organize all of rhetoric — the audience, the thing spoken about, and the speaker. There is, first, one connection between the prince and his subjects that should always be avoided: that relation where the prince is hated and disdained (p. 153). No matter how a prince acts, hatred and disdain will cause his downfall because they are the two emotions which inevitably separate the prince from his subjects, his sources of power: "Whoever reflects on the discourse written above will see that either hatred or disdain was the cause of the downfall of the emperors mentioned earlier; and he will also understand how it comes about that, though some acted in one way and some in a contrary way, whatever the way they acted, one came to a prosperous, the others to an unprosperous end" (ch. 19, p. 171). Aristotle introduces his treatment of the emotions in book 2 of the *Rhetoric* by saying that the speaker must understand them in order to produce the goodwill and friendship (εὐνοία καὶ φιλία) that bind audience to speaker, showing that the speaker is on the side of the audience and to be followed and trusted (2.1.1378a23): hatred and disdain are emotions of separation between speaker and audience rather than of affiliation or identification.

Second, fortresses and possible sources of power distinct from both the prince and his subjects are things which sometimes cause security and sometimes insecurity; the one definite assertion possible is that if material things are taken as a substitute for action they will cause the prince's downfall. To the extent that the prince relies on them, they cause a disconnection between the prince and his real source of power, the people: "I shall commend him who builds fortresses and him who does not build them; and I shall reproach any one who, placing his trust in fortresses, places little value in being hated by the people" (p. 183). The categorical nature of Machiavelli's condemnation of reliance on fortresses is represented in the *Discourses* by the way he turns, in a highly uncharacteristic manner, to direct address: "I will discuss this subject in a more familiar manner. Prince or republic, you would either keep the people of your own city in check by means of fortresses, or you wish to hold a city that has been taken in war. I shall turn to the prince and say to him that 'nothing can be more useless than such a fortress for keeping your own citizens in check'" (2.24.364).

Finally, after stating precepts about the people and about fortresses, Machiavelli can say something about how the prince himself can act to become secure. The consequences of actions are unpredictable and hence not a source of security, but continually doing great things and getting "fame for being great and excellent" is always useful, and indeed always the most useful of things. Doing glorious things is the solution to the problem of how to make the people depend on the prince without weakening them, and hence is his most secure source of power. Instead of proving to the people that you are on their side—the point of Aristotle's goodwill and friendship—always acting nobly and gloriously makes the people want to be on your side, makes them want to become followers.[28]

Chapters 22 and 23 treat the prince's ministers and flatterers in just the same way that chapters 12–14 dealt with the armed forces and 15–21, with the prince's subjects. The prince must avoid becoming dependent on ministers; he must make them dependent on him without thereby weakening them. He must ensure their loyalty, make them act for his advantage and not for theirs (ch. 22), and he must compel them to speak truly and not as they suppose he wants to hear (ch. 23). When the prince succeeds in reversing the relations of dependence, "we may say that the prudence of the prince does not come from the advice given him but, on the contrary, good advice whatever be its immediate source, has its true origin in the wisdom of the prince" (p. 204). What these chapters mean for the relation between the prince and the author of *The Prince*, and consequently for how this text is to be read and, more generally, for the role accorded to practical intelligence, will have to be considered in detail in subsequent chapters.

Throughout chapters 12–23 Machiavelli has been presenting general methods for making innovations secure. Throughout, his problem has taken a single form, while the content has varied from armies through citizens to ministers. Formally, the problem has been to make specific and practical the apparent conclusion of the first eleven chapters, that stable innovation comes from the prince's depending on nothing outside himself, his making everything as much as possible a function of his own action. Giving content to that formal conclusion has meant finding ways for the prince to make himself secure by making something outside himself dependent on him without weakening it. How to make the army strong without becoming its slave, how to be supported by the people without being dependent on them, how to have servants of independent mind dependent on him—

these are the specific ways Machiavelli treats the problem of how an innovator can be secure, and with it, the more general problem of how to
organize and make intelligible changing particulars. The problem throughout
those chapters is one of finding suitable material for the formal operations of innovation. Since Aristotle, rhetoricians have distinguished between supplies of ready-made arguments, "composed beforehand and laid up for use," and the faculty of inventing arguments in a
given situation.[29] Were the prince acting in a stable world of traditional
rulers, subjects who did not question their customary rulers, and other
states whose resources and ambitions were similarly fixed, ready-made
modes of action would suffice; since neither the prince nor the world in
which he operates have that kind of stability, the prince needs the ability
to construct, to invent, relations to other states, his army, his citizens and
ministers, instead of presupposing such relations. It is this ability that
Machiavelli offers him in chapters 12–23.

Integrating the last three chapters of *The Prince* with the rest of the argument has always been difficult for commentators; the reason for the difficulty should now be apparent. The argument of the first twenty-three
chapters has been one whose formality I have tried to stress. That formality has three related functions: (1) to dissociate the key terms, *virtù*
and *fortuna*, innovation and stability, from their conventional connotations in order to state and solve the problem of stable innovation; (2) to
invent and explore exhaustive sets of possibilities, in order to give a systematic unity to the argument; and (3) to structure the techniques that the
prince is learning, making a series of examples and precepts into a systematized art, which gives technical meaning to *virtù* and *fortuna*, innovation
and stability, and thereby gives autonomy, self-rule, to the prince. That
formality has made the argument of *The Prince* into one of increasing
generality; at each stage the generalization is motivated by the need to keep
the formality from degenerating into useless display oratory. Thus, to re-
capitulate, the first chapters gave examples and maxims that were hypothetical, tied to some supposed specific situations of acquisition. Machiavelli then discusses general methods of acquisition and preservation useful
in all situations. Within the special cases of chapters 1–11, he first takes
the kinds of states prior to acquisition (chs. 2–5), and then generalizes to
the modes of acquiring states (chs. 6–11). Within the general methods of
chapters 12–23, he first deals with the proper places of the useful, the honorable, and the just, and then generalizes to the topics of things always

dangerous, sometimes useful and sometimes dangerous, and always useful for further action. At each stage in the argument, it is the hypothetical character of the precepts, their dependence on the supposed situation, which makes the utility of the advice questionable and which is thus the motive force behind the advance of the argument. At each stage, unless the argument continued, Machiavelli's advice to the prince would have been, "Do your best." *The Prince*, however, ends with three chapters that establish propositions differing from those of the preceding chapters. Instead of being hypothetical, the propositions of the last three chapters are assertoric: they make assertions that are not conditioned by any hypothetical situation. Machiavelli's invention is finished; the last three chapters are a judgment, a comparison of Machiavelli's accomplishment with what he started with.[30]

Chapter 24 begins by comparing the new kind of stability that is a function of an art of innovation with the traditional meaning of stability: a new prince who prudently observes the "things mentioned above" becomes more secure than one who derives his security from tradition. The fact that the new prince is more closely observed seemed at first to be a source of insecurity, but now it can become a source of stability: "When [his actions] are recognized as good actions, they win men over and hold them in allegiance much better than ancient blood" (p. 205).[31] The princes who have lost their states have trusted to tradition and now blame fortune, but their trouble is failing to recognize that "those methods alone are good, are certain, are lasting, that depend on you yourself and on your *virtù*" (p. 207).

The first step towards completing the education of the prince has been to compare the new, technical meaning of stability with the traditional one. The next step is to compare old and new meanings for *fortuna*, old and new relations between fortuna and virtù. The conventional meaning of *fortune* is an external cause outside our control: with the new meaning that depends on the art of innovation, fortune has become matter for the prince's form. The title of chapter 25 has two parts: "How much fortune can do in human affairs and how to contend with it." Asking for a metaphorically quantitative answer to the question raised in the first half of the title shows that fortune is taken as good or bad luck, an external cause to be "weighed" against ability as an internal cause, while asking how to contend with it is asking how to treat fortune as material to be used by virtù. Knowing how to contend with fortune cannot be a knowledge tied to particular situations: one cannot know the details of the operations of fortune until too late; hence, no one can be wise enough to adapt to changes in fortune. The answer to the question posed in the title to this chapter is, accordingly, the first assertoric imperative: "It is better to be impetuous than cautious, because fortune is a woman" (p. 215).[32]

Finally, completing the education of the prince with a rather difficult and comprehensive examination is the exhortation to liberate and unify Italy. Like any good final examination, it is a test both of the teacher and of the student. Less dramatically, it is a test of whether the art of constructing novel stabilities is possible; nothing could be a harder test, but for that reason no other success could give stronger evidence that it was due to an ability founded in art rather than to fortune.[33] Chapter 26 has always seemed *ad hoc*, not truly of a piece with the rest of the argument, but its difference in tone and apparent disjunction from the rest of the text ought to provoke questions about the relations between discourse and action, between intellectual and practical success. *The Prince*, as I have analyzed it, promises to teach prudence through imitation of Machiavelli's argument itself, but the typical reader's reaction to the last chapter should serve effectively to provoke questions of whether the abilities the prince can acquire in this way enable merely discursive success or practical power in a more general sense.

2 DISCURSIVE VIRTUOSITY AND

PRACTICAL VIRTÙ

My first chapter shows how Machiavelli uses rhetoric to articulate the possibility of stable innovation and prudence, and shows how crucial aspects of his argument are invisible when one neglects his rhetorical techniques. Pocock, Mazzeo, and McCanles, for example, have stressed the formality of virtù, but the formality they attribute to *The Prince* is not as systematic and thorough a formality as the one I have elaborated, and so is easier to dismiss as merely stylistic and not touching on the heart of Machiavelli's project. The literature on imitation and the use of examples in the Renaissance is voluminous, but the availability of acknowledged methods of imitation threatens to trivialize the problem of prudence and autonomy by making them susceptible to purely discursive, even stylistic, solution.

Each of those two insights, into reflective imitation and into the formality of *The Prince*, requires further inquiry and a consideration of rhetoric as something more than a series of techniques for verbal and argumentative manipulation. While my exhibition of Machiavelli's argument should have put beyond doubt its formal qualities — completeness, elegance, architectural solidity — to attach a practical rather than aesthetic value to those qualities should not be conceded without further argument. (The topic of the practical and the aesthetic is one whose variations require, and will later receive, attention, in Chapter 4. Similarly, the analysis of Chapter 1 contends that the new prince must imitate Machiavelli's discursive practices, translating an argumentative, text-generating, and text-interpreting prudence into a prudence connected with deeds beyond words, moving from the intellectual project Pocock describes as "rendering the particular intelligible" to the prince's innovation of a new state to render "political actions viable and political structures stable in time."[1] But such translation depends crucially on the conversion of Machiavelli's rhetorical techniques for imposing literary form on matter into methods for imposing virtù on fortuna, and that is a gap whose enormity must not be minimized.

That imitation is a principle of education both in acquisition of verbal style and in learning how to act is a Renaissance commonplace.[2] But regardless of how common it was in the Renaissance, a too easy inference from verbal fluency to practical intelligence must be resisted: not only is it inherently implausible that something as difficult as seizing a state, or, tougher still, establishing stable rule over a powerful and resistant people, could be won as simply as acquiring a style of discourse, but the ethical and intellectual objections cut deeper.[3] The project of imitating great examples is undermined by Machiavelli's strategies of presenting contradictory examples, and examples of contradictions, but a fairly simple meaning of imitation could still be saved by a more penetrating analysis of just what in the great should be imitated: it is rare that people have thought that imitating Christ requires trying to walk on water, and Machiavelli's exhibition of contradictions could be taken as stimulus to finding stable principles of greatness beneath those contradictory appearances.

But in Machiavelli's case these dissonances between and within examples point to a deeper problem when the object of imitation is virtù: imitating the great deeds and heroes means becoming like them, but the contradictory recipes for success and failure leave nothing for the new prince to become "like." The exemplars of virtù did not proceed by imitation, so how could Machiavelli's reader acquire it through imitation? Not for the first time, Machiavelli's response to this difficulty seems to make things worse:

> Not altogether able to stay on the path of others nor arrive at the ingenuity [virtù] of those they imitate, a prudent man should always take the path trodden by great men and imitate those who have been most outstanding, so that, if his own ingenuity does not come up to theirs, at least it will have the smell of it; and he should act like those prudent archers, who when the target they are aiming at seems too far off, aware of the capacity of their bow, set their sight a good deal higher than the desired target, not to reach such a height with their arrow but rather to be able, with the help of aiming high, to reach their target. (Ch. 6)

The archery metaphor, drawn from a very old commonplace, is incompatible with the idea of imitation, and consequently must leave one wondering how to imitate, or to aim at, Cyrus, Romulus, Theseus, and Moses. (Indeed, instead of imitation, the metaphor seems to enjoin self-deception.) The trouble with acquiring a tinge of greatness, as Machiavelli says in the passage quoted above, is that the result is most unlike its exemplar; when Machiavelli substitutes the imitation of his argument for imitating individual examples, he forbids the outcome of imitation to be "like" the thing imitated, but at the cost of creating new problems of imitation, problems symbolized at the beginning of the *Protagoras* when Hippocrates wants enthusiastically to learn eloquence, and therefore political power, from the Sophists, but is embarrassed at Socrates' suggestion that if he learns from them, he will become a Sophist himself. The prince must develop some prudential powers in reading and interpreting *The Prince*, but needs a different sort of prudence to acquire and keep a state.[4]

Such an extension of the realm of rhetoric beyond verbal devices and their effects threatens to trivialize the problem of prudence by making it amenable to a purely intellectual or discursive solution. The danger of trivialization will take different forms as the argument proceeds, but here it is worth noting one feature of Aristotle's rich distinction between rhetoric and the sciences: "But in proportion as anyone endeavours to make of Dialectic or Rhetoric, not what they are, faculties, but sciences, to that extent he will, without knowing it, destroy their real nature, in thus altering their character, by crossing over into the domain of sciences, whose subjects are certain definite things, not merely words [ὑποκειμένων τινῶν πραγμάτων, 'αλλὰ μὴ μόνον λόγων]" (*Rhetoric* 1.4.1359b18f). Aristotle's distinction between words and things is no eternal prohibition against rhetorical manipulation of "definite things," but it does mark one of the obvious apparent differences between arts of words and methods of practical achievement: words are manipulable, through rhetoric, while facts are usually taken to be just those things that are not subject to such easy manipulation but have some large measure of recalcitrance about them. Machiavelli is interested precisely in manipulating the facts, but we need to be mindful about the seriousness of such a project.

The difference between the recalcitrance of language to stylish virtuosity and the recalcitrance of other sorts of manipulable, resistant material — other men's passions and actions, one's own *persona* and character, even the external world generally that Machiavelli personifies as Fortuna — to persuasive virtù suggests the need for more extended treatment. (To recall the parallel I drew initially between Machiavelli and Descartes, the easy manipulability of language is grounds for Descartes to separate arts of words from a method for the sciences by constructing a mathematical method that, unlike many more recent variants, is not one of symbolic manipulation, and to restrict as much as possible the material on which the method can operate.) Machiavelli must present the transition from verbal to practical imitation as a glorious task, and not minimize its difficulties, but he cannot make either his success or the prince's depend on extended philosophical reflection.

Where Machiavelli directly presents both the difficulty and the possibility of glory, my task of providing a full view of the presuppositions and implications of his project, placing it in a history of prudence, does demand a more reflective argument. All the central claims I have been making about imitation, his enjoining the imitation of argument rather than individual *exempla*, his offering the use of examples for reflective consideration and practice in prudential judgment, are easy to state negatively: one must not imitate examples slavishly, not assume that because human nature does not change, what once worked will work again. But it is difficult to explicate a positive side to those counsels of avoidance, and therefore the theme of the relations between principles and cases becomes focal as the argument proceeds. Without pushing the argument farther, the Machiavellian development of prudence would fall back on the commonplace contrast between simple-minded and reflective examples and imitation, which defines reflection negatively and incompletely, and suggests that the alternatives are either rules instantiated by cases or cases standing alone, once again reviving algorithmics and heuristics as an exhaustive distinction. Even Bacon—whose account of the probative method I earlier cited because it captures Machiavelli's construction of an argument as object for imitation—falls back into taking as exhaustive the distinction between two possible relations between example and argument: "It hath much greater life for practice when the discourse attendeth upon the example, than when the example attendeth upon the discourse."[5] But that latter alternative is not Machiavelli's, and so the imitation he recommends is not like the uncontrolled meditation on emblems. The assumption that either cases or rules must govern, common as it is, plays into the hands of the traditional rulers and their intellectual defenders, since it usually follows that the only alternative to action as the exemplification of approved principles is action whose rationale comes from its successful consequences rather than its valued principles. There is nothing remarkable about wanting to avoid that dichotomy, but there is something unusual about Machiavelli's strategies for doing so. Instead of directing attention to either principle or consequence, Machiavelli focuses on the relations between rule and case, and on the *acts*—discursive or not—of bringing rules and cases together. Making connections between rules and cases are the prudent acts presented for imitation in *The Prince*; and for just that reason its argument is itself, for both Machiavelli and the new prince, an instance of prudence. Nevertheless, it remains difficult to understand more precisely the connections between prudent discursive acts and prudence more generally.

Consideration of Machiavelli deepens our understanding of the relation between verbal decorum and practical intelligence, makes the commonplace alliance between stylistic decorum and practical appropriateness into a topic for invention, because he on the one hand prevents the simple interpretation of verbal imitation and eloquence substituting for practical habituation and efficacy,[6] and on the other makes it possible to take more seriously the possibility that *in this case* there is a verbal object whose imitation does afford instruction in practical abilities worth acquiring. The example of *The Prince* permits us to sidestep more general arguments

Discursive Virtuosity and Practical Virtù

about the relation between discursive virtuosity and practical virtù, literary and ethical decorum, to raise the more particular question that will occupy us in the ensuing chapters: What does it take to construct a verbal object whose imitation would induce practical prudence and not just verbal decorum? The strategy of my first chapter has been to use the stylistic surface of *The Prince* as evidence for the more practical dimensions of rhetoric and prudence; continuing that strategy here would invert my question into, Why should Machiavelli present the surface he does, of contradictions both within and among examples? What does that surface have to do with the purpose I imputed to him — teaching prudence?

Because prudence consists in a reflective and problematic relation between rules and cases, Machiavelli must not just tell the prince, Be wise, avoid imitating too mechanically and stupidly, but must replace such exhortation with something that is itself an act of prudence, which an exhortation certainly is not. Other writers in other times may have thought themselves entitled to show what prudence is and even teach it by more direct and straightforward modes of discourse, but Machiavelli has undercut the conditions that would make that easy enterprise possible. (He will return to consider the possibility of restoring such conditions in the *Discourses*.) The new prince must aim at innovation, at autonomy, at finding stability *within* flux. He could not find rest within individual examples or maxims without becoming as conservative as the old rulers, and then his role — being other than a hereditary monarch — would contradict his moving smoothly in established grooves. Instead he must imitate Machiavelli's argument, because it is an instance of finding stability within flux, generating a stable, intelligible argumentative structure within shifting particulars. *The Prince* teaches prudence by presenting its own argument as an example of prudent action which forces the reader to engage in a prudential activity: the argument of *The Prince* is itself an articulate and accessible example of what it would mean to combine flexibility and continuity, to make practical intelligence responsive to circumstances. And to do that, Machiavelli must also problematize the relations between discursive and practical imitation — and between writer and reader, between reader *qua* reader with his illocutionary uptake and reader *qua* ruler with the work's perlocutionary effects — lest the imitation of an argument create too easy a homology between discourse and action. Instead of having either rules or cases to live up to or imitate, Machiavelli offers only the relation between rule and case, the prudential relations found in acts such as reading the past and applying knowledge to action, and in terms such as *judgment, tact, decorum,* and *taste.*

Making the connection between rule and case into the object of imitation accounts for the sort of formality so evident in the stylizations and the innovative purposes of the text. The formal conception of virtù, recall, begins as one case among others, one formal relation between acquisition and preservation. Machiavelli then appears to make virtù not a case but a principle, that which lies behind success in almost any practical situation. That result was not obviously satisfying, though, because Machiavelli shows that there is no single mode of action always characteristic of virtù. Consequently Machiavelli carries the argument a step further, and turns to an analysis of virtù as an ability to organize appropriate material — the most formal conception possible. The sense in which virtù is and is not one method among others will point to a deeper problem requiring examination in the next chapter, and ultimately is a function of the paradox at the heart of the Machiavellian project, the paradox of an art of prudence, the attempt to make virtù and hence potent political action subject to an ability or technique.

I think that the way to advance the argument and develop a better understanding of prudence, and in particular the extradiscursive action that can be the result of the prudent imitation of *The Prince*, is to notice that in a crucial sense, my analysis to this point has been unrhetorical: while stressing Machiavelli's use of rhetorical techniques and his rhetorical purpose of aiming at stable innovation, I have temporarily bracketed the fact that this text has an author and some readers, a purpose and an intended effect. In the same way, my introductory exposition of three kinds of rules was dialectical, not rhetorical, since it abstracted the relations of rule and case from the political functions and practical strategies connected to choices among the kinds of method. We can avoid making writing and reading into prudent activities in too easy a fashion by raising questions about the relation between what is said and what is talked about, between what is said and the fact that it is said.

I am not asserting that these questions must be asked because of some general thesis about the nature of rhetoric; Machiavelli forces these questions on the reader by constructing a dissonance among alternative purposes and audiences. There is no easy way to reconcile the explicit motive, the stated intention, and whatever one could reasonably ascribe as an intended effect. He offers as a motive a goal I find it hard to take seriously: getting his job back. The preface ends: "And if Your Magnificence from the summit of his high position will at some time move his eyes toward these lowlands, he will know to what extent I unjustly endure the great and continuous maleficence of fortune." His stated intention is to present the great examples of the past; how to measure its accomplishment should now appear more problematic than it may have seemed initially. And finally, there is some sort of anticipated effect—just what it is, is something that we will have to work out—on the unspecified wider public who may be expected to read the work. There are a number of ways of responding to such dissonances. As I suggested above, many commentators too quickly take the easy way out and put them down to hesitations and confusions in the mind of the author. A more sophisticated response, and one more grounded in Renaissance practices of creating meaning through indirection, would be to distinguish a public from a hidden teaching for the text. Machiavelli, though, refuses to separate what the prince is supposed to make of the text from how the unspecified wider audience is to interpret it, refuses to allow an interpretation that finds two meanings and attributes them to what just happens to be a single expression in *The Prince*, as though Machiavelli could have written two texts to express his two messages, but just happened to write a single one that does double duty. *The Prince* is not a secret teaching available only to the prince but not his subjects, nor is what the prince is to learn from it simply identical to its intended effect on a wider audience, in the way the straightforward moralizing of earlier Mirrors for Magistrates could afford to be. Aristotle points out that the means a speaker uses to present a certain character are just what he uses to understand and manipulate the character of his audience (*Rhetoric* 2.1.1378a15f); along those lines, the production/reception distinction, the contrast between a rhetoric of speaking persuasively and one of interpretation and criticism unmasking the pretenses of opponents, becomes unstable because Machiavelli must teach the prince to speak by teaching the audience to read, forcing his readers to engage with Machiavelli in a cooperative performance.

Most critically, Machiavelli's treatment of the emotional ties between ruler and ruled presents resources available, in different ways, to both ruler and ruled.[7] Consequently we will be able to understand how this text can reasonably be thought to aim at extradiscursive practicality by looking more closely at its rhetorical properties as a text, connecting what the text says not only with how it is said but with the fact that it is said, connecting text to possible authors and readers.[8]

The most common sign of misreading, which will point by negation to what it means to read Machiavelli prudently, is a reading that sees Machiavelli's texts upholding a new set of values rather than focusing on the connection between values and action. As we have seen, the more seriously one tries to limit oneself to such a doctrinal surface, the less solid that surface appears, not because of sloppiness or hesitation on Machiavelli's part, and not because he is saying one thing to the prince and another to potential subjects, but because Machiavelli wants to insure that his new politics not be taken as a new ideology replacing the old, with a new set of heroes to imitate, a new set of duties for prince and subject, a new set of values, a new paradigm for normal politics to replace the old after a temporary revolution and interregnum. In fact, Machiavelli will find it easier to uproot old *political* allegiances by exposing the connection between the old politics and practical failure, than he will find altering old *intellectual* allegiances to values such as anonymous reading and writing, considering discourses without attention to the circumstances in which they are generated and received. But if Machiavelli is only half successful, weakening the hold of old political habits while failing to teach new methods of reading, his teaching will be seen as a reduction of intelligent action to cleverness in opposition to the authoritative and algorithmic old politics; should it replace that politics and itself become authoritative, its values would then become the principles of new algorithmic reasoning.[9] Machiavelli, unlike the ideologue, whether conservative or revolutionary, is not saying, "The obvious connections you make between character and action, between policy and consequences, are wrong; I shall offer new but no less obvious connections," substituting a new set of principles to ground algorithmic thinking. Instead, he draws attention to the relation between rules and cases, values and actions, by forcing a redescription of political discourse — the pronouncements of rulers and the text of *The Prince* itself — as a series of actions rather than the statements of doctrines or evident matters of fact.

Machiavelli does not present a new method for succeeding practically, based on a new set of political values. That strategy, first, could not work; if the old paradigm were what people mean by politics and ethics, then a new one would not be taken as a version of ethics and politics at all, but as something else: the replacing of ethics by calculated self-interest and of politics by force and fraud, of rhetorical persuasion by propaganda, a reading that accounts for much of Machiavelli's public reputation. (Later in the history of prudence characters will appear whose innovations work in just that way. The contrast between those two kinds of revolutionaries will be the subject of the next chapter. Here, as is often the case, "progress" in the history of thought consists in doing what was, by older standards, impossible. Machiavelli's use of rhetoric means that he cannot, and need not, be revolutionary in the way Mandeville and Hobbes, for example, will be.) Machiavelli's new prince would be doomed to staying a usurper, and vulnerable to newer usurpers, instead of appearing "as old as" the traditional ruler, as he claims in chapter 24; he could seize power only at the cost of having that power cease being political. And second, even if the strategy could work, it would not be an improvement over the old regime; once again, Machiavelli's rhetorical critique of the old politics, unlike later ideological revolutionary manifestos, will not declare that we now know that honesty and stability are bad things to be replaced by more up-to-date ways of acting, but will instead try to undermine the supposedly transparent connection between thought and action, between values and practice.

Machiavelli pushes into the background the values political actors hold, since purity of intentions is no mark of virtue or cause of success; on the other hand, fortune makes success itself too undependable to erect into a principle, and so Machiavelli attempts to direct the audience's attention to the connections between values and action, principles and consequences, rules and cases. Successful ethical action depends not so much on affirming the right principles—that part is easy—but on learning how to bring those principles to bear on action. The bearing principles have on a case becomes subject to argument, to deliberative and forensic rhetoric, and the main achievement of Machiavelli as educator will be to redirect attention —as I have tried to do—to the relation of principles and cases. Algorithmic and heuristic methods can afford to be stated as doctrines, separating what is said from who says it to whom, separating the meaning from the force of an utterance. (Hence the context-free autonomy of Descartes's algorithmic thinker is not the kind of autonomy Machiavelli's man of virtù can have.) The art of rhetoric domesticates, makes subject to method, those aspects of the use of language treated as extralinguistic pragmatics by studies of language based on the other kinds of rules. Politics, then, is necessarily argumentative and rhetorical; the subject of politics and practice is the essentially contested, and the purpose of Machiavelli's new politics is not to erase the old from memory but to join it in argument.[10]

The Prince and the *Discourses on Livy* are necessarily rhetorical works, then, but not because they present a rhetorical "view" of politics or use a rhetorical method or outward rhetorical form. *The Prince* and the *Discourses on Livy* are rhetorical because their purpose is to initiate political discourse, not just discourse *about* politics but talk and texts which embody commitments by the speaker and aim at practical consequences. Machiavelli holds that the old politics has, by making debate about politics impossible, also made politics itself impossible; he wants to reinstitute politics by provoking reflection, debate, and, through them, deliberation and prudent judgment. Instead of looking at Machiavellian texts as the statement of doctrines, then, we have to read them as performances.[11]

Making politics argumentative and rhetorical rather than ideological and ceremonial cannot be done by proclamation; although constructing a rhetorical politics is a public accomplishment, a performance, it is not one of those performative utterances whose success is achieved in the appropriate performance, like "I accept your bet." Making politics rhetorical can be done only by engaging one's opponent in debate, and by engaging one's readers in judgment and action. This is no easy task because Machiavelli's opponents have good reasons to try to avoid appearing in a debate; the traditional politics he opposes is antirhetorical in the sense that it does not work by argument, and is indeed undetermined by argument. Therefore, making politics into rhetoric requires that Machiavelli figure out the proper allotment of shares of that work among his own texts, a variety of intended readers, and even his opponents, the partisans of the old politics, and requires that we take such a division of labors into account in our readings of Machiavelli's enterprise.[12] As a result, Machiavelli's texts will have to be treated not merely as performances, but as public performances. The idea of a public performance, of *The Prince* as the representation (or, in classical theory, an *imitation*) of an act of teaching, supplies the means of connecting the two audiences of *The Prince:* the internally specified audience of Lorenzo and the indefinite public who can watch that represented act of teaching and learning. (All these relations between internal and external audience will have to be reconsidered when we turn to the *Discourses.*)

Since regarding Machiavellian texts as doctrine, as constatives, produced instability — their examples could not in any straightforward sense be imitated, and on those occasions when their precepts were clear, Machiavelli immediately undercut them — I suggested that we instead be attentive to the performative dimensions of *The Prince* as an act of teaching the prince, of disputation against the old politics. But Machiavelli's rhetorical politics is constituted not only by fighting against the old politics, but more precisely by fighting against it before the bar of his readers. *The Prince* and the *Discourses* are designed to be overheard as well as heard, publicized as well as read. If Machiavelli could present his arguments in an already determinate rhetorical situation, then a performative reading would be enough to do justice to his rhetorical politics. But Machiavelli must at the same time both treat politics rhetorically and create an audience before whom politics can be actions; the reader must imitate Machiavelli's argument. Finally, he must imitate it not just *qua* argument but *qua Machiavelli's* argument; the new prince must not only follow Machiavelli's advice but be seen to follow Machiavelli's advice. Machiavelli and the new prince must not just engage in debate against the old politics, but must conspire together to show the public that that debate is rhetorical, and that politics consists in such debate, even though the prince's role in such debate will be far from one of equality with his subjects: Machiavelli's making everything subject to debate does not make politics any more democratic, at least not in any obvious sense.

Machiavelli can provide an example of prudential argument in *The Prince* and can construct a text that teaches prudence to its readers and requires prudence from them. But not just any reader can learn prudence in any context; successful teaching of prudence must either presuppose or construct a situation in which there is a possibility of prudential action, including but certainly not restricted to the prudential acts of reading and writing.[13] I claimed earlier that Machiavelli shows how the old politics made action impossible by making debate about action impossible. Unfortunately, though, the converse of that proposition does not follow, and is not even true. Participating in Machiavelli's argument does not automatically make someone into an active political participant. If all prudence required was exhibiting, or considering, both sides of an issue, it would be easy, and prudence could be taught by relying on traditional methods of the rhetorical schoolroom. Giving and receiving good advice is another primary prudential intellectual activity, but if one could teach prudence by moralizing, "The best-laid plans sometimes don't work," even supplementing that with "Treat fortune like a woman," and "Rely on things inside your own control," "There's nothing new under the sun," "Things aren't what they used to be," and the other maxims Machiavelli appeals to and dramatizes, prudence would again be easy to practice and easy to learn. Machiavelli must show what it means to take such precepts prudently. If reading, or learning, is to become a prudent activity in *The Prince,* that will not be a victory won so cheaply. Making action possible, restoring ancient freedoms and virtues, is not simply a matter of discovering a true doctrine, nor yet can it be an illocutionary act, something completely accomplished *in* the saying, nor, finally, is it simply a matter of persuasion either, at least in any obvious sense of persuasion, because it is not a matter of decision, and prudence and rhetoric are both concerned with things within our power. Conversely, the attenuated perlocutionary effects posited by the dramatic framework of *The Prince* — the author trying to win a job, the reader supposedly going on to unify Italy — should make us hesitate before embracing the idea that *The Prince* is intended to be a consolation for impotent but deserving intellectuals, a strategy whose appeal comes from the fact that such literary doings and undergoings, writings and readings, are almost automatically — regardless of context — within our power. (The unstable and incomplete character of Machiavelli's texts is one means of blocking that sort of literary "satisfaction" and inaction.)[14] Restoring ancient freedom and making thoughtful action efficacious can be effected neither by true doctrine nor correct performance.

One is therefore tempted to say, Well, then, restoring the possibilities of action is not a rhetorical problem amenable to argumentative treatment at all, but a military one, or perhaps a constitutional one. Discourse about action is something the writer can control, but whether action itself is possible (and whether such discourse will be an instance of political action) depends on circumstances outside his control. If one of Machiavelli's jobs is carefully to demarcate what he, or the new ruler, can accomplish, and what must be left for the reader, or one's subjects or fellow citizens, to do, it might seem plausible to draw that line between discursive conditions and effects and extradiscursive ones, between illocutionary acts and per- locutionary effects. If instances of political rhetoric—for example, *The Federalist Papers* or *The Communist Manifesto*—can be read today as so many interesting "theories," while something as innocent-looking as Livy's *History* can become a text participating in political discourse, it is tempt- ing to argue that whether or not some text is practical depends on its extra- argumentative context. Machiavelli's reading of Livy in *The Discourses*, certainly, can be read as mere epideictic narrative, assessing credit and blame, balancing arguments on both sides of subjects, and being quite dis- connected from practical action. If it—and *The Prince*—are to be docu- ments with political consequences, that cannot depend on some intrinsic properties accessible to observation.

But Machiavelli does not accept that devaluation of the power of dis- course, with its easy distinction between talking and acting; instead he uses rhetorical methods to expand what will fall under the discursively accessible. He wants *The Prince* to initiate not only talk about politics but political discourse among its readers, that is, discourse with political con- sequences, with commitment by the speaker and something more than mere uptake, in the narrow illocutionary sense, by the readers; for that objec- tive, Machiavelli must find inadequate the translation of the question of the relation of political argument to political action into a question of the relation between political argument and *motion*—nonargument, extra- argumentative consequences. That formulation begs the question of the relation between thought and action, but begging the question in this case is more than a fallacy to be identified and rejected. It is, rather, a func- tional error, one that contributes to the ineffectiveness of discourse about politics and to a satisfaction with elegantly formed but practically detached discourse. Algorithmic, nonrhetorical politics depends on taking as ex- haustive the distinction between ideology and force, making everything outside discourse (or even some preferred form of discourse, sacred or scien- tific) as extradiscursive, irrational force, and so implying that the only way of making connections between speech and action is by discourse bringing off physical effects, as in the simple distinction between an illocutionary act, promising or warning, commanding or threatening, and a perlocu- tionary effect, being in debt, being scared, obeying or cowering.

But rhetorical politics finds room between words and physical effects, replacing the sort of illocutionary act that does something with words and is thus successful in the act of speaking with illocutionary acts done by a speaker with the cooperation of an audience, and replacing physical effects with conventional effects (conventional, as illocutionary forces are, but effects, as in the perlocutionary dimension of language). The power of rhetorical politics is to civilize by conventionalizing the practical, converting it, as much as possible, from a realm of force to one of argument. Such an easy distinction between words and deeds, between principles and consequences, suggests a division of the world into a realm of intelligibility and a realm of contingency. Guided by such a distinction, one can easily distinguish an action from its consequences and define action so narrowly that a principled act is never wrong, never even unsuccessful; it's just that overwhelming outside forces got in the way of its success in the material world. Either we need not be concerned about such supposed failure, generating stoic resignation, or we can use the weapons of that world in that world; in either case one keeps principles pure by keeping them ineffectual (as the ideological politician surreptitiously used heuristic force and fraud distinct from his own proclaimed method). In the more complicated rhetorical world, it is always debatable which consequences flow from which principles, and thus where to draw the line between acts and consequences, and those complications bar such stoical inferences from the possibility of failure. (Recall, for example, Machiavelli's appeal to the image of the archers aiming too high in order to reach a distant target. To follow that analogy, I could try to take power in a small city like Lucca by imitating Cyrus and hoping that by aiming too high I hit the target. But how could anyone tell whether I have successfully imitated Cyrus, while falling short, or whether that imitation was the cause of success or overambitious failure?)[15]

To return, though, to my claim that rhetoric civilizes the realm of praxis by converting it from a world of force into one of forceful argument. Aristotle noted the difference between human and animal communities, and tied that difference to the uses of language in his often quoted remarks in the *Politics:*

> Man alone of the animals possesses speech. The mere voice, it is
> true, can indicate pain and pleasure, and therefore is possessed by
> the other animals as well . . . but speech is designed to indicate the
> advantageous and the harmful, and therefore also the right and
> the wrong; for it is the special property of man in distinction from
> the other animals that he alone has perception of good and bad
> and right and wrong and the other moral qualities, and it is part-
> nership in these things that makes a household and a city-state.
> (1.2.1253a6–18)

Language civilizes praxis by transforming battles about pleasure and pain into disputes about justice and utility. Pitkin sees Machiavelli pointing to a similar transformation in a flourishing republic and, unlike Aristotle, seeing the threat of degenerating from the human world to the bestial world of pleasure and pain:

> Such a city offers each Citizen, each class of Citizens, the genuine possibility of fulfilling individual needs, pursuing separate interests, expressing real passions; it does not depend on sacrifice, either voluntary or enforced. Yet the selfish and partial needs, interests, and passions brought into the political process are transformed, enlarged, brought into contact with the conflicting needs, interests, and passions of other Citizens and ultimately redefined collectively in relation to the common good — a common good that emerges only out of the political interaction of the Citizens.[16]

Given that possibility of using rhetoric to civilize and domesticate the passions, and given the threat of the return to barbarism, Machiavelli has two jobs. First he has to initiate discourse about politics, a task he can accomplish in the act of writing. But secondly, he must make discourse about politics into political discourse, discourse which is itself a political act. This second job, without which the first is just stylized play, is the difficult one, and the one for which Machiavelli's strategies deserve our attention. Machiavelli's attacks on the old politics have made problematic the relation between their principles and action, but his tactics are telling against much more than just that specific target; he has made problematic the relation between any discourse — including his own — and action, and so has made it difficult to say when any discourse is practical and how any discourse can become practical. His problematizing achievement has been to focus attention, and suspicion, on the connections between text and action, converting the connection between decorous and prudent imitation from a bridge into an obstacle.

Traditional ethics and politics are ideological, and they lead to impotence. They have made action impossible by removing the possibility of argument about action: in ideological politics and ethics there is nothing to argue about. The problem is how to increase the possibilities for action through reinstituting debate about action. If debate about actions does not automatically lead to action, how it can lead to action at all? One would expect Machiavelli to show that, once false consciousness is destroyed by a critique of ideology, and illusory obstacles to successful action removed, then the field of the practical will be expanded; since more becomes possible, people will be able to act more effectively. But what we see instead of that hopeful line of reasoning, in both *The Prince* and the *Discourses,*

Discursive Virtuosity and Practical Virtù

is a surprising and substantial constriction on the range of the practical, a lowering of the estimate of how much can be accomplished by politics, and by human action in general. Although Machiavelli indeed claims that reading The Prince will make the new prince more successful, and even more explicitly in the preface to the Discourses says that his purpose is to make action possible by converting people's relation to history from an epideictic awarding of praise and blame to active participation, his texts nevertheless present a drastically restricted estimate of the effectiveness of human action. To summarize the experience of constraint, of the limited efficacy of intelligent action, in The Prince, we have already seen that

— Machiavelli both advocates and undercuts the idea of success through imitating the great heroes of the past.
— He endows the prince with powers that will make his own position as advisor superfluous.
— While telling the prince that he must study military strategy above all things, and place strong arms and military valor at the foundation of the secure state, he refuses to assimilate politics to strategy. As a consequence, the matter of first importance to political success falls outside of politics.
— He dramatizes the unstable relation between discourse and action: the fable of the lion and the fox initially shows that human action depends on the possibility, or threat, of merely being covering for animal brutality, but the figure of the fox, as we shall see in greater detail in the next chapter, utimately points in the reverse direction. By ascribing human qualities to animal species, the fable makes both inevitable and problematic the thrust of human action outside its own boundaries.
— His treatment of fortune, while seeming to open up the possibility of mastery and domination over fortune, ultimately discovers fortune at the very center of human action: the sort of character a person has is a matter of luck.

To anticipate the analogous effect of constraint in the Discourses

— Machiavelli shows that the solutions to practical problems depend on impossible conditions (e.g., Lycurgus starting from a tabula rasa making laws), or "where corruption has penetrated the people, the best laws are of no avail, unless they are administered by a man of such supreme power that he may cause the laws to be observed until the mass has been restored to a healthy condition. And I know not whether such a case has ever occurred, or whether it possibly ever could occur" (1.17; see also 1.18 for a similar and longer argument).

—He points to the importance of the operations of chance (2.29: "Men may second Fortune, but cannot oppose her; they may develop her designs, but cannot defeat them").[17]

—He shows the operations of historical necessity outside human control (e.g. 1.2.114, showing "the circle which all republics are destined to run through").

—Not only does he show that each of a pair of contradictory actions can lead to success—chapter 22 in book 3 is entitled "How Manlius Torquatus by hardness, and Valerius Corvinus by gentleness, acquired equal glory"—but more specifically he sometimes counsels moderation ("We see one man proceed in his actions with passion and impetuosity; and as in both the one and the other case men are apt to exceed the proper limits, not being able always to observe the just middle course, they are apt to err in both," 3.9) and sometimes shows how moderation leads to disaster ("Either . . . go away from [princes], or . . . attach yourself very closely to them, 3.2).

—He demonstrates the impossibility of effective action because its conditions and consequences are related in a vicious circle (e.g., 1.18: "As good habits . . . require good laws to support them, so laws . . . need good habits on the part of the people").

—He shows how effective action can require an ethically incompatible pair of talents in a single agent (e.g., 1.18: "The reformation of the political condition of a state presupposes a good man, whilst the making of himself prince of a republic violently presupposes a bad one.")

—He makes that last observation even more damaging for the possibilities of successful action by barring the notion that that single agent might for a time possess or use one skill or character trait, and then use another: "That we cannot . . . change [our characters or mode of action] at will is due to two causes; the one is the impossibility of resisting the natural bent of our characters; and the other is the difficulty of persuading ourselves, after having been accustomed to success by a certain mode of proceeding, that any other can succeed as well" (3.9). Not only will we not be able to succeed; we cannot even blame our failures on natural character.

—He shows how effective action depends on abilities that most men do not possess (e.g., 1.26: "Men generally decide upon a middle course, which is most hazardous; for they know neither how to be entirely good or entirely bad").

—He gives advice that is impossible to follow: "He errs least and will be most favored by fortune who suits his proceedings to the times . . . and always follows the impulses of his nature" (3.9). The first half of this precept, Machiavelli shows elsewhere, cannot be followed while the second half cannot fail to be followed.[18]

Discursive Virtuosity and Practical Virtù

The image of the archer aiming above the target undercuts the idea of imitation of the ancients; similarly, the medical analogies Machiavelli employs to picture the use of intelligence in action makes effective practice impossible: not only, it seems to follow, do symptoms become apparent only after treatment will no longer work, but it may also be reasonable to infer that the more one understands human affairs, the less one can act in them. (The opposite side of that possibility, also to be considered in more detail below, is that it is precisely one's inability to act that makes deep reflection possible.) While expanding the range of practical affairs one can argue about, he has constricted the range of things one can do something about. Above, I noted the way that Machiavelli, by making problematic the relation between political discourse and action, destroyed any transparent relation between knowledge of the past and present action, and hence between past and present: it is equally mistaken to think that the past is immediately "relevant" and easily imitated and to think that all great things have already been done; here I am pointing to its generalization, that there is at least an apparent disjuncture between the enabling practical purpose of *The Prince* and the embodied strategies of restraint. At the beginning of this section I pointed to the difference in manipulability between language and the extralinguistic, and that added recalcitrance of the nonverbal has emerged to set Machiavelli's problem at this stage. To this point in the argument, however, constraint is found in the material on which the prince and Machiavelli work, and therefore in their prospects for success, and not in their methods. It is this latter task that Machiavelli must engage in, and its sign is those dissonances between intended purpose and the means at his disposal.

That ultimate dissonance, though, between practical purpose and his strategies, points the way toward a solution. I have referred briefly to Machiavelli's destruction of old intellectual habits as a critique of ideology, and I now propose to take that title more seriously. The interplay between the internal and external audience of *The Prince*, between a rhetoric of reading and interpreting and one of producing and persuading, will show how complicated a prudent critique of ideology must be.

3

THE POLITICS OF

RHETORICAL INVENTION

Chapter 1 treated rhetoric as a set of resources for creating and exploiting ambiguities, for finding or creating discursive stability in the absence of the firm extralinguistic undergirding supplied by transparent reference to uncontested examples. But rhetoric traditionally supplies a method of persuasion as well as an art of ambiguity and invention, and the persuasive dimensions of rhetoric deepen our sense of Machiavelli's project of articulating prudence. Therefore in the last chapter I pointed to the two instances of persuasion that organize *The Prince* — Machiavelli's inviting the new prince to act prudently and the new prince's convincing the people to follow him. If "prudence" or "doing the right thing" were a straightforward notion, it would then make sense to talk about Machiavelli's persuading or convincing the prince to do something. When the object of choice is recognizable, then persuasion consists in convincing someone that that object ought to be desired and aimed at, but if Chapter 1 has established anything, it is that there is no such object, and consequently Machiavelli's act of persuasion requires a closer examination.

Once the idea of persuasion is problematized, the other parts of the text and its context shift correspondingly. Machiavelli's explicitly stated purpose is to get his job back, but he undercuts that possibility, not only by stating it — a curious tactic that could be called, in modern language, perlocutionary suicide — but also by rejecting the value of such a role in the discussion of counsel and advice that appears in chapters 22–23. Instead of achieving that narrow goal, though, he has shown the more general need for the kind of intelligence he represents, by showing what happens when it is not present, when either the imitation of the past or the instantiation of eternal values is taken to be an easy task. The remaining dimensions of Machiavelli's act of persuasion must similarly be transformed as imitation and success become more questionable and virtù becomes more abstract and formal. In the same way, the second case of persuasion in *The Prince*, the prince's relation to his subjects, requires further scrutiny both because it relies on more than merely verbal resources and because taking seriously the idea of the new prince as orator will create new dangers for prudence that we have yet to consider.

The Politics of Rhetorical Invention

In Chapter 1, as in most of the history of the reception of *The Prince*, the main danger to prudence was its threatened collapse into villainy and opportunism. This took the form not only of the notorious Machiavellian immorality but also of its abstract intellectual equivalent, the difficulty of differentiating Machiavelli's new form of stability from the instability expressed by the moral that one's eye must always be on the possibility of failure and that one must always aim at short-term success, the difficulty of distinguishing prudence from heuristics. If anything can be an example for anything, then method would seem to consist in the heuristic enterprise of assembling as large a repertoire as possible of techniques that might be employed in an unexpected situation: "If one could change one's nature with time and circumstances, fortune would never change" (ch. 25). When Machiavelli turns from acquisition to defense in chapter 12, he similarly turns from examples and reasoning from case to case to enthymemes and reasoning from general rule to case, but that form of reasoning has problems of its own, to which we must now turn.

Our investigations thus far have left us with two connected fundamental problems in using Machiavelli to explicate prudence: we are left with what was necessarily an extremely problematic set of relations between discourse and action, and we need in addition to develop further the abstract characterization of prudence as a peculiar relation between rules and cases, principles and consequences. To get farther along with the difference between prudence and other uses of knowledge in action, I want to make a different cut and talk about the place of knowledge in action with a different typology that will permit a more fine-grained analysis; that analysis will, in turn, uncover new enemies of prudence besides its conflation with villainy and opportunism. Algorithmic thinking, and the search for a kind of knowledge stable enough not to require negotiation, generates an antirhetorical way of governing; the separation of ruling from rhetoric suggests a perspective from which we can differentiate kinds of rhetorical politics, and therefore distinguish rhetorical from sophistic and immoral opportunism. (After I explore the possibility of ruling without rhetoric in the current chapter, the next chapter will raise the next threat to prudence, rhetoric without rule, ineffectual rhetoric.)

Rhetorical and Antirhetorical Politics

Not every large association of people is a state, and not every mode of ruling and being ruled is political. Political rule is based on a ruler's authority and on a subject's or citizen's loyalty, consent, obedience, and obligation. While just how large a role persuasion plays in developing and maintaining those relations of ruler and ruled will vary from state to state, no regime can be fully political without at least partially tying authority and its correlatives to persuasion. (Thus, Aristotle accuses Plato of building so much unity into the ideal state that he destroys its political character, making it nothing more than a large family. The ideal state that Plato describes permits only a modest role for effective discourse and persuasion: wisdom — not rhetoric — tells the rulers what to do, and they then must convince the other classes to obey without understanding why they must act as they do.) Rhetoric, as the art of persuasion, is for that reason a part of politics, an elaboration of techniques and resources for ruling and being ruled. Quantifying how large a part of politics rhetoric occupies has only a limited utility: the language of the more and the less would permit us to say that rhetoric has a larger role in Aristotle's state than in Plato's, and a larger one in a direct democracy than in a tyranny, but not much more. I find it more useful to see the different parts or offices of rhetoric — invention, judgment, style, and memory — offering a taxonomy of fundamental persuasive activities and ties between ruler and ruled, basic ways in which a ruler can make himself an authority and make his subjects loyal and obedient. Machiavelli's advice to a usurper presents a kind of politics which is based on invention as the principle that defines judgment, style, and memory and assigns them their proper roles in supporting the prince's rule. In other kinds of politics, rhetoric can have a role without making the principal problem of politics one of stable innovation.

The Prince forces consideration of a politics based on a rhetoric of invention, since Machiavelli clarifies the nature of such inventive political rule by a pair of polemical contrasts, first to traditional rule founded in a rhetoric of style and then to rule not grounded in persuasion at all but in military strength; only then, starting with chapter 15, is he able to treat directly the inventive relations between prince and subjects. (Just to avoid misunderstanding, neither of these opponents should be identified with heuristic opportunism or villainy; instead, I shall argue that both traditional rule and the reduction of politics to warfare represent forms of algorithmic thinking. These other kinds of politics *include* rhetoric, but only a politics in which prudence is fundamental can be called a *rhetorical politics.*)

The stated purpose of *The Prince* is to use great examples from the past to teach the prince how to acquire and preserve a state, but we have already seen how the relation of past event through general practical rule to a chosen action — a relation summed up in the term *imitation* — is not as simple as one might like. An unreflective imitation assumes that similarities between past and future are evident, and hence that any past success carries obvious prescriptions about what to do. The great deeds of the past carry no direct advice about what to do, not because human nature has changed — it has not — but because such a simple-minded conception of how to learn from the past depends on a deeper and even less justified assumption, that successes and failures are easy to identify — in other words, that no great moral or intellectual powers are needed for recognizing which past or future actions exemplify which general values (including the general value of success), which particular conclusions about how to act fall under given universal major premises about what is good. The traditional accusations of immorality against Machiavelli come from his rejection of such subsumption.

Above I claimed that it was easy to condemn literal and unreflective imitation, but not trivial to pose an alternative — nor, as we shall see, is it all that easy to make those condemnations very penetrating. (Heuristics is reflective only in inviting the learner to sit back and reflect; reflection in that case has no more positive definition than the abstract recommendation that one pause between past and future, between example and new act.) I argued that the object of imitation was neither precepts nor examples but Machiavelli's argument itself as it mediates between rule and case, and suggested that this transformation of imitation into something demanding greater intellectual and moral powers — that is, prudence — made much more problematic the relation between the discursive success of following Machiavelli's argument and the practical success of stable usurpation.

The analogies between what Machiavelli is doing in the argument and what the prince is supposed to do when he learns from it create these dangers, but they also suggest one way of addressing them. It is difficult to conceive the relation between speaker and hearer in The Prince, difficult to see what Machiavelli is trying to accomplish and what the aspiring prince reading the document is supposed to do as a consequence. Rather than treat that question directly — and we will return to treat it directly — the analogy suggests that we can turn instead from the sorts of persuasion that connect Machiavelli and prince to the persuasive relations between prince and subjects. Since the purpose of the Prince is to teach the prince how to act by presenting great examples from the past, Machiavelli is, among other things, a historian, one who fits perfectly John Ward's description of the Renaissance historian, for whom "history is made, not revealed . . . [history is] a 'case' made out by the historian who is free to locate himself in time and use rhetorical techniques of contrast and comparison, opposition and resolution, argument and emotion, to demonstrate the validity of the perspective to which he has nailed his literary identity."[1] Just as I began this chapter by asserting correspondences between kinds of rhetoric and kinds of politics, here to every such historical "perspective" and every such use of rhetoric corresponds a version of politics; the varieties of history will be the middle term we can use to make more specific and evident the relations of politics and rhetoric. Hayden White offers a simple and suggestive typology of two different ways history can be related, via general rules, to action; he distinguishes two kinds of history, defined by their relations to audience and language (two factors too often neglected in investigations of practical reason):

> By "straight" history is meant . . . that form of historical writing which does not, in the course of constructing its account of the past, make appeal to anything but what might be called the "common wisdom" of the group for which it is written. . . . This implicit appeal to the *consensus gentium*, manifested in the professional historian's distaste for jargon or any technical language and reflected in the philosopher's uniform distaste for any "metahistory" (which could almost be defined as the tendency to try to substitute special language for ordinary educated speech) is the mark of "straight" history as against every form of metahistory.[2]

White's distinction has rhetorical antecedents. In Cicero's *De oratore* philosophy and rhetoric were in conflict over whether to use ordinary or esoteric language, a conflict which White rediscovers in the dispute between metahistory and straight history: "The subjects of the other arts are derived from hidden and remote sources, while the whole art of oratory lies open to view, and is concerned in some measure with the common practice, custom and speech of mankind, so that, whereas in all other arts that is most excellent which is farthest removed from the understanding and mental capacity of the untrained, in oratory the very cardinal sin is to depart from the language of everyday life and the usage approved by the sense of the community" (*De oratore* 1.12).[3] Each of these kinds of history has a kind of politics associated with it: the public authority to which the straight historian appeals makes him conservative, while "to espouse a radical version of history is to be willing to use radical language, a language which, by its very nature, brings under question the conventions of ordinary educated speech of the society under attack. . . . Anyone who tries to change society in *politically* radical ways will be forced to articulate what the philosophers call a 'metahistorical' system. . . . I am suggesting that the term 'metahistorical' is really a surrogate for 'socially innovative historical vision.'" Finally, "the dispute between the 'ordinary historian' and the 'metahistorian' is precisely over who will determine the rules for looking at history in socially responsible ways," a dispute which, when thus formulated, clearly involves Machiavelli and his readers.[4]

White's typology reveals the importance and difficulty of Machiavelli's

The Politics of Rhetorical Invention

rhetorical contribution to politics. Machiavelli has to be politically radical — aiming at innovation and writing for the new prince — but by White's linguistic criteria he clearly does not proceed metahistorically. Instead, he conservatively appeals to the *consensus gentium* and undercuts claims to specialized knowledge and language in political, as opposed to military, affairs. White's correlation between history and politics presupposes that there are exactly two possible forms of practical reason: to be conservative is to think that connections between past and future are smooth because general values have transparent relations to their instantiations, while to be a metahistorian is to be politically radical by subverting such connections by making them the subject of esoteric, specialized knowledge, and thereby subverting existing values. It is my thesis that Machiavelli's ability to be politically radical while conservatively continuing to appeal to common wisdom — and hence to be radical while remaining *political*, rather than "metapolitical" and accomplishing political ends by nonpolitical (scientific or military) means — depends on rhetorical invention for articulating a more complicated form of practical reasoning than either of White's alternatives. More complicated connections among *exemplum*, general value, and prescribed action, permit reflection while barring appeals to esoteric knowledge and authority derived from expertise.[5] It is not just that complicated relations are better than simple ones, that reflection is better than unhesitating action (or better than a reflection whose only mark is hesitation), but that Machiavellian prudence must problematize the relations between past and future, between case and rule, if the prince is to eat his cake and have it too, if he is to be radical and usurpatious while remaining political.

White constructs a dilemma that evokes a problem rhetoricians have always had to face. For White, to be radical is to appeal to standards and values beyond the beliefs and values of the people — and thereby appeal to things outside the resources of the politician *qua* rhetorician — while to be political, to limit one's appeals to opinions already validated by the public, is automatically to be conservative: either lead the people by bringing a new and learned revelation or follow the people by acting according to their antecedent values. The choice seems to be either to find a kind of knowledge outside rhetoric — metahistory and metapolitics — or to use a debased form of rhetoric that fulfills Socrates' depiction of it as flattery. Rhetoricians have always had to devise ways of avoiding the apparent dilemma of either telling the audience what they already want to hear or of having their message fall on deaf ears, and so White's contrast would be enriched by bringing in a traditional rhetorical distinction used to evade that choice, the difference between topics, often called commonplaces or clichés, used as ready-made parts to be inserted into a speech when needed, and topics used for invention: topical invention is a way of appealing to common wisdom rather than to esoteric knowledge that permits action that would be at the same time radical, even usurpatious, and still political. Rhetorical revolutionaries — including, as I shall show, Machiavelli — must always claim to come not to destroy the old law but to fulfill it.

Bacon's distinction between Topics and Promptuary is especially apposite here: "Provision for discourse may be procedured in two ways. The places where a thing is to be looked for may be marked, and as it were indexed; and this is that which I call *Topics;* or arguments concerning such matters as commonly fall out and come under discussion may be composed beforehand and laid up for use; and this I will name the *Promptuary.* This last however scarcely deserves to be spoken of as part of knowledge, consisting rather of diligence than of any artificial erudition."[6] White's straight historian is the rhetorician using a promptuary art, appealing to the past as a source of such "arguments . . . composed beforehand and laid up for use," a description closely resembling accounts of "scissors-and-paste" historians and the politicians who see the past as consistent and affording obvious lessons. Such commonplaces offer the rhetorician and his audience a simple homology among past *exempla,* general rules or morals, and future application. Since Pericles, or Cato, acted this way, honesty is the best policy, so you should act that way too. Imitation means performing actions that have been thus certified by the past: the past is the criterion for legitimacy and the guarantee of success; actions algorithmically inherit their value from the deeds they imitate and the principles they embody; and the metaphor of the Mirror for Magistrates is the best image for learning from the past. White's contrast makes it appear that the only way of avoiding such a simple homology is through the subversive tactics of metahistory, which substitute a scientific, and no less simple, homology; in what follows I shall show the way topical invention, and a politics of invention, offer an alternative to both straight history and metahistory, both conservative politics and metapolitics.

Rhetorical Politics versus the Traditional Politics of Style

Straight history and promptuary rhetoric are not *bad* history and rhetoric, as would be easy to infer from Bacon's contrast of promptuary to topics. Machiavelli shows that a simpleminded sort of imitation — an unreflective connection between past successes, universal values, and future acts — would be disastrous for the new prince. The traditional ruler appears to have no such problem; he need simply observe and imitate outward forms of ruling inherited from his ancestors: "It is sufficient not to transgress ancestral usages" (ch. 2). Prudence, unlike wisdom, is not a use of intelligence everywhere useful or appropriate; as an intellectual virtue dealing with the variable and practicable, its own utility and appropriateness are similarly variable. Straight history and promptuary rhetoric are the kind of history and rhetoric needed by a hereditary monarch, who rules by ceremony, by *style* rather than invention, and for that reason such history and such rhetoric come in for attack in the first eleven chapters of *The Prince*, as Machiavelli undercuts algorithmic praxis to create a need for prudence.[7] A hereditary monarch is better off relying on a promptuary art and a correspondingly straight vision of a past which simply reveals truths and duties, while someone who is to *achieve* authority has to employ topical invention to manufacture relations between past action, general value, and future action; the *Discourses on Livy* is dedicated to "those who . . . are worthy to be princes" as opposed to "such as are princes" and, as Machiavelli develops that contrast, to those who exhibit their princely qualities in action as opposed to those whose ruling qualities are imputed atechnically, by virtue of office, relying "rather [on] diligence than [on] any artificial erudition." As Struever points out, it is the legitimating function of style, of status and ceremony, that will be destroyed by Machiavelli's practice of imitation and his use of history: "The spare and precise political *exempla* are the result of a process which strips the exemplary statement of every condition and capacity of rule which simply acts in a self-fulfilling manner."[8]

All a hereditary monarch has to do is act like a king, while there is nothing for the new prince to act like. Consequently, the kind of imitation appropriate in his world is what Greene has appropriately called "sacramental":

> The simplest imitative strategy . . . [a] reverent rewriting of a hallowed text[,] bespeaks an almost ceremonial veneration for the "sacrosancta vetustas." . . . The version of history implied by this imitative strategy might be called *reproductive* or *sacramental*; it celebrates an enshrined primary text by rehearsing it liturgically, as though no other form of celebration could be worthy of its dignity. . . . Under this sacramental myth of history, writing becomes analogous to ritual as Eliade has described it; our conduct is referred to the archetypal beginning, *in illo tempore*, which in this case is the composition of the original poem.[9]

Machiavelli's prince must act in a world where style no longer carries automatic legitimacy with it; his problem is how invention can be the source of legitimacy: must not legitimacy in rulers be as it is in children, something inherited and not something one can do something about for oneself? (It is easy enough to invent, to act in novel and even successful ways, but those actions will not be political, and therefore in Machiavelli's opinion will ultimately not be stable, unless they somehow carry legitimacy with them.)[10]

The first eleven chapters of *The Prince* define the new prince's situation, and all his initial problems are generated by this contrast to rule by style: where style rules, the new prince has no room for action, since anything he did would be bad form; but where style does not authorize rule, politics seems reduced to the insecure use of force. It appears that Machiavelli's new prince will be driven to the alternative posed by the politics consonant with White's metahistorian, substituting force, often backed by expert knowledge, for truly political rule. But both Machiavelli's strategy in attacking traditional politics and straight history, and his alternative to them, are in fact more subtle. We saw in the first chapter how Machiavelli rejects simple dichotomies between ruler and ruled, acquisition and preservation, appearance and reality, inner and outer, ability and luck; that destructive rhetoric uncovers a delicately balanced and narrow wedge between authority based on traditional rule and style — the vicious circle that the king rules because he is called a king and acts like one — and the temporary and merely apparent rule based on force and violence — the vicious circle that the ruler is the strongest, and the strongest is he who rules.[11] Between traditional authority and short-lived force lies virtù, which cannot be simply identified with force or with anything else, because located between such tautologies the definition of virtù can only be formal: virtù is "that by which order is imposed upon *fortuna*" or "the quality which enables a ruler to attain his noblest ends."[12]

And so, in finding that White's pair of alternatives are not exhaustive, we also have discovered that they are not all that different from each other. Dialectically, each represents an algorithmic conception of the straightforward relations between rule and case: the choice between the conservative politician with his straight history and the radical's metahistory is a choice between a conventional language — embodied in unthinking customs, straightforward, unproblematic reference, and inference — and a novel, scientific language whose reference and inferences are just as straightforward and unproblematic.[13] If reference and inference were not so obvious, the straight historian could not be so conservative — he would have to see that tradition offered possibilities and ambiguities for further action — and the metahistorian would not be so radical — he would be forced to acknowledge that translation of principles to action might have to take place *via* the *consensus gentium*. By rejecting ambiguity, rejecting the notion that either history or science might not offer straightforward prescriptions for action, and by assuming that all reasoning must be algorithmic, the politics of style and the scientific antipolitics of metahistory both remove the possibility of prudence.

Moreover, in removing the possibility of prudence, both the politics of style and scientific antipolitics destroy the place that can be occupied by political rhetoric, because both think that their foundations, in authoritative history or science, replace rhetoric by something more dignified. In fact, though, each has to rely, to an extent greater than it can admit, on force and fraud unconnected to, and hidden by, their source of legitimacy. Consequently, conservative politics and metapolitics are similar not only dialectically, by identical conceptions of the relation of rule and case, but also rhetorically, by undermining the conditions in which deliberation can go on. Conservative politics and straight history replace rhetoric with debased rhetoric, with flattery and pandering, with the ruler telling the people what they want to hear and doing what they ask; metahistory and radical politics replace rhetoric with the scientific manipulation of their audiences, manufacturing consent through esoteric knowledge and secret operations. (This is a familiar contrast in Marxist debates about the spontaneous will of the masses versus the scientific leadership of the party.) Just as chapter 15 of The Prince attacks "theoretical" accounts of politics — that is, political language that ignores the way people really are — The Prince as a whole attacks the traditional politics that constitutes the practical counterpart of such theory, the impotent rulers who think they inhabit the world described in those theories and convince their subjects that they live there too. The old politics depends in that sense on a theory whose work it is to suppress the existence of theory, as art conceals art. Machiavelli's new politics is designed to associate such theories with the sort of stability that can be achieved theoretically only in the imagination, and practically only at the cost of leaving reality and, hence, of an impotent retiring from the field; the new politics then has to carve out a new sense of stability, not just a new means of attaining it.

My classification of three kinds of rules — algorithmic, heuristic, and prudent — and three consequent ways of acting according to rules, displays affinities between modes of action usually distinguished in political theory, as it distinguishes between reasonings often assimilated. Although they look like enemies, both traditional politicians appealing to historically embodied standards (including the traditional ruler Machiavelli seeks to overthrow) and those whom White calls "metahistorical" politicians, who rely on scientific laws which underlie and govern overt historical events (including those who would make politics into war and political understanding into military science) embody an ethics of principles and algorithmic methods which celebrates the distance between principles and circumstances. The politician who appeals to straight history legitimizes his actions by appealing to authoritative, traditional standards; this action is right because it conforms to the right authorizing principles. The metahistorical politician appeals to scientific laws outside history, and so he too acts rightly when he acts according to right principles.

Because of their reliance on an ethics of principles, I call both kinds of politicians ideological, although each would deny the epithet: ideology is precisely the method of practical thinking that depends on subsumption of particulars under general truths and, conversely, the employment of algorithmic methods on practical affairs. Ideology here consists in putting forth political claims as authoritative, because justified either by tradition or by science; ideology restricts debate by claiming to put certain principles, and their meaning and application, beyond debate. In the first eleven chapters of *The Prince*, the object of Machiavelli's polemics is the ideology of the hereditary ruler, while he begins the second part of the book, in chapters 12–14, by distancing his new politics from the ideology of military strategy.

The ideological politician must be tempted to infer that since his principles make his actions right, they should make those acts successful too. And that is an expectation that will inevitably be disappointed by the outcome of events, generating accounts that exemplify the following genre of narrative: a politician first simply does what is right, and then finds it necessary to embed that action in a more complicated context and describe it as doing the right at the cost of sacrificing success. Next, seeing that sacrifice as the cost of rightness, he will come to feel cheated, since legitimacy ought to imply success, and he must then find something other than those principles to blame. Finally he will justify any auxiliary action as bringing the success he already deserves. And so the ideological politician almost inevitably becomes a ruler by force unconnected with his principles. To the extent that one can determine the rightness of actions prior to action, outside of argument, outside a community, to that extent one will "enforce" the right by any methods available. Hence the ideological thinker, finding that algorithmic methods are never alone adequate for successful action, turns to heuristics, to success at any price. Whereas in the Introduction I pointed to the way algorithmics and heuristics are used in smooth alternation in the sciences, because each stipulates a gap between general rules and particular applications, the political analogon is the ideologue's surreptitious reliance on force and fraud. Although neither the ideology of traditional rule nor the ideology of legitimacy justified by metahistory has room for villainy and heuristic methods, both eventually must employ methods they cannot acknowledge. Far from recommending villainy, Machiavelli in fact shows the traditional ruler that it is he who must act villainously to remain in power; if one wants to avoid paying a villainous price, one will have to give up on the ideological thinking that faithfully transmits rectitude from principles to actions, and construct the kind of community in which prudence, the forgotten alternative to both ideology and villainy, is possible and desirable.

That dramatic inversion, though — that those whose political systems have no place for villainy and heuristics, and for whom prudence represents an immoral compromising of moral principles with brute reality, are those condemned to rely on modes of force outside their intellectual ken — offers the opportunity for prudence and rhetoric to become something more than compromises, second-best methods, inconveniences, and embarrassments. I have claimed that Machiavelli presents the argument of *The Prince* as an instance of prudence to be imitated by the new prince as he learns to be prudent, but I also noted that the new prince's success required that imitation here be something odd, almost unrecognizable as imitation, because the stable usurper must imitate Machiavelli without looking and acting "like" him. We can now make a bit more sense out of those conflicting demands. The function of topical invention in the first eleven chapters was to locate the new prince, to articulate the difficulties and opportunities of his situation; and this determination of the field of prudence was carried out by means of contrasts to the politics of style. But, although Machiavelli *employed* a rhetoric of invention to find a place in which the new prince might successfully operate, the result so far is not a *politics of invention* as opposed to the politics of style; nothing that definite has yet emerged. Conversely — and this is where a closer scrutiny of metahistorical, algorithmic, antirhetorical politics has led us — a politics of invention is the means of crossing the line from discursive facility to practical virtù. When the subject of *The Prince* shifts, starting with chapter 12, from acquiring a state to maintaining the new prince in power, the place of rhetoric in *The Prince* alters accordingly: for the prince to succeed at maintaining the regime he has taken, he must not only learn from and imitate Machiavelli's topical invention — which may be sufficient for acquiring a state — but must hold the state, must rule, by practicing topical invention of his own; he must not only find some means of persuasion or a situation in which those means operate, but must actually do some persuading. While Machiavelli can employ traditional rhetorical devices of invention in chapters 1-11 to explore the different possible ratios between acts of acquisition and the kinds of states acquired, when he turns to showing general methods of stability, he — and the new prince — must develop a politics of rhetorical invention. Therefore, there is a corresponding shift in the kind of politics in contrast to which the politics of invention is developed;

comparisons with the politics of style and so with straight history are re-placed by attacks on nonrhetorical bases for politics; Machiavelli's oppo-nent changes from the conservative politics of style to the metahistorian's alternative version of politics.

Rhetorical Politics versus the Metapolitics of Military Strategy

Once Machiavelli shows in chapters 1–11 that anything can become an example for anything, the marking of similarities and dif-ferences opens up a field for argument because he has undercut any ob-vious case to case reasoning. He undercuts any specific major premisses that may justify inference from a past success to a future deed: he makes ambiguous all the categories that could form the terms of such premisses – ruler and ruled, acquiring a state and keeping it, force and fraud – leaving only the most abstract possible major, the uniformity of human nature, a premiss that can justify any mode of conduct whatsoever and can itself generate none. In so doing, he also undercuts the normative majors that take for granted the subsumption of acts under values: one cannot choose Machiavelli's usurpatious attitude towards the past and hence towards gen-eral categories for describing human action without thereby choosing a similar attitude towards general moral categories and values. Therefore he must move, in what follows, either to a field outside debate, such as mili-tary science, or to showing new ways of subsuming acts under values, ways that permit a continuing debate but an enabling, practical debate, not a scholastic debate whose indecisiveness makes it remote from practical con-cerns. If he fails, he will have inadvertently ratified the ideology of conser-vative politics, which claims that even if standard, conventional practices of inferring from rule to case contain arbitrary directions for subsump-tion, those directions are best left tacit, because if removed or exposed, all control and all morality disappear.[14]

As I noted in the last chapter, chapter 12 announces that it will treat general methods for preserving states, and Machiavelli immediately says that preservation means securing the foundations of the state. Of the two sorts of foundation – laws and military power – the latter is truly funda-mental: "There cannot be good laws where there are not good arms, and where there are good arms there must be good laws." Good arms are the ideal subject for the metahistorian, who sees beneath the superficial causes of order and disorder, good laws, and instead learns to control the un-derlying military forces hitherto thought outside the political system alto-gether. Therefore – it is natural to infer – Machiavelli's hard-headed new politician will ignore the legalisms of White's "ordinary educated speech" and learn the radical vocabulary of military strength.

The trouble with the metahistorian's "realism," his radical vision that strips away illusion and recognizes the martial foundation of civic power, is that there is one crucial phenomenon invisible and nonexistent in that vision: stability. That is no minor oversight, since stability in maintaining a state is the new prince's purpose. Mercenaries and auxiliaries are inevitably undependable; even if they help you to win a battle, their use will ensure that that victory will not be worth much. The prince has to use his own troops, "would rather lose with his own men than conquer with forces of others" (ch. 13). Therefore, despite the fact that military matters are the one crucial place where metahistorical *study* is apposite — "A prince should therefore have no other aim or thought, nor take up any other thing for his study, but war and its organization and discipline" (ch. 14) — that study depends for its successful use on the prince's relations to his subjects: topical invention will give content to the formal ideal of virtù — content in the rhetorical sense of general methods — by connecting virtù, as the metahistorian cannot, to the traditional virtues in chapters 15–21. That military knowledge differs from prudence is apparent from the fact that it must be *applied* to be used; prudence, unlike either algorithmic or heuristic methods, permits no simple separation between the possession of knowledge and its application. (If it did, incontinence — knowing the better yet choosing the worse — would be a lamentable fact of life, not a philosophical puzzle. There is no mystery about possessing scientific knowledge or an artistic skill and not applying it, and so such abilities differ from prudence, where, as Aristotle points out, the idea of intentional error cannot apply.)

The metahistorical vision of stable truths lying somewhere behind the flux of circumstances becomes increasingly appealing as the circumstances in which one finds oneself appear increasingly unpredictable and disadvantageous. When there is no automatically stable or legitimate action, no action certified by style and status, then it is tempting to infer — and commentators have typically imputed this inference to Machiavelli himself — that success is the only possible goal, security being out of the question and legitimacy simply certified by success: remove practical reason in the simple and smooth sense, and we are left with irrational opportunism in which anything can be an example for anything. (Such a reading replicates the inference that the only alternative to algorithmic thinking is heuristics, that if rules do not govern cases, then cases must govern rules.) In such a situation, the metahistorian can discover the hidden laws of past success and show the prince how to act on those laws: one of the appeals of metahistory is its consoling message that if stability cannot be found in the world, at least it can be located in our knowledge of it.

This is the Machiavelli who teaches the prince how to act in a world without stability or legitimacy as he tries to "to maintain himself in the position of power and insecurity which innovation has brought him. . . . *Stato* means that one's eye is always upon immediate dangers; *virtù* is that by which one resists them, not that by which one is emancipated from the need to fear them."[15] The trouble with this reading of *The Prince* is that, just as Machiavelli shows that the hereditary monarch's standards of action are inappropriate for the new prince, so he shows how metahistorical focusing on success is equally self-destructive for him. Simple success or failure in an immediate crisis is not the criterion for effective or desirable action; on the contrary, the source of power—in this case, one's own troops rather than mercenaries—is the criterion of success and failure because it is the measure of stability. Win or lose, mercenaries decrease the prince's power of acting, and so chapters 12–23 show that one's eye must *not* always be on immediate dangers. The algorithmic conception of practical reason stands Parmenides on his head: the straight historian, following the way of opinion, proclaims a world of stable rulers and eternal values, while the metahistorian's way of truth is a world of becoming.

The moral of the discussion of mercenaries and other military resources, that stability cannot be won except by one's own resources, translates into the rhetorical advice that the prince should avoid *atechnoi*, avoid appealing to resources outside his art. For Machiavelli, things outside the prince's own power are a resource a prince might be tempted to use, and therefore they must be condemned, not because they are not inventive—that would be like enjoining a lawyer not to use a confession, because he simply has to use it and not invent arguments about it—but because they lead to instability. Machiavelli is thereby making the first move in the long process, which will occupy us for the rest of the book, of finding constraints in action and the rhetorical arts to replace the abandoned constraints supplied by the old politics' moralizing.

Therefore, by attacking these external *topoi*, these external resources for action, Machiavelli shows that it is possible for the prince not only to acquire a throne but to find some stability there; by attacking the external *topos* of mercenaries, Machiavelli shows that there are general methods of preservation. Not all invention leads to stability, and hence not every temporarily successful act is desirable, and virtù will not be defined simply as the cause of success, as a heuristic ethics of consequences would do. The consideration of mercenaries permits Machiavelli to make a categorical condemnation; for the first time, he does not have to say, Whether or not this is good depends on circumstances and luck. The ceremonial precepts of the hereditary monarch are far too specific for the new ruler trying to find some security in a world of flux, but Machiavelli has to find maxims at least more specific than the pure opportunism of, Do your best. While the injunction to avoid mercenaries is not earth-shaking, it provides at least one stable truth in the world of change.

The judgment Machiavelli makes about mercenaries is not a categorical judgment every politics of invention must make; it is a political judgment applying, categorically, to the new prince in these particular circumstances. Machiavelli is not saying that mercenaries and anything else which draws on resources outside oneself are always bad; he is not advocating some sort of purity, if not of motives, then of art and actions, a purity which would once again collapse prudence into an ethics of principles, where the value of an action derives from its source. To read the condemnation of mercenaries as that sort of categorical judgment would give a fixed meaning to the topic of the internal and the external, whereas *The Prince* uses this topic as a formal device for inventing arguments and discovering just what the prince's own resources are. As we shall soon see, making his subjects among the things "within the prince's power" is the prince's greatest challenge. It would be fatal to assume that they either are or are not within his power, since his job is to make them so. The reason mercenaries, and the suspect fortresses and ministers of later chapters, are so tempting is that the prince may think they are within his power, and Machiavelli's argument redefines what is within the prince's power, and so redefines *virtù*. The condemnation of mercenaries is a judgment that in employing them the new prince would forfeit his one chance of stability and be forced back into the world of instability.

Machiavelli's discovery of this initial stable truth in the world of instability and risks differs in important respects from the sort of stability metahistory offers. Metahistory condemns the new prince to the world of instability, since according to physical law any finite force is always liable to be overcome by a greater one. Metahistory can offer the prospect of stability only by positing an end of history in which all conflicts have been resolved and the state withers away. Before that time, metahistory offers stability only in its lessons, not in what they apply to; its truths are stable because they are scientifically certified and so not capable of being refuted by events, not subject to counterargument.

Machiavelli's prudent judgments, such as the condemnation of mercenaries, on the other hand, can be refuted, because their reasons are so closely tied to the particular circumstances in which the new prince operates; rules of prudence are defeasible and do not guarantee either rectitude or success. His judgments are both stable — albeit impermanent — results of argument and a stable feature of the prince's rule. In the case of mercenaries, Machiavelli discovers — and there will be further instances as the argument of *The Prince* proceeds — a way for the prince's rule to be stable while still responsive to circumstances. In this way, the first subject treated by Machiavelli's "general methods" is an initial instance of a rhetorical conclusion, an initial instance of how the rhetorician, while always able to assemble arguments on both sides of a question, is nevertheless able to end in assertion rather than doubt. The danger, though, is that in repudiating metahistory and the search for stable foundations for politics outside of politics, the reader will be led to the opposite extreme, from algorithmic thinking to heuristics: after reading that Machiavelli makes politics into war, the reader is next led to think that Machiavelli takes morality out of politics by making action a matter of what you can get away with.

We now can see Machiavelli's solution to the problem of prudent imitation, how the prince can imitate this argument without thereby resembling Machiavelli. Machiavelli not only employs topical invention, as the section on general methods for stability proceeds; he also shows the prince how to use topical invention, so that he does not have to be content with the results of Machiavelli's invention. But there is one princely function which calls for something other than topical invention, one place where the prince is told to learn from the past, *res gestae*, rather than from tradition and its publicly certified past, *historia rerum gestarum*, the material for topical invention. In chapter 14 Machiavelli tells the prince to study military history. The prince is not here supposed to invent anything, but to acquire a large repertoire and know how to use it. Unlike the strategic decision of whether to hire mercenaries, or of whether it is better to be loved or feared, which do call for topical invention, here is one situation which calls for nonrhetorical methods — there is actually something to know here, and the test of knowledge is not the verdict of the public, a rhetorical judgment, but success at arms. Since there is no rhetorical invention or judgment called for here, Machiavelli has nothing to say about military strategy in *The Prince*, other than to recommend study and application. Just as hereditary rule, on which he had little to say, is the appropriate field for straight history, military strategy is the appropriate field for metahistory.

What, then, is the relation between military science and rhetorical politics? Aristotle's *Rhetoric* suggests a useful analogy. In its primary meaning and application that art of rhetoric, unlike many later versions, is a "restrained" rather than a universal art, covering only those subjects — the realm of the practical, things that can be otherwise through our actions — for which rhetoric is not a second-best method. It admits, in a secondary sense, of the existence of a "rhetoric of science" or of other settled bodies of doctrine; in such cases rhetoric is a method of expounding truths that are certified by a superior means. Rhetoric is then appropriate because of the constraints of time or the weaknesses of the hearers. Similarly, the prudent art of stable usurpation that Machiavelli teaches to the prince has a limited subject matter and range of appropriate utility that will be political in a narrower sense, and military matters are a more established body of knowledge that can be known by more studious, more esoteric means. The prince *qua* military leader does not have to worry about whether what he knows accords with the *consensus gentium*.

The Politics of Rhetorical Invention

The prince's problem in relation to his subjects, by contrast, is one that does call for topical invention, not only by Machiavelli, but by the prince as well. Here in chapters 15–21, the prince must not simply learn from the past, but must present himself as the heir to the public version of history.[16] His understanding of the past cannot be metahistorical because the public, the *consensus gentium*, decides the rightness of his understanding. If all he were interested in was success and novelty, he could afford to be a metahistorian discovering hidden laws, but to succeed in stable innovation and legitimacy, the prince must appear to the authority of tradition.

Scholars have often debated whether or not Machiavelli assimilates civil to military problems, as some quite coherent political theories and versions of Machiavellianism do.[17] Viewing *The Prince* from the perspective of the rhetoric of politics, we can see that such debate turns on the relation of nonrhetorical, metahistorical methods of governing, which Machiavelli claims are useful for military affairs, to politics based on rhetorical invention, which it is Machiavelli's own great innovation to apply to civil matters. Out of the materials of the sentiments and beliefs of the people, the prince *invents* stable and legitimate rule over them: his method is one of topical invention, and the test of success is by rhetorical judgment by his subjects. The overt enemies of prudence in chapters 15–21 are villainy, amorality, and opportunism, but the more subversive danger comes from assimilating politics to warfare, rhetoric to metahistory, prudence to science.

Machiavelli lays out his plans for the prince's topical invention in chapters 15–21 when he discusses the prince's relations to his subjects and shows how invention permits the prince to construct relations to his subjects that are stable connections of true political rule — rule by authority and not by force. As Struever points out, White's *consensus gentium*, which she calls "common humanity," is topically defined in terms of accessibility, as "an appeal to tactics the audience and speaker share and command which allows discursive mastery of a range of shared issues. . . . The topics appeal to an available repertoire of civil behavior."[18] Common humanity, a rhetorical rather than an esoteric audience, defines and offers a shared understanding of what counts as victory, success, glory, and therefore security and legitimacy. While accessibility makes the methods of the prudent new prince differ from those of the metahistorian and metapolitician, that accessibility does not make such methods, unlike the devices available to the traditional ruler, easy or available without learning, application, and virtù. In Chapter 1 I showed the way Machiavelli lays out four formal possibilities combining ease and difficulty of acquiring and preserving states, and locates virtù as the combination of acquired with difficulty and therefore easy to hold; here, that combination is reflected in the need to combine two apparent opposites, that the methods of virtù and the politics of rhetorical invention be both generally accessible and yet achievable only by a few. These two criteria, accessibility and difficulty, show that prudent, rhetorical politics must respond to the dilemma with which Socrates confronts Protagoras when he asks how virtue can be taught: if virtue, unlike the arts, cannot be a matter for specialists (and so Zeus tells Prometheus to distribute the gifts of prudence and eloquence equally throughout the community), how can there be teachers such as Protagoras? Protagoras, like Machiavelli and the new prince, must carve out for himself a practical role for the kind of intelligence he advertises; when he responds to Socrates' doubts about the teachability of virtue by claiming that it is a gift of the gods to all mankind, he seems to be denying himself a function. If virtue, or prudence, is not a specialty, how can there be teachers, and why should its possession seem so rare? One of the dimensions of this combination of difficulty with accessibility we will have to consider later is the extent to which virtù can be an art susceptible to formulation in the precepts of method; at this point, though, articulating a politics of rhetorical invention turns on showing how the prince as persuader uses topics persuasively to consolidate his rule.

Received Values and Topical Values

So far I have claimed a consonance between topical invention as a rhetorical office and Machiavelli's political purpose of making secure innovation possible, making a new prince legitimate, a task impossible on either of White's kinds of history. Machiavelli's politics of stable innovation drives a wedge between eternity and eternal flux, between Pocock's realms of grace and custom, in the same way that prudence opens up room between algorithmic and heuristic methods, between an ethics of principles and one of consequences. The connection between political purpose and rhetorical activity can be strengthened and the activity of topical invention clarified further by turning from Machiavelli the historian to the prince opening up room between a conservative politics of style and the obvious but villainous alternative.

If the prince's prudent stability depends on his constructing relations between ruler and ruled that are grounded in topical invention, then understanding Machiavelli's project depends on our being able to give some depth to the usual commonplaces about how rhetoric uses topics for invention. Both the new and the old prince appeal to the values held by their subjects to create and consolidate emotions and habits of loyalty and obedience; and both *rule*, that is, they use the desires and powers of the audience to accomplish their own ends, which are not necessarily those of the audience. In what sense, then, does the new prince use rhetorical invention, while the old prince relies on an etiolated version of invention appropriate to a politics of style? Kenneth Burke offers "value" as his preferred translation of *topos*; taking that hint and recalling Bacon's distinction of two kinds of provision for discourse, we can distinguish topical from promptuary *values*.[19] The values Machiavelli advocates are formal and abstract, topical rather than promptuary. Not only are they established in argument by abstract means; the values themselves are formal in the sense that they require action to be realized, and consequently their use in argument, including the persuasive arguments with which the new prince appeals to his subjects, must differ from the use of values in epideictic argument and the politics of style. These new values do not contradict traditional values and make evil into good; they transform values from being eternal objects waiting to be exemplified into *agenda*, things that need to be done. In that sense, the new values are inherently ambiguous: not only morally dubious from the point of view of the old values, but ambiguous in the practical sense of its being unpredictable what sort of actions will realize them. Just as the straightforward imitation of past success has its dangers, so the old values criticized are bad, not in the sense that they praise what should be blamed, but because they, and their attendant method of understanding the past, give a false and misplaced sense of concretion. Duties such as "always keep your word" and "pay your debts" remove the need for invention and judgment.

I want to explore this idea of values as things to be done by looking briefly at Aristotle's development of the idea of good action as its own end. Sequences that connect means to ends do not always work out as planned, and people before the Renaissance did not need a revelation from

Machiavelli to notice the fact that all the things they hoped for and desired were not always obviously reconcilable with each other. Aware that the pursuits of pleasure, honor, money, and knowledge can often lead in conflicting directions, and unwilling to join Plato's search for an ultimate end that will subordinate things men think are already ultimate ends, Aristotle used the looseness of connections between actions and their results to discover intrinsic values adhering to actions and not only the things those actions bring about.[20] There are no ends "more final" than the objects men do in fact pursue as ultimate ends, but the intrinsically valuable *activities* people engage in while aiming at those good things are capable of organization, harmonization, not by being subordinated to a more final end but by being incorporated into a good life. Virtuous activities become Aristotle's primary ethical solution to the problem of multiple ultimate values, for they incorporate ultimate values without subordinating them. Aristotle is not the only pre-Machiavellian thinker to recognize the existence of plural final goods, and therefore to find a need for prudence, deliberation, and rhetorical argument to negotiate the practical problems set by their ineliminable plurality. Prudential, deliberative reasoning and the rhetorical discourse it requires take different forms through history, but they are a necessary part of the equipment of the good man whenever practical action has dimensions beyond doing what everyone knows is right. Aristotle can face this problem against a relatively stable background; whether historically accurate or not, he acts as though for the most part virtue is rewarded, and so he does not have to confront radically anomalous juxtapositions of appearance and reality, means and ends; prudence and rhetoric will, as a consequence, have a more restrained role to play in good action for him than that suitable for Machiavelli. As a consequence, Aristotle is able to locate primary values in activity without thereby making those values ambiguous, as Machiavelli must. Morally virtuous activities were Aristotle's primary ethical solution to the problem of plural final goods; in addition, he locates in political constitutions, and in the intellectual virtues (including the virtues and methods of deliberation), resources for the continuing problem of inserting ultimate values in a world of human action rather than relegating them to a Platonic heaven of self-existent values and ideas. But where Aristotle subordinates rhetoric to politics, placing deliberative activity within a context of stable constitutional arrangements, Machiavelli makes such argument the center of his solution to the problem of plural ultimate value. Because of the destructive effects Machiavelli's rhetoric has on the ideology of stable values, the possibility and efficacy of both heroic action and stable institutions become derivative —in both *The Prince* and the *Discourses on Livy*—from efficacious practical argument: while action that is its own end was interpreted by Aristotle to mean acting for the sake of the noble, in Machiavelli it will mean acting for the sake of glory.

In the first chapter I showed how Machiavelli used rhetoric to distinguish things within from things outside the prince's power. Here that distinction is rhetoricized further by making activities the fundamental locus of value, making these achievements a function of the prince's art of rhetoric, not just Machiavelli's. The values *The Prince* advocates are not different values in the sense of competing answers to the same question, as in the radical politics of the metahistorian or the scientific, esoteric philosopher; instead they exhibit a different structure of openness and definiteness, formality and ambiguity, a structure appropriate to stable innovation, and not to the traditional alternatives of stability and innovation. For example, success is a value, a good thing, preferable to failure. But, as the case of mercenaries shows, simple success or failure cannot be the end of action and the criterion for good action; instead success is the derivative of a more fundamental value, that of acting from one's own power: while military success can be recognized apart from the actions that brought it about, civil security cannot. Acting from virtù is not a new and competing value because it functions differently from a traditional value such as success: virtù necessarily rejects the separation of means and ends encouraged and even required by traditional values.[21] In the same way, liberality and mercy—princely actions that evoke favorable sentiments and judgments from the prince's subjects—are good things, and the prince should wish to perform them, but, as we saw earlier, they are not *therefore* automatically to be chosen. On the contrary, the extent to which the prince can safely choose actions that lead to military success and actions that his subjects will praise is the best measure of his security. In hereditary monarchy and straight history there is an algorithmic homology among *exemplum*, value, and act; in what Machiavelli calls villainy anything goes, success is the only value, and there is no relation at all between other values and recommended action; in topical invention, by contrast, all traditional values are maintained but are made to depend, for their being carried into action, on virtù: the old values are still valued, but we cannot know what they mean in action until they are done, and they cannot be done successfully unless the prince can do them by his own virtù. The old values are still valued to the extent that they can be accomplished *in* action, not as the results of action distinct from themselves. The moral of the Cesare Borgia story is not, Act like this, or, Don't act like this, but, Virtù is the only source and measure of security.

Machiavelli has complicated the relations between values and actions by introducing a different sort of value—virtù, or relying on one's own power—a value it would be tempting to call a second-order value or a metavalue if those terms had any determinate meaning, instead of being sophisticated ways of evading the issue. Virtù is a criterion both for when other values can safely be adopted as ends and for which means one can safely use to attain those ends. In this sense Machiavelli's virtù then serves the same function in argument as does the virtue of justice in Aristotle's *Ethics*, although virtù may look more like injustice and its motive, *pleonexia!* "[The goods] on which good and bad fortune depend, . . . though always good in the absolute sense, are not always good for a particular person. Yet these are the goods men pray for and pursue, although they ought not to do so; they ought, while choosing the things that are good for them, to pray that what is good absolutely may also be good for them" (*Ethics* 5.1.1129b3–7).

Such an interposition of virtù between value and act — between rule and case — must be seen as threatening by established morality, but it need not itself be immoral or amoral. Socrates, thus, makes the same sort of reversal between virtue and money as Machiavelli makes between stable power and military resources: "Virtue does not come from money, but from virtue comes money and all other goods things to man" (*Apology* 30d). Both Socrates and Machiavelli look immoral not only because they show that existing values must sometimes be overridden — if the charge that Socrates introduced new gods has any meaning above the stock accusation he says it is — but because each, in quite different ways, invites questions about what would happen if everyone acted that way. Each challenges not only an existing community of values — and both are fairly contemptuous of those given communities — but may challenge *any* community of values, unless it is possible for there to be a community of Socratic inquirers or Machiavellian princes.

Just as in Socrates' case, making acts the loci of value opens up a series of problems that will occupy us for the rest of the book. I do not propose to explore Socrates' encounter with that sort of problem of universalizability here, but I do think that problem worth exploring for Machiavelli. In Chapter 5 I will raise the question whether such a community can exist, and in Chapter 4 I will return to the question of the relation of new and old values by subsuming it under the question of the commensurability of the old and new politics. Here, instead, I propose to offer the following abstract way of approaching the problem of new values, new major premisses for prudent action: is the topical invention that Machiavelli has been employing really a kind of invention that can be part of a complete rhetorical art, something teachable and something that comprises not only invention but judgment, style, and memory? The Machiavellian enterprise will succeed only if rhetoric is not just a series of devices but a discipline, a limited power for finding and assembling available resources and achiev-

The Politics of Rhetorical Invention

ing ends in action. In substantive terms, if topical invention allows the new prince's rule to be stable, can we be confident that it will really be recognizable as *political* rule? Machiavelli's new mode of action will be political if and only if it is rooted in a full art of rhetoric, not just some devices, and that is possible if and only if the other parts of rhetoric follow from the principles of rhetorical invention. All the parts of rhetoric must be present in some form in any fully developed rhetorical art, and in any fully developed political system based on a relation between tradition, values, and policy. In particular, the rhetorical criterion of accessibility and appeal to the *consensus gentium* demands a treatment of the new kind of style corresponding to a politics of rhetorical invention: if Machiavelli's critique of ideology and exposure of the arbitrary nature of traditional rule does not lead to an unrestricted vision of a deeper reality, what does it mean to be confined within this domain of artifice?

Force, Fraud, and Prudence

Machiavelli's hard-headed realism, taking men as they are and not as they ought to be, is celebrated for breaking through the pretenses of terministic screens by which we dignify and legitimate our selfish, covetous, envious attempts to gratify our desires, and is praised, or condemned, for replacing partial and illusory vocabularies with a scientific Last Word. It follows on that reading that he proposes a new set of values appropriate to human nature and human behavior instead of the pious fictions of how people should act. As we can now see, that reading of Machiavelli makes his critique of ideology a metahistorical one that exposes and sees through the false consciousness of the *consensus gentium* and replaces it with the scientific study of men as they are, along the lines of the Cartesian dictum of accepting no ideas but those about which no error is possible, or, even more analogously, of Bacon's project in the *New Organon* of first destroying the idols and then building secure science on the basis of an undistorted access of reality. (Recall that Descartes exempts moral and practical ideas from at least the initial reach of his method, and consequently recommends a conservative provisional morality of obedience to custom and accepted ideas.) It is true that by making them discursively accessible, Machiavelli domesticates ambition, force, and fraud, but they are not civilized and pacified by the construction of a scientifically and morally neutral vocabulary for them. My insistence on the difference between Machiavelli's exposure and criticism of apparently natural but actually deeply conventional practices and that usual caricature is brought to a head by a consideration of the most notorious putative example of such reduction of action to motion, the assertion in chapter 18 that the successful prince must learn not only the methods of man but also of the beast: "There are two methods of fighting, the one by law, the other by force: The first method is that of men, the second of beasts; but as the first is often insufficient, one must have recourse to the second. It is therefore necessary for a prince to know well how to use both the beast and the man."

But that reduction of man to beast cannot be complete, and so Machiavelli's realism, or pragmatism — his Machiavellianism — is no behaviorism, no dissolution of the political into the military. After separating human from animal methods of fighting, he distinguishes a pair of bestial methods: "A prince being thus obliged to know well how to act as a beast must imitate the fox and the lion." In literal and traditional language, the prince has to rely on force and fraud. We have seen how Machiavelli pointed to the importance of leonine, military methods earlier in *The Prince*. The methods of the beast which Machiavelli actually writes about in *The Prince* are really confined to one bestial method, that of vulpine fraud; the body of chapter 18, as its title states, is only about the method of the fox: "In What Way Princes Must Keep Faith."

But while lions really are strong, foxes are not actually "great feigners and dissemblers" but merely a natural symbol for the specifically human activity of fraud. So Machiavelli has divided methods into the human and the bestial, but then finds that at the heart of the animal is an essentially human way of acting, deception. Fraud must be classified as bestial because no honor attaches to it, but here is a particularly human sort of animal behavior. Hence, mere motion will never do, and the reduction of politics to force is incomplete without the reduction of force to fraud. The human world, the world of politics and rhetoric, is ineliminably restored after all.[22]

The conservative politics of the hereditary ruler depended on kinds of conventions whose power came from their remaining hidden, while the radical politics associated with metahistory depends on exposing those conventions and relying on scientific force instead; Machiavelli becomes the champion of the third alternative, fraud, as the argument of *The Prince* carves out room for the necessary operations of fraud, and extends its meaning by dramatizing the inadequacy of the traditional ruler who acts by merely "human" methods and the inadequacy of the mercenary or other purely military figure who follows the lion. Along those lines, fraud becomes expanded to include everything not covered by either human or leonine methods:

When Machiavelli talks of force he means coercion, the explicit and ultimate form of power. When he talks about fraud he is also talking

The Politics of Rhetorical Invention

of power but in its covert forms, the forms it takes when it is either insufficient to reveal itself nakedly or when it can afford to dissimulate its appearance because of a voluntary obedience of its subjects. Fraud includes the power and genuine authority Numa gained when he fraudulently founded a religion which the Romans believed in and which justified in their eyes the power he claimed but did not safely possess until he gained it in this fraudulent way. . . . Where we today talk about myth, convention, social fictions and the like, Machiavelli used the single term "fraud."[23]

With the possible exceptions of Alexander Borgia and Savonarola, no one ever thought that fraud by itself could be enough to ensure success, while the other two methods had their traditional partisans. A political method grounded in fraud will be either a sophistical politics relying on heuristic opportunism or a rhetorical prudence, and Machiavelli carves out room for this latter alternative, a prudent possibility besides blind obedience to traditional rulers and the scientifically grounded opportunism represented by naked force, by destabilizing the topic of appearance and reality so that it can be used for topical argument. (Sophistical heuristics, by contrast, destroys the appearance/reality distinction by making everything into appearance, so that there is nothing to choose between appearances except how well they "sell.") Sometimes the prince must appear bad in order really to be good, as in sacrificing short-run popularity for long-run stability, but the reality there is just a more stable appearance; conversely, he who appears good may in fact be bad. Thus, Machiavelli denigrates the importance of both appearance and reality, arguing that it is more important to appear good than to be good, not in order to deceive but because ultimately an appearance that lasts long enough is the only reality, the only effectual reality. As McCanles points out:

Throughout the second half [of *The Prince*] Machiavelli progressively dispenses with the reality/appearance differential and substitutes for it a conception of political interaction wherein there simply are no realities save signs. That is, "reality" is constituted of signs whose only function is to refer to other signs, or to evoke in the beholder his own text composed of signs. Instead of a political world wherein words are "backed up" by force Machiavelli gives a world in which physical power exerts no force until it is textualized.[24]

That the ultimate Machiavellian reality consists in signs merely reconfirms the specifically human character of the methods of the fox; if the signs were disguises of nonlinguistic realities — if, for instance, they were merely signs as "symptoms" of desires, or instruments towards the fulfilments of such desires—then the difference between man and beast, politics and warfare, would be "merely conventional," that is, apparent in the sense of unreal. The fact that this apparent reduction of human action and motives to bestial forces undercuts itself by introducing a specifically human kind of action in the vulpine allegory shows that Machiavelli's invocation of the lion and the fox is not in this respect so different from Cicero's earlier use of the same fable. Cicero too needs to give some intelligibility to a world in which rules and cases interact in unexpected ways, and in seeing how "circumstances alter cases," he invokes two criteria: equity and common sense, and "prudence and necessity. In particular, political life frequently requires us to apply the latter rule. We should conduct war and peace without guile or violence, if possible. But, while such strategies are bestial rather than human, we may have to use them as last resort. This is the context in which Cicero mentions the famous analogy of the lion and the fox."[25]

The rhetorical force of this critique of ideology shows why *The Prince* cannot be taken as saying one thing to the prince and another to his subjects and its other readers. This critique exposes the domain of artifice only to show that it has no alternative, no reality standing behind it in which we might live if we were smart enough, or brave enough, or good enough. Still, it is far from clear how a better understanding of the operations of fraud help us to live better.

If the exemplary prudential act to be imitated is the argument of *The Prince* itself, then this exercise of prudence, like any good action, may become its own end, done for its own sake. But when an act of reading or writing becomes its own end, there is a possible interpretation available not readily applied to acts of other kinds: a literary end in itself is "literary" in the aesthetic sense of the term—its own end and hence an object of contemplation and enjoyment rather than, in Burke's phrase that captures the rhetorical use of literature, "equipment for living." Rather than the analogies between discursive and practical acts protecting the act of reading and imitating *The Prince* from such an aesthetic interpretation, the analogy opens up the threat of inference in the other direction, so that the resultant further acts that reading *The Prince* empowers threaten to become aesthetic as well. As Struever puts it, the problem Machiavelli faces is "raising discourse to history," rather than "reducing history to discourse, 'fetischizing' discourse."[26]

If the activities of the fox are conventional human actions in general, then what does Machiavelli tell the prince, and the rest of his audience, when he says that the prince must learn such methods? What is the force of such exposure, such domestication, such tough talk? Even if "prudence" and "fraud" refer to a single set of denotata, making them synonyms must be an outrage. Machiavelli responds to this predicament, of exposing the conventional nature of crucially human acts without pointing to any natural reality apart from such convention, in a way that wavers between — or mediates between — the autonomy of the aesthetic and the autonomy of the practical. If one cannot escape from history by seeing through the ideological distortions of history to a clearer perception of reality, then the two next most plausible possibilities are, first, an appreciation of the empowering resources history offers to the prudent politician, an appreciation with an evident practical dimension, as one's ability to act increases, "appreciates," through studying great deeds of the past, or, second, a purely aesthetic or ironic "appreciation," as one learns to withdraw and contemplate the drama of ignorance, folly, and vice. Rather than either of those actually characterizing the force of this destructive rhetoric, this exposing of the fraud that underlies forceful and even apparently glorious action, those two set the limits inside of which Machiavelli can respond.

Starting on the poetic side, Machiavelli teaches his audience educated responses to the theatrical qualities of people acting out of base motives with bestial methods. He poetizes the way we look at politics, narrowing the scope of vision by excluding motive and effect to focus on style, as conscious and shared artifact. Machiavelli fills in the motives of the prince with fairly empty terms like honor and glory, and with the vain hope of unifying Italy, so that he can explore the space between motives and consequences. This poetizing, then, has a profoundly practical function, since narrowing the scope of vision offers room for practical maneuver. Such aesthetic and decorous appeal does duty for traditional moral constraints, as that which cannot be appreciated remains irretrievably bestial. A strict moralizing and a conservative politics must be repelled by Machiavelli's enjoining the prince always to do great and glorious things, but that appeal to glory restrains the new prince as it distinguishes prudent action from truly bestial, or scientific, military methods.[27] Glory thus not only prevents a reduction of politics to military tactics, but also blocks a distinction between practical and aesthetic. If politics is reduced to military success, then aesthetic values become identified with the useless and must be distinct from practical values, which become narrowed to the merely useful.

To recall my claims at the beginning of the chapter: the traditional five parts of rhetoric — plus the antirhetorical possibility of metahistory — offer a typology of political regimes, and Machiavelli's new politics could then be characterized as a politics of invention in opposition to the traditional ruler's politics of style. Although lacking in rhetorical invention, the hereditary monarch did have a surrogate which served the function of invention — promptuary action. Correspondingly, the new prince acts primarily through invention, and such action generates its own new kind of style: the last of the chapters on the relations of the prince to his people treats of glory. Even in a world where success is always unpredictable, one can count on the appropriate reception from the civic audience for doing things with style, and so the prince should continually do great things and get "fame for being great and excellent."

I noted that while Mazzeo may be right in claiming that Machiavelli expands the idea of fraud to include all conventional acts, nevertheless, even if fraud and convention, or fraud and prudence, refer to the same set of objects, it would be absurd to take them as synonyms, and the idea of glorious fraud ought to cause some hesitation. In fact, Machiavelli's exposure of convention without relying on a contrast between convention and something more stable outside it undercuts the idea of reference altogether.[28] On the other hand, such performance by the prince really is fraudulent, and not just "conventional," even if the audience realizes it is a fraud. To quote McCanles again: "Yet in order for the prince successfully to exploit the Machiavellian reduction of history to discourse, the assumption of a domain of power beyond the boundaries of discourse must remain inviolate. People will respond to the power textualized in discourse only as long as they believe that such an entity as power distinct from discourse exists, and remain ignorant that the prince being always an emperor with no clothes on, becomes powerful only when they dress him in that power."[29]

This deconstructive side to the symbolic emotions that bind ruler and ruled — that it is not force but the fear of force that counts, but that that fear depends on the force actually being available, that reference, while undercut, is still indispensable — is a solution to the earlier rhetorical problem of how a ruler can derive his power from the people without depending on them, and hence to the subsequent problem of how there can be an alternative to both the conservative politics that relies on established order and a radical politics that ignores it. Machiavelli's treatment of the emotions, and its back-reference through the lion to arms as well as the man, exhibit the conventional character of just those aspects of human activity most likely to be taken as natural. While it is tempting to identify the distinction between the subject matter of science and that of prudence with the difference between nature and convention, the fable of the lion and the fox makes it impossible to rest content with such a simple identification. Whereas Aristotle rejects that identification at *Ethics* 3.3, using the letters of the alphabet as an example of something that is conventional yet not something we deliberate about, Machiavelli instead dramatizes in chapter 25 the possibility of making conventional rather than natural one's own character, taking something that seems to be given and making it subject to choice, or at least subject to debate. The arguments on both sides of *that* question are the last things Machiavelli can say in other than future tense in *The Prince*, and they demand a closer look.

4   PARADIGMS AND PRINCES

The previous chapter focused on chapters 12–23 of *The Prince* and the way Machiavelli complicates the relations between general rules and the cases to which they apply by destabilizing the relations between appearance and reality, appearing good and being good, seeming strong and being strong. While the earlier chapters of *The Prince* problematized rhetorical induction or reasoning by example, rendering questionable the project of serving up for imitation great examples of the past, this next part of the text turned to a use of rhetoric the prince himself must practice, and not simply learn from: the enthymeme, the translation of universal precepts and values into practical decisions and acts. Machiavelli begins this section by pointing to the real and nonnegligible value of algorithmic thinking and its easier relation between rules and instances, but he limits its use to military, as opposed to political, affairs — the methods of the lion, but not the fox — a limitation which can be used polemically to expose as empty the ceremonial politics of style and certified rules and examples that the old politics depends on. We have seen how the politics of style and metapolitics both remove the need for prudence and for rhetoric by positing an unproblematic relation between principles and cases. Machiavelli attacks the algorithmic thinking of the old politics by laying bare the assumptions without which those inferences from principle to policy could not be so smooth. (To anticipate, there is another sense in which *The Prince* as a whole focuses on reasoning from example, teaching the prince how to exploit examples of great actions and of prudent imitations, while *The Discourses* embodies an enthymematic reasoning that explores and offers frameworks for particular exemplary actions. Within the argument of *The Prince*, though, that same relative contrast between actions and contexts, or general methods, holds.)

But this rhetorical critique of ideology, with its strategy of undercutting noncontroversial and direct reference to motives and consequences, opens up the danger that debunking will become a general, unrestrained intellectual habit, as Socrates' young followers became indecorous questioners whose purpose was merely destructive; the corresponding practical consequence is, of course, that the new prince's success would make further usurpations easier and more likely. Without some constraint on the calling into question of foundations, rhetoric once again threatens to degenerate into opportunism and sophistic.[1] To recall once more the parallel places occupied by Descartes and Machiavelli in the respective histories of theoretical and practical reason, where Descartes's proclamation of the autonomy of theoretical reason freed it from the traditional restraints of established custom and belief, Machiavelli's autonomy of practical reason seemed to remove the restraints tradition placed on immoral, selfish, corrupt behavior; and if constraint cannot be supplied by an art of rhetoric, it is difficult to see how it can be supplied at all.

Unlike the metahistorical critique of ideology, Machiavelli's argument has appealed to the appearance/reality distinction only to problematize it: reference to a bestial reality underlying courtly, decent appearance only serves to highlight the need to ground such references to reality in appearances, in what people—subjects, citizens, and opponents—think. The ontological-sounding distinction between appearance and reality has been transformed into the more linguistically centered opposition of the implicit and the explicit, or the pragmatic one of suppressing and exposing (recall, for example, Dewey's claim that the real problem in philosophy is not so much appearance/reality as appearing/disappearing), and therefore one must ask what difference it makes in prudential politics, as opposed to metapolitics or a traditional politics of style, to have one's foundations exposed, to lay bare the sources of one's power.

The philosophical form of Machiavelli's latest problem is this. Rhetorical self-consciousness has limits and constraints only if prudence and the articulation of practical principles have a *function;* consequently, if theory, or whatever more modest title one should accord to Machiavelli's own contribution, is not automatically liberating, as a metahistorical stripping away of illusion is, then what is the use of prudent reason, and especially the prudent perception of the ultimate reality of appearance, in action? (Science does not need restraints beyond those offered by its reality, but an art does if its practitioners are to have any integrity.) Earlier, I noted the disjunction between Machiavelli's liberating purposes and the constraint that appears in the substance of his advice, the way he shows that increases in knowledge and self-knowledge are not automatically liberating, but could instead lead to a recognition of the severe limitations on thoughtful action. To find a definite, while limited, function for prudence is precisely to internalize those constraints, so that they are not conceived, incoherently, as the force of external circumstances (without which one could act freely and without limit?) but as consequences of the function of practical reason itself. (Further dimensions of the prudently ambivalent status of self-consciousness will become prominent in later chapters.)

I think that the way to treat this destabilizing of the distinction between the implicit and the explicit—a destabilizing that is not simply a destruction of that distinction, since Machiavelli also shows that we cannot live without it; we just cannot pin it down for very long—is by turning to the other distinction made problematic in prudence, that between principle and case. Not only has that distinction been problematized, but so too has one critical instance of it, the relation between a particular ruler and the kind of politics he represents or exemplifies. Machiavelli must be concerned, on behalf of the new prince, that some individual hereditary monarch not be overthrown while his politics remain inviolate. For the new prince's usurpation to be political, the new prince must be seen as a politician, and that requires that the old, overthrown prince be seen as defeated not only as an individual but as a representative of a kind of politics. On the other hand, just as the great strength of the old politics is the way it permits a distinction between the regime, the kind of politics represented, and any particular ruler and embodiment of that politics, so conversely it is difficult to see the usurping new prince as representing anything other than himself, the embodiment of personal rule. He is the gambler always eager to stake everything on a single bet, always ready to call any test a crucial experiment, while the conservatism of the traditional politics depends on its ability to resist such challenges, turning away from crucial experiments. If the critique of ideology were therapeutically liberating, it would not only produce the scientific freedom and ability to act without constraint, but it would also thereby produce radical individualists who, to the extent that they did not represent anything, could not be characterized and hence had no character; reading Machiavelli's lessons as advice for usurpation without constraint results in precisely such a loss of character. This threatened loss of character is the ethical form of the problem that mere particulars by themselves are unintelligible; when a person becomes radically individualized, he has no being, no character. (It has often been noted that utilitarian ethics of consequences have no room for character or even the discreteness of agents. If the locus of value is in conditions of the world instead of activities, instead of even the actions that produce those conditions, then it becomes hard to attribute any value to individuality, integrity, or autonomy, beyond their tendency to improve the state of the world. Individual agents and actions are valued and are intelligible only as connected to those results.)

The old politics, then, derives its strength and continuity from the distance between a kind of politics and a particular regime—a strength Machiavelli will convert into a weakness—and the act of pure usurpation derives its flexibility from the way it has no principle, is not an instance of anything else. By contrast, in some way yet to be specified the relation between *The Prince* and the prudential politics it "represents" must become subject to debate and judgment. In the language that Aristotle uses to develop his conception of prudence, the difficulty is as follows: sciences and arts have rational formulae, *logoi,* that can be explicated in algorithmic methods. While prudence has an *orthos logos,* that right rule cannot be stated apart from its embodiments in particular modes of good action, such as, in Aristotle's own exposition, the moral virtues. (To complete the triad, sophistic opportunism has no right rule at all, and is in that quite literal sense *unprincipled,* and the sophist, like the classical figure of Proteus, has no character.) Machiavelli's task is to show that the rule of a new prince has a principle, and that his rule is therefore political, without being able to formulate that principle, as can the hereditary ruler, apart from its embodiments. (If he could, then virtù could be a method, and virtue could be taught.)[2]

If Machiavelli cannot make his new politics at least to that extent rational, then it once again will collapse into opportunism, the danger we encountered initially in Machiavelli's need to give virtù a meaning beyond exhorting the new prince to do his best. Nevertheless, if traditional rule is weakened when its grounds are explicit, it is hard to see how Machiavelli's new politics of usurpation and invention would not equally be weakened by being tamed and domesticated, as revolutionary leaders traditionally disappoint their followers by allowing themselves to be restrained by following stable, public procedures. Making explicit the relation of rule and case seems to weaken politics based on both algorithmic or heuristic uses of principles.

The problem of the explicit and the implicit is a fundamental aspect of the more general problem of the use of intelligence in politics, the relation of reason to action, because it raises the question of what use an understanding of politics is, what could be the use of making explicit the relation between the exercise of power and its source. The problem's specification into that of the relation between any ruler and the politics he *represents* points to one possible function of intelligence in action, that of making evident — to subjects, citizens, other states, and other candidates for rule — that the kind of action inspired by Machiavelli is in fact political.[3] This pair of connected questions — What happens when the foundations of rule become open to view? and, How does one make a new, or at least a newly rationalized and methodized, mode of action rationally defensible by common standards and thereby political? — does more than just invite an exploration of further dimensions of prudence and rhetorical politics. In addition, it has clear and fruitful connections to current problems of incommensurability, and the refinements of that latter debate give a language for exploring some of the complexities of Machiavellian prudence. Machiavelli demonstrates the political character of his new politics by making it commensurable with the old; that act of comparison also converts the old politics from politics as such into one kind of politics among others. Recent discussions of commensurability have shown the way rhetoric is a way of thinking especially appropriate to periods of revolution or interregnum, where more straightforward, scientific, or algorithmic methods fail; and I consequently think it useful to turn to the last three chapters of *The Prince* and treat them as three ways in which Machiavelli makes the new politics political by making it join the old in argument.[4] If, as we saw in the last chapter, chapters 12–23 of *The Prince* made the prince more active by presenting a kind of rhetoric he must practice as well as learn from, these last three chapters force some sort of activity on the readers, who must judge between the two politics.

It would be hard to find two fundamental orientations towards action more unlike each other, less likely to understand each other or find common ground, than Machiavelli's new politics and the old politics he wants to supplant. The hereditary monarch commands habitual obedience by acting as princes are expected to. The old ruler sees himself, and expects to be seen, as a ruler because he has inherited the throne; his actions, similarly, are right as their rightness is inherited from the principles that justify them. The new prince sees himself as a ruler because he is successful in seizing power, and his actions are right to the extent that they succeed: consequences, not principles, are the measure of value.

Rhetorical Argument and Making the New Politics Political

If the presentation of exemplary achievements together with directions for their imitation counts as an initial criterion for a paradigm, then when Machiavelli dedicates *The Prince* to Lorenzo de' Medici and says that he is presenting him with "the knowledge of the great deeds of the past," he is offering *The Prince* as a new paradigm for politics. The first twenty-three chapters can be read as developing a new "normal" politics; the last three chapters of *The Prince* are a series of interparadigmatic comparisons between Machiavelli's new politics and the old politics he exhorts the prince to overthrow. Machiavelli does not merely hold up for comparison and weighing the two kinds of politics, but broadens the object of our attention from the comparison itself to the longer processes by which contending parties sometimes try to force their competition to join in such a contest, and sometimes try to avoid submitting to a comparison and decisive judgment. Those writers who regard as simple the whole question of whether paradigms are commensurable or not, who think that all paradigms are either obviously commensurable or obviously incommensurable take for granted those preparatory acts and assume either that the battle can always be joined or always avoided, while Machiavelli is forced to devote more attention to those preliminaries, converting the question of whether the competing versions of politics are comparable or not into a practical question.[5]

Exemplary achievements and the methods for imitating them can of course be compared, a fact that Machiavelli exploits to his advantage, but such comparisons serve only to demonstrate that examples and methods can survive without the world views that give them depth. A world view such as that possessed by both the old politics Machiavelli attacks and the new politics he promotes is a fundamental orientation towards the world, general enough to contain criteria for applying what once were called the transcendentals, for saying what is real, true, and good. Machiavelli finds that a successful reorientation of politics towards prudence requires joining the battle against both the world view of the old politics and the paradigm — the exemplary achievements together with directions for their imitation — he associates with it.

Ptolemaic astronomy and the other examples usually appealed to in the literature on scientific paradigms may be transfigured by being systematized, but that change is minor compared to what happens to traditional politics when made explicit; the old politics depends for much of its effect on being implicit, so the very act of making it explicit will call it into question and thereby weaken it. Traditional rule is in that quite strong sense therefore antirhetorical: it depends for its success on being beyond argument and must contain ways of preventing itself from becoming discursively accessible.[6] While the logical transformation of the implicit into the explicit, of unarticulated modes of experience to their systematization, may be a relatively harmless operation in modern science, where the implicit is always assumed to be the *potentially* explicit, the relation between implicit and explicit is far more tenuous in politics, where there may be specific values at risk in the process of making things explicit. Roger Scruton, for example, has recently claimed that conservative politics forfeits its character in the act of articulation, in effect asserting that a conservative *orthos logos* and a conservative prudence cannot be articulated, that theirs is a virtue that cannot be taught:

> Conservatism may rarely announce itself in maxims, formulae or aims. Its essence is inarticulate, and its expression, when compelled, sceptical. But it is capable of expression, and in times of crisis, forced either by political necessity, or by the clamour for doctrine, conservatism does its best, though not always with any confidence that the words it finds will match the instinct that required them. . . .
> . . . Conservatism — as a motivating force in the political life of

the citizen—is characteristically inarticulate, unwilling (and usually
indeed unable) to translate itself into formulae or maxims, loath to
state its purpose or declare its view. . . . Indeed, if it is true that
conservatism becomes conscious only when forced to be so, then
it is inevitable that the passage from practice to theory will not be
rewarded by any immediate influence from theory back to what
is done.[7]

As Machiavelli points out in chapter 24, close scrutiny of the new prince
works to his advantage—"A new prince is much more observed in his actions than a hereditary one, and when [his actions] are recognized as virtuous, he wins men over"—while the more closely we look at a traditional
ruler, the more arbitrary and groundless his rule becomes. Certain ideas
and modes of action are destroyed by self-consciousness, while others are
strengthened by scrutiny. We have to wonder whether making both kinds
of politics explicit is a test fair to both sides. Machiavelli does not need
to worry about whether his new politics will be compared with the old;
princes, subjects, and future readers can hardly refuse to see them as alternatives. What is in doubt, though, equally in Machiavelli and in the recent literature about paradigms, is whether such a comparison, and such
a choice, can be rational, fair, neutral, or disinterested, whether there is
anything that can be called common ground for such comparisons. Instead of that theoretical formulation of the problem, Machiavelli must face
the practical problem of whether his new prince will be *seen* as a prince
and not just a usurper, whether his new politics will be *acknowledged* as
a new version of politics rather than as a violent replacement of politics
by something else; what Machiavelli lacks in philosophical and methodo-
logical sophistication he makes up in practical urgency. Defeating old states
on the battlefield is not good enough, just as a new science out-predicting
and out-performing the old is never by itself sufficient for it to inherit the
rights of orthodoxy. The new prince, while successful on the battlefield,
can be dismissed as a usurper who has placed himself outside politics, just
as scientific discoveries found by unconventional methods can be ascribed
to creative and irrational intuition. The new prince must find a way of
showing his new politics to be discursively and intellectually superior, of
becoming the victor in debate as well as in war; he must become the *legitimate* victor over the old politics.[8]

Machiavelli's problem is a practical one of how to make the two politics
comparable, and the task is especially difficult because the usual common
ground for talking about different political systems, common moral standards, is not readily available to him. Indeed one of the functions of any
revolutionary rhetoric—including the rhetoric of scientific revolutions—is

to show that grounds once thought neutral, common, and fair are in fact ideologically loaded.[9] In Machiavelli the obvious and famous sign of the loss of self-evidence and of the unproblematic attitude associated with normal science is in relation to conventional morality, but Machiavelli's critique is more general than that, focusing on the relation between intention and effect, desire and success, appearance and reality, all the connections that were taken for granted and are now made questionable. If neither military victory nor a common morality will serve as a test of the two politics, what will?

Kuhn talks about the situation in which one paradigm replaces another as a revolution, but that term is not available to us, since one of the competing paradigms sees politics as permanently revolutionary, while the other sees revolution as antipolitical, the opposite of politics. The historical schema of alternating revolutions and establishments presupposes that algorithmic thinking — puzzle solving — is characteristic of normal science and stable regimes while rhetorical thought applies only in those temporary transitions between one stable period and the next; so better than characterizing interparadigmatic competition as a revolution, it is more appropriate here to call it a *state of war* — not actual fighting but the condition in which might makes right.[10] Within any paradigm or established regime, rights are a limited and authorized species of might, which by being authorized is not seen within the paradigm as a form of force at all, but the antithesis of force. Eloquence, age, birth, popularity, are forms of might which some political communities recognize as right rather than might; for this reason Aristotle, in his discussion of justice and equality, recognizes the incommensurability among such claims to right and rule:

> Suppose someone is superior in playing the flute but much inferior in birth or in good looks, then, even granting that each of these things — birth and beauty — is a greater good than ability to play the flute, and even though they surpass flute-playing proportionately more than the best flute-player surpasses the others in flute-playing, even so the best flute-player ought to be given the outstandingly good flutes; for otherwise superiority both in wealth and in birth ought to contribute to the excellence of the performance, but they do not do so at all. Moreover on this theory every good thing would be commensurable with every other [πᾶν ἀγαθὸν πρὸς πᾶν ἂν εἴη συμβλητόν]. (*Politics* 3.7.1282b35ff.)

But outside some political community or some paradigm, there are no authorized forms of force, and so all kinds of force are seen simply as force: might has to make right because there is nothing else which could certify right: that is the force of Thrasymachus' challenge to Socrates. Prior to the establishment of a single paradigm, right is not yet separated off from might, and rationality is not yet, in Levi-Strauss's term, *domesticated;* the distinction between the rational and the irrational is the political consequence of such an establishment.[11]

Rhetoric offers a way of making such situations intelligible because it traditionally refuses to accept as given any distinction between rational and irrational appeals, but instead shows the way the distinctions between legitimate and illegitimate, artistic and inartistic, proper and improper bases for judgment, must be negotiated. Rhetoric, in addition, is the traditional storehouse for the strategies paradigms employ to avoid confrontation and commensuration. No system of thought or action could survive for long without having some such strategies available. Indeed, the whole current elaboration of paradigms and related objects in the philosophy of science was designed not only to overthrow the myths of rationality that made science into the steady accumulation of facts, but equally the myth that contests between theories are typically settled by crucial experiments. (There is a need to make epistemological sense out of the military idea of reserve troops.) Since *The Prince* ends with something that looks like a crucial experiment—the unification of Italy—these protection-and-avoidance strategies become all the more important. From the standpoint of Machiavelli's new paradigm, the old ruler is not much of a ruler at all, but a parasite on the people, someone who has not earned his throne. The new prince offers welfare, rule based on success (what could better prove the right to rule than a manifest ability to rule?), and even glory. Of course, from the point of view of the traditional paradigm, these considerations are not reasons for loyalty but the false inducements of the usurper and demagogue. How could such diverse views of the nature of politics be commensurable?[12]

Interparadigmatic Judgments and the Usurpation Of Tradition

Interparadigmatic comparisons are less straightforward than judgments within a single paradigm because the standards of judgment are themselves open to question; a sign of how different matters stand once one steps outside any particular paradigm is the way the most self-evident truths appear to one's opponents as empty tautologies.[13] The hereditary monarch has the right to rule because he is a hereditary monarch; although any particular ruler may be vulnerable to the predations of an aspiring new prince, the kind of politics which he exemplifies cannot be overthrown, or even challenged, so easily—one can overthrow or refute an instance, but one does not thereby destroy the rule, nor is it clear that Machiavelli should *want* to refute the principle of which the hereditary ruler is a case. He faces a dilemma: he has to expose the vacuously circular character of claims to rule based on hereditary rule, while at the same time forcing a reinterpretation of such a principle so that the subjects of the new prince can pay him the homage and obedience due to the traditional ruler. The problem—how to overthrow a particular rule without appearing opposed to political rule as such—suggests that Machiavelli's best line of argument would claim that, unless the new prince be admitted as a legitimate political ruler, the principles of politics will be empty, contemptible tautologies; the circularity between claims to rule and actual ruling can be avoided only by accepting the new prince. It becomes to the old ruler's advantage to recognize the legitimacy, the political character, of the usurper's challenge, and to that extent the old politics can be a participant in its own downfall.

Therefore chapter 24 is entitled "Why the Princes of Italy Have Lost Their States," but it begins, not by answering that question about the failures of the old politics, but by asserting, "The lessons above taught . . . will make a new prince seem old, and will soon seat him in his place more firmly and securely than if his authority had the sanctions of time." The meanings that the two politics ascribe to the fundamental terms of politics —security and authority—are, consequently, commensurable because the fundamental legitimating, authorizing, term of the traditional paradigm, tradition itself, has operational equivalents in the new paradigm: the new prince can seem as old as traditional ones. The new prince will not only be more secure and powerful than the old; he will even seem older. Tautology is avoided by making everything a matter of appearance.

But for the new prince to seem old may not be by itself enough to achieve commensurability for the two paradigms. Among the alternatives to commensuration, divided allegiance, trimming, hedging one's bets, and neutrality are serious possibilities—and easily available and attractive meanings for prudence. In the present case, the prospect that subjects and citizens should simultaneously prefer a successful new prince while still retaining allegiance to the old political paradigm is perhaps the most likely outcome of all. All those alternatives to commensuration are ways of circumventing prudential thinking by making the realm of practice into something else, and the interest that Machiavelli holds for investigating prudence comes from his rejections of these methods of solving the problem of prudence by defining it away. For example, one can evade conflicts of right against right, ultimate value against ultimate value, avoid having to make difficult choices, by segregating final goods from each other and supposing, for example, that the values of rectitude and of mercy will never conflict.

Such divided loyalty is one of the most common readings of Machiavelli, in which he is taken to be making public certain modes of conduct people had been already following but not acknowledging; on that reading, such people would be capable of a divided allegiance to public moral standards and to unadmitted but actual ways of acting; a clear conscience would require that such people see those two politics as incommensurable, occupying distinct realms, and "prudence" would consist in acting by self-interest while preserving as far as possible the proprieties dictated by decorum. And so people have distinguished, and found that Machiavelli distinguishes, between the public and the private, what people say and what they do, the moral and the political, values appropriate to acquiring a state or to revolution and those relevant to holding one. Machiavelli is often read as employing a containment strategy, seeing politics as a state of nature, a war of all against all, but thereby protecting private morality, or morality *simpliciter*, from contamination, or, in a more sophisticated reading, seeing the acquisition of states as governed by different standards than their maintenance. Crick contends that Machiavelli's "fundamental distinction was between personal or princely rule, relevant to times of crisis — the best way to save corrupt old states or to create new ones; and republican or political rule, relevant to normal conditions in states with a large middle class — the best way to preserve states through time."[14] Berlin rejects this comfortable interpretation of Machiavelli: "For the defenders of the *raison d'état*, the sole justification of these measures is that they are exceptional — that they are needed to preserve a system the purpose of which is precisely to preclude the need for such odious measures, so that the sole justification of such steps is that they will end the situations that render them necessary. But for Machiavelli these measures are, in a sense, themselves quite normal."[15] Someone who says that the best form of government depends purely on appropriateness to circumstances is asserting that different forms of government are not commensurable because they are not true competitors, a kind of contextual relativism. Such a strategy threatens prudence because it suggests the segregation of competing values into separate realms, in each of which the inference from principle to policy, rule to case, is therefore smooth.[16] As I pointed out in the contrast of Machiavelli's new politics to metapolitics, the segregation strategy would not suit his purposes because it would doom the new prince to being a permanent usurper; prudence is destroyed when the world is divided into the kingdom of right and the kingdom of expediency.

There is obviously nothing logically impossible about divided loyalty —

rendering unto Caesar is not an incoherent position – but Machiavelli thinks that he can make the unstable world of Italian city-states into a situation which will *force* a comparison and prevent divided allegiance and other compromises.[17] First, there are obvious considerations the new prince can present: more security, more prosperity, and more glory. Second, far from being irrational, these appeals are relevant grounds – in fact the only available grounds – for standing outside any particular kind of politics and choosing between competing political systems. Within an established political system, as I suggested above, safety, prosperity, and glory are illegitimate and corrupting appeals – that is, they are bribes and threats, to be rejected in favor of rational, legitimate reasons for action. Obeying the law and deferring to authority are the decent ways of knowing what is the right thing to do, while consulting self-interest or private conscience is not.

Even if these common inducements of safety, prosperity, and glory make a choice between competing paradigms possible by making evident the way the two politics both are "politics," they still do not compel a choice. A community may decide, in effect, in favor of some particular new prince but not thereby in favor of the new politics, just as a scientific community may accept some particular result but withhold approval to the theory that supposedly generated it, prudently dissociating rule and case. Such a split decision appears especially likely for the new prince, since it is far from clear that there is a "politics" apart from his personal powers and qualities: the old politics can survive the failure, and even the incompetence, of particular rulers, but if a new prince fails, is there any "politics" to survive him? The trouble with heuristics and the politics of opportunism associated with it is precisely such instability, not only the practical instability of permanent susceptibility to further usurpation, but the intellectual instability of nothing but successful results without any grounding. Machiavelli has to make a vote for the new prince into a vote for the new politics as well, and his strategy here is quite canny. Authority in traditional politics is strongly associated with tradition, since the right to rule is based on inheritance: the hereditary monarch has the right to rule because he is a hereditary monarch. The new ruler can appear old when he presents himself as the heir to the great deeds of the past presented in *The Prince:* the new prince usurps states that previously were either free or belonged to hereditary monarchs to the extent that Machiavelli can usurp the great heroes of the past that used to belong to the lineage of the old politics, and so the new prince's success depends not merely on making attractive a new world view, and not merely on possessing new methods for imitating great examples, but on the systematic articulation of examples, methods, and a world view in Machiavelli's argument. Moses, Romulus, and Lycurgus may not have been aware that they were allied to Machiavelli's new politics, but he makes them into part of the new prince's pedigree. If the first function we can point to for rhetorical prudence is to make the new politics appear political, then the first way in which Machiavelli exercises that function is by permitting the new prince to usurp not only the throne but also the heroes of the old politics.

Showing how the two politics share examples is still not enough to make them commensurable, though. The two paradigms seemed incommensurable because the methods by which each ruler becomes secure were as different as usurpation and inheritance, because the principles and consequences justify actions from opposed directions. But Machiavelli shows that neglect of the methods of the politics of invention is the answer to the question posed in the title of the chapter, why the old princes have lost their states. The two politics are thus comparable because where the new methods are present, any ruler, old or new, is secure; where they are absent, there is unstable rule. Hence the chapter ends with the presentation of the result of that comparison: "Those modes of defence are alone good, certain and lasting, which depend upon yourself and your own worth." Moreover, the community judges entirely on the basis of appearances: the new prince is successful if he appears old, that is, if he commands obedience as unconsciously and habitually as the traditional monarch. This appearance is not the appearance *of* some deeper reality; the subjects "know" that the new prince is an innovator and are not fooled into thinking him venerable, but this knowledge does not weaken their obedience. Where the old politics' hold on its subjects may be weakened by a critique of ideology, the new prince appears not to be threatened by increased understanding.

That is what it means for the new prince to appear old.[18] This sort of appeal to the community and its standards of value and tradition is indispensable and cannot be reduced to judgment by external facts; Machiavelli's new prince cannot be a ruler if he successfully commands instant obedience through intimidation rather than relying on a subject's sense of value and tradition, just as, again, no one would be counted a scientist if he produces correct answers by consulting an infallible oracle or a black box instead of appealing to what is taken to be science. Machiavelli has offered good rhetorical reasons for preferring the new politics: it has the heroes and it has prospects of success on its side. Moreover, while it is tempting to regard such rhetorical appeals as a second-best resource, to be used only when one does not have more straightforward, objective, or scientific reasons at one's disposal, Machiavelli inverts those standards of evaluation and, by making the new prince seem old, makes the reasons behind his appeal into good reasons.

It might seem that the new politics has won its battle with the old simply by showing up at the fight, since the old politics depends for its success
on not being thought of as one kind of politics among others, as some
paradigms seem to require that they not be thought of as paradigms but
as inevitable ways of thinking forced upon us by the external world. The
old politics depends on not having to justify itself, and to ask it for justification is itself unfair. The old politics, unlike the new, becomes unstable
simply by being challenged. Machiavelli has seduced the old politics into
competing with the new — if it did not, then its principles would become
vacuous circularities — but the old politics must lose once the new prince
seems old. I argued earlier that the old politics is weakened by being made
explicit, and Machiavelli stresses the opposite side of that by saying that
the fact that a new prince is new makes his actions more closely watched,
and so affords him the opportunity for quickly seeming ancient. Machiavelli now tells us that the old politics cannot rely on tradition but must
practice the same methods as the new. But the old politics has its revenge.

Fortuna as the Fickle Guarantor of Commensurability

After the judgment of chapter 24 is rendered against them,
the partisans of the old politics can still maintain that that decision was
merely a victory for the new prince's "methods," strategies, ways of acting;
the new prince cannot claim to be the legitimate heir of Romulus, Moses,
and Lycurgus while the old politics still has exclusive title to the proper
way of seeing right and wrong, truth and reality. The old prince may have
to learn these new ways of fighting to stay in power, making things depend
on his own resources as much as he can, but the new prince has to give
up his opportunism as soon as he takes control and must try to look like,
and govern like, a hereditary ruler. Logically, the commensurability between old and new can be read in two opposed ways: emphasizing the
way the new politics absorbs the old by offering methods that everyone
must now use, or emphasizing the way the new politics must appear old
in order to become fully political. Machiavelli turns to Fortune to learn
which way to read the equation.

Machiavelli begins chapter 25 by saying that many people believe that
Fortune governs everything and that human actions have no effect, and
says that he too thinks so some of the time. On the other hand, the whole
thrust of *The Prince* has been to train the new prince to regard human
action as all-powerful. Correspondingly, the prince must learn to regard
Fortune as inert matter to be shaped according to forms induced by human

Paradigms and Princes

action. Machiavelli's problem is to judge between these two attitudes towards the external world: is it the unpredictable and radically contingent, or is it material waiting to be shaped? Is the relation between virtù and fortuna a relation between two competing forces, or between form and matter? The two possibilities generate two sorts of "hope" for the future in Machiavelli and two notions of how *The Prince*, and the *Discourses*, can be "practical." One can either think that the miraculous actions of the savior-prince can permanently remove Italy from history, or think that heroic action can provide a solution to good action by devising a realm in which doing what is right cannot fail. But both these hopes are, strictly speaking, impractical because Machiavellian prudence rejects the Stoic solution to good action of escaping from the possibility of failure, and Fortune is the symbol, as much for Machiavelli as it was for Aristotle, of that rejection.[19]

Machiavelli suggests that the "solution" to the problem of Fortune, of how much Fortune can do and how to oppose her, must be metaphorical rather than literal; immediately after giving the misleadingly literal formulation that Fortune controls about half our lives, he turns to a series of comparisons, first to a river, an image which is supposed to serve for fortune "in general," and then to Fortune as a woman. Machiavelli has to construct a situation in which the judgment between the two politics is rendered by the external world. In competing for the allegiance of princes, subjects, and future readers in chapter 24, Machiavelli had to prevent a split decision, had to prevent a judgment of incommensurability, through confining the new politics to the acquisition, not the rule, of principalities. In trying to secure the judgments of an external, objective nature, Machiavelli has to guard against the eclecticism of thinking that both kinds of politics offer useful methods, and the best ruler will be he who can avail himself of either, the eclecticism that seems to follow from Protean adaptability such as the following:

> Two men, acting differently, attain the same effect, and of two
> others acting in the same way, one attains his goal and not the other.
> . . . No man is found so prudent as to be able to adapt himself to
> [changing times and circumstances], either because he cannot de-
> viate from that to which his nature disposes him, or else because
> having always prospered by walking in one path, he cannot per-
> suade himself that it is well to leave it. . . . If one could change one's
> nature with time and circumstances, fortune would never change.
> (Ch. 25)

Since there are many good things, and one cannot have them all, the best policy must be to forfeit some pleasure for the sake of duty, and not be an ascetic, a pharisee, but recognize that duties should be generally, although not universally, observed: prudence then is a reasonable compromise between principles and consequences, duty and inclination. It is easy to say that such a strategy is intellectually incoherent because there can be no right amount of each that is being compromised, but its intellectual emptiness does not stop it from being appealing, and so Machiavelli shows that it is practically unsuccessful as well. Berlin captures Machiavelli's strategy here when he observes that, according to Machiavelli, "Compromise with current morality leads to bungling, which is always despicable, and when practiced by statesmen involves men in ruin."[20] Commentators from Guicciardini through Halifax to Berlin have thought that such moderation should be the practical implication of Machiavelli's original proclamation of the existence of plural goods, but—even if he should—Machiavelli clearly does not draw that inference. To quote Berlin again, Machiavelli's "intellectual consequences, wholly unintended by its originator, were, by a fortunate irony of history (which some call its dialectic), the bases of the very liberalism that Machiavelli would surely have condemned."[21]

Tempting as such eclecticism is, Machiavelli knows why it offers no serious option. Each kind of politics contains claims to exclusivity designed to prevent such eclecticism, and even framing it as a possibility requires a stance outside any possible practical situation, a contemplative distanced view in which one can see times and tempers shifting, sometimes suiting each other and sometimes not.[22] And when such eclecticism is excluded, so too is the appeal of identifying prudence with moderation and compromise.[23]

The history of degenerating states in *Republic* 8 and 9 is an account of a series of failed compromises, as each successive state mixes ethics of principles and consequences in unstable ways. No politics can permit such eclecticism; moreover, no individual can act from such an Olympian standpoint, and no practical actor can so completely ignore his own character: such success would depend on literally having no character at all, and so there would be success without anyone to do the succeeding.[24] It is hard to see how such a compromise, with its quantitative language, makes any sense. Either fortune rules over an unpredictable amount of our lives— and to say an unpredictable amount is as good as saying that fortune rules over all our lives, since we cannot make provisions against a force whose strength and mode of operation is unknowable—or it does not rule at all, and chance is just another name for human ignorance and failure.

Not only is it difficult to see how Machiavelli's proposed compromise could make sense, but one must also wonder why he offers such a compromise at all instead of offering arguments for the superiority of the mechanical, scientific view of the external world. Such arguments would not, after all, be hard to find; the message of *The Prince* and its advocacy of the abstract quality of virtù would seem to promote treating the external world as an unpredictable force, towards which one should act as though subject to mechanical control. Machiavelli concedes that fortune controls part of our lives, and then makes things much worse by saying that our characters are themselves not a function of education but of fortune. Where before it appeared that fortune had been domesticated, made into matter and potential, now it seems that human action and human character have been made into chance. What is outside the control of method shifts from the river that needs to be dammed to one's own individuality. Why should Machiavelli thus elevate fortune, in apparent contradiction to his prior teaching?

Treating fortune like a woman is a mode of action that is defensible, on different grounds, in each paradigm. A woman, in Machiavellian imagery, is halfway between a person and a thing, and so treating fortune like a woman is a compromise between the anthropomorphizing attempts at domination and the industrial habits of craft. Grabbing Fortune by her forelock requires a modern, compromising term like *management* to replace mastery of subjects or manipulation of things. To treat fortune like a woman is to view fortune as an independent power, and hence is a superstitious attitude, appropriate to a hereditary monarch; at the same time, to treat it like a woman is to act mechanically, seeing fortune as nothing but matter waiting to be formed, and hence is a mode of action appropriate to the innovator.

Tactically, striking a compromise is Machiavelli's way of making the new politics seem to inhabit the same world as the old, but we still have to see how compromise is possible, how one can intelligibly say that fortune rules half our affairs, or maybe a little less. I suggested above that neither world view could accommodate such a compromise, but I have also claimed that there can be no third world view Machiavelli can offer within which the old and the new politics appear as special cases: when politics is conceived of as a merely instrumental means of satisfying private desires, then eclecticism and compromise could be useful political devices, but to the extent that politics is an activity that offers criteria for deciding what is real and what is good, that eclecticism is unsatisfying. Heuristic eclecticism and opportunism, while they may be stable modes of action in the sciences, cannot last practically without a more rational backing, and so such hedging and compromising must receive philosophical elaboration as part of an algorithmic decision-theory in order to be political at all. The practical analogon to such a metatheory that houses the two given theories is the discovery of a "more ultimate" good to weigh and resolve the conflicting claims between the things that people in fact regard as absolute values, as in Plato's idea of the good representing a reality that lies behind the apparent goods that people pursue. Machiavelli presents a way of acting that includes the two competing theories of final good just because it is no theory at all: far from being at a higher level of abstraction than the two given theories, Machiavelli's advice to treat fortune like a woman is more closely related to action than either of those. The Machiavellian way of moving from greater abstraction to greater concretion is to situate fortune inside, rather than apart from, the prince's character, so that one must be fortunate to have the right character to cope with fortune, whereas the eclectic solution must depend on detachment from character. Attempts to "unpack" the metaphor of grabbing Fortune by the forelock and to substitute a literal statement of what treating fortune like a woman means would lead back to one or the other competing paradigms. Instead of the magical and traditional or the mechanical and novel habits of mind, Machiavelli here considers two ways of acting—caution and daring—which correspond to the two politics, since the magical mind is usually cautious and conservative, while the mechanical mind is more daring.

But that correspondence is only a habitual, not a logical relation: modes of action are not strictly tied to world views, and even the hereditary monarch can act audaciously. Machiavelli decides that impetuosity is better than caution, but only to a slight extent, that little bit more than half our lives that is governed by man rather than fortune. Machiavelli's solution seems to be to advocate an end to ideology, telling us pragmatically to use whatever methods are available, and not to worry too much about supposed ideological rationales behind those methods. Instead of trying to show how the new prince really inhabits the political world as defined by traditional politics, as he did in chapter 24, Machiavelli here makes both forms of politics inhabit a new practical world purged of old superstitions about legitimacy. Treating fortune like a woman is advice which could be followed by a hereditary monarch, but at the price of making him into a new politician.

It looks as though the compromise really gives victory to the new politics. The innovator can choose to treat fortune like a woman, but the hereditary monarch cannot. A traditional ruler might happen, by luck, to *be* daring, but he cannot *choose* to act audaciously, because his world excludes the very idea of choosing how to face fortune. In other words, Machiavelli's tactic has been to show that world views and modes of action are not connected by ties of strict necessity, but rather by the kind of motive-act connections that involve intentionality. The old politics must think that world views and modes of action are bound by necessary ties: if you know what is true, good, and real, then you know how to act. The new politics wins this trial by transforming itself into a practical position, while the old politics, once Machiavelli has elevated it from a habit of action into a paradigm, has become impractical because it has become ineffectual. The external world, Fortune, does not give a definitive judgment between the two politics—her verdicts are impermanent, unpredictable, and obscure—but in submitting themselves for judgment the two politics show that, although the issue is not fairly decided by Fortune, only the new politics is capable of bribing the judge to decide the case in its favor. The victory of the new politics comes in taking over the territory traditionally occupied by the old: the new politics can recognize an anthropomorphic truth, and a truth which the old, supposedly anthropomorphic politics cannot—namely that the supposedly neutral judge is not a disinterested one.

Even if it gives the wrong answers to practical questions, the new politics at least can give answers, while the politics of style cannot. Therefore, the fact that caution and confidence are more matters of one's nature, and of luck, than of education and choice, is not a capitulation of the new politics to the old and a victory for the operations of fortune, as it appeared. But fortune, and the old politics, seem yet again to have the last word. Since the judgments of fortune are unpredictable, the victory of the innovator is not worth very much. And since whether one is daring or cautious is more a matter of one's natural character, of fortune, than of education and choice, the victory belongs, not to someone who loyally follows Machiavelli's teachings, but to someone who happens, by good fortune, to have the right character for the times. The new prince may as well be superstitious and pray that he has that right character. The heuristic solution of flexible techniques and the algorithmic appeals to a single method would not work, but the prudent solution of a fortunate character does not seem to be an advance.

Having the right character, the taking one's character as an ultimate datum, is in fact just the resolution that Berlin attributes to Machiavelli: "What if [men] found that they were compelled to make a choice between two incommensurable systems, to choose as they did without the aid of an infallible measuring rod which certified one form of life as being superior to all others and could be used to demonstrate this to the satisfaction of all rational men?" Berlin thinks that Machiavelli in fact takes this stand: if someone chooses Christian virtue, Machiavelli has nothing to say to him: "There was no problem and no agony for him; he shows no trace of scepticism or relativism; he chose his side, and took little interest in the values that this choice ignored or flouted."[25]

Before turning to the last chapter of The Prince, and from there to a more detailed analysis of the sort of impossibly radical choice that Berlin sees as the moral of the text, I think it important to put this discussion of character in the context of the abstract problems of prudence with which this book began. In the Introduction I quoted Williams' interpretation of Socrates' variation on the theme of stability and flexibility; Williams sees Socratic wisdom as finding a stability invulnerable to the vicissitudes of fortune by distinguishing between incident and constitutive luck:

> There has been a strain of philosophical thought which identifies the end of life as happiness, happiness as reflective tranquility, and tranquility as the product of self-sufficiency — what is not in the domain of the self is not in its control, and so is subject to luck and the contingent enemies of tranquility. The most extreme versions of this outlook are certain doctrines of classical antiquity, though it is a notable fact about them that while the good man, the sage, was immune to the impact of incident luck, it was a matter of what may be called constitutive luck that one was a sage or capable of becoming one: for the many and vulgar this was not (on the prevailing view) an available course.[26]

Setting aside the question of whether Socrates subscribed to such a doctrine — his interpretation of the Delphic oracle would seem to eliminate constitutive luck even more decisively than incident luck — the turn in chapter 25 of *The Prince* precisely seems to make the ability to withstand incident luck into a matter of constitutive luck. Without such complications in the relations of inner and outer, the positing of character outside the realm of action is the final way of avoiding the full dimensions of practical reason and action. Throughout this chapter, I have suggested that problems of incommensurability were generated not only by Machiavelli's desire to qualify the new prince as a fully political agent, but equally could be understood as coming from the problematic and perhaps unstable relations between principle and case characteristic of prudence, as they apply in particular to the relation between a ruler and the politics of which he is a representative. Machiavelli has turned the virtù/fortuna distinction on itself by making one's character apparently a matter of luck, and prudential relations of principle and case can help us to make sense of that development. In algorithmic thought, cases are mere particulars. The particles studied in physics are nothing but what they are *qua* solutions to physical equations; they have no properties besides those relevant to being studied by the physicist. Hereditary rulers, similarly, are nothing but their office. (Recall the distinction drawn in my Introduction between algorithmic methods, in which no data not admitted in the premises can be allowed to infect the conclusion, and prudential reasoning, where the possibility of new data remains open throughout the process of reasoning.)[27] Traditional monarchs, as Machiavelli describes them, have no character in the sense of individuality, and so make choices and act only in private roles, not as princes: they have only to follow the customs and avoid drawing attention to themselves to succeed. On the other hand, the opportunist who never fails dominates fortune by failing to have a character too: "If one could change one's nature with time and circumstances, fortune would never change." Given that attitude, then Berlin's radical choice, itself a denial of character and hence of choice in that sense, is the only reasonable response.

The Inescapability of Prudence

What does the last chapter of *The Prince* have to do with all this? What does an exhortation to liberate Italy from the barbarians have to do with the questions of whether the old and the new politics are commensurable or not? Why should Machiavelli turn from the proliferation of metaphors and images for framing the relation of virtù and fortuna to an exhortation?

After all the complications of chapters 24 and 25, the reader must be relieved to arrive at the hopeful simplicities of the final chapter of *The Prince*, "An Exhortation to Liberate Italy from the Barbarians," if only they could be taken seriously. That relief comes from the way chapter 26 parallels the chapter on ecclesiastical monarchies, chapter 11, which brings to a close the first, exemplary, section of *The Prince*. Both ecclesiastical principalities and a unified Italy offer ways of avoiding permanent commitment to the world of prudence, of deliberation and difficult choices, but raise the possibility only to show how remote that prospect is. In a quite reasonable sense, this last chapter does continue the series of interparadigmatic comparisons initiated by making the new prince seem old. Where chapter 24 made competing theories appeal to the appropriate audience, and chapter 25 made them appeal to a nature outside the control of either theory, chapter 26 makes the two theories judges of each other by pointing to a crucial experiment both sides must be glad to submit to. Whereas in chapter 24 the new prince forced the old to submit to a common judgment by appealing to their common source of power — the subjects whose judgment constitutes power and authorizes rule — here in chapter 26 the new prince uses not force but an inducement: here is a goal everyone would like to accomplish. Uniting Italy is unquestionably a good thing, not just something one party can do and the other cannot — all along we have seen some of the techniques for not counting a local victory as winning the war — but an accomplishment so great that no one would question its value and therefore the value of any method that accomplishes it. A crucial experiment is decisive only if both parties allow it to be so — in the *Discourses* Machiavelli mocks the folly of those who propose that a battle be settled by each side picking a champion to fight it out — but unifying Italy is an achievement that cannot be discounted.[28] The present servile and fragmented condition of Italy is not an anomaly that appears as a minor embarrassment to either paradigm, nor is it a puzzle that either would ever claim within its scope; failing to unite Italy does not count against either paradigm because unifying Italy cannot be counted as something any decent ruler ought to be able to do. Instead, unifying Italy is an achievement, glorious precisely because it was hitherto thought beyond the range of any human ruler. So, once again, the new politics is seen as superior to the old. And, once again, the victory is an ambiguous one, since Machiavelli's last chapter is indeed an exhortation, as its title indicates, not even a prediction, let alone the statement of an accomplishment.

Even if I can offer such an allegorical reading of chapter 26 and make it continue the enterprise of interparadigmatic comparisons of the previous two chapters, that interpretation does not account for the striking shift in mode that makes so many readers regard the last chapter as special pleading. Instead of metaphorical language, we have the promise of future benefits, the expectation of salvation in the future.[29] In short, one can leave allegorical language at the cost of resorting to another sort of nonliteral language, the anagogic. Of course, the anagogic mode here offers not the promise of future spiritual benefits in the next life, but the promise of future material benefits in a paradise on earth, a unified Italy.

This last chapter is not only a final variation of the theme, which I have stressed, of interparadigmatic comparison, of Machiavelli's making the new politics *political*. It builds on and goes beyond the preceding two chapters in exploring further the location of political action between goals and resources, legitimizing principles and successful consequences. It follows the strategy of chapter 25, the strategy of exhibiting the incompleteness of the technical or methodical line of argument of chapters 1–23 by making success depend on impossible conditions, and consequently continues the enterprise of trying to make the new politics *political* at the price of making *The Prince* increasingly, at least apparently, impractical. The last two chapters symbolize the ultimate dissonance created in Machiavelli's argument by his appealing to a pair of banal clichés — that fortune is unpredictable and that it would be wonderful if Italy could be united and free from the barbarians. Machiavelli employs those clichés as topics not, this time, of invention but of judgment. That pair of clichés is a rhetorical representation of the way in which prudential methods are necessarily incomplete. Earlier I showed why Machiavelli's prudential methods must be grounded in rhetoric, since they must appeal to the *consensus gentium* as the ultimate source of legitimacy; rhetoric, though, proves opposites, and hence rhetorical arguments and methods are necessarily incomplete. The systematic elaboration of a science may be *in fact* incomplete — there can be things outside its ken — but that state is considered temporary and superable. (To complete the triad, the antisystematic opportunism of heuristics is complete only by addition.) The need, however, and the methods of making allowances for incompleteness differ between theoretical and practical methods and circumstances: a theory based on algorithmic methods must be alive to the possibility of anomalies and counterexamples, but a practical method grounded in prudence is always threatened by defeat, by the possibility that doing one's best will not be good enough. In science one can always say after the fact what one should have done, known, or said, but in practice one can have acted as one should and still fail.[30]

These different understandings of incompleteness issue ultimately from the different relations of rule and case embodied in the three kinds of methods, as each kind of thought employs methods to avoid refutation, and each mode of action tries to avoid defeat. First, the distance between algorithmic rule and case permits some flexible adjustment of the critical relations of subsumption and reference that permit a scientific theory to avoid refutation. Kuhn, along these lines, recognizes the need for a flexible application of rule to case: "What from one viewpoint may seem the looseness and imperfection of choice criteria conceived as rules may, when the same criteria are seen as values, appear an indispensable means of spreading the risk which the introduction or support of novelty always entails."[31] Such adjustment, it should now be clear, requires an informal, implicit, and often surreptitious use of prudential judgment, so the question is not whether or not to employ prudent judgment — *every* method will use prudent judgment, if only in the application as opposed to the enunciation of principles — but whether one can, and should, build a whole way of acting around it.

In practical reasoning, the purpose is not to introduce or support novelty, as Kuhn claims for scientific reasoning, but there is still good reason why morality too finds it advantageous to spread the risk. Keeping the connections between principles and cases flexible, and hence spreading the risk, has a different function in moral judgment from what it does to advance scientific progress, but in both cases it is an indispensable means for avoiding the undesirable alternatives of instability and enforced stability; in the practical case it is the only way to avoid the otherwise inevitable sequence of fidelity to principles and their obvious applications: failure, followed by reliance on force unconnected to principles and unlimited by them. If a moral decision followed algorithmically from its principles, and if that decision led to an action one later regretted, those principles would be in serious jeopardy. As difficult as it is to abandon scientific principles, the price of giving up a moral principle must be much greater because one's moral principles are tied to the individual character as technical principles are not, and so we have very strong reasons for wanting to keep moral rules irrefutable and permanent: we can't say, "Evil be thou my good," and transvalue our values very often. If our principles are to be effective in action while still protected from bad consequences, then the ties between principle and act must be loose. (It is just this desire to use and at the same time protect one's principles that Pascal ridicules in the Seventh Provincial Letter.) If those connections are not loose and flexible, then they must be rigid, and hence liable to fracture.

One can deny that one's principles could ever lead to bad action, since they are the criteria for good and bad results—that is what I called the ethics of principles in the Introduction, most strikingly represented in its extreme form as *Fiat justitia, ruat coelum*. Taking that denial seriously removes any room for prudence, because once moral principles have no consequences in action, morality must be supplemented by an amoral efficiency; morality is locked in the best parlor, to be used only on Sundays and other important occasions, and kept away from the rest of the business of life.

Consequently these last two chapters force prudent reflection on incompleteness in the face of unpredictable external and internal nature and unreachable goals: in addition to the unforeseeable "out there," there is also the irrational within the heart of practice in the possibility that intentions and consequences may not line up, that one can act successfully only to discover that what was aimed at was not so desirable after all. Chapter 25 made the new prince's success depend on the impossible internal condition of the chameleon, able to respond instantly to every fluctuation of fortune, while chapter 26 makes the escape from instability depend on the impossible external opportunity of unifying Italy. Machiavelli dramatizes these impossible boundary conditions as hopes and dreams, instead of simply offering their logical roles as paradoxes undercutting the pretenses of method, but their rhetorical function is to refute Machiavelli's basic premiss of imitation.[32] The messiah of chapter 26 is the counterpart of the founders cited earlier—Moses, Theseus, and the other exemplars of virtù—and like the chameleon of chapter 25, the savior too attempts to break out of the world of permanent insecurity, and the need to find stability within contingency, by escaping from the world of shifting particulars into a realm of easier intelligibility and easier success.[33] Therefore, the function of the last two chapters is double: it shows that most people have no choice but to operate prudently, and it makes it unlikely that prudence can be subject to methodical control. Rhetorically, the chameleon and the savior are two argumentative tactics that seek to undermine rhetorical discourse by finding something better, more directly successful, through direct access either to successful consequences or unassailable principles. The chameleon who defeats fortune by luckily having no character inside himself that can be out of tune with the times represents what Aristotle says happens when we cure or persuade by any means: we gain victory by sacrificing the continuity provided by art. The prince who can unify Italy will be in the same position as Aristotle's orator who "hits upon [ἐντύχη] first principles," and "will no longer be [practicing] Dialectic or Rhetoric, but that science whose principles he has arrived at" (*Rhetoric* 1.2.1358a25) — and who takes seriously Aristotle's invocation of luck, *tuche*. Should one find himself able to achieve the heaven of a unified Italy, one cannot turn down the chance. If Machiavelli's first loyalty were to his art, to politics insofar as it is teachable, then these alternative methods would come in for condemnation and he would recommend that the prince avoid them. Instead, Machiavelli, while primarily concerned with those dimensions of politics that are teachable (namely, the discursively defensible, the rhetorical), acknowledges the others as extra-artistic resources that the prince sometimes is lucky enough to have available — the founder or savior — and is sometimes desperate enough to have to use — fraud and force which, when separated off entirely from virtù, become villainy.

5 THE *DISCOURSES ON LIVY*

VIRTÙ UNIVERSALIZED

Everyone knows that it is difficult to integrate chapter 26 with the rest of *The Prince;* at the very least there is an obvious shift in tone, and at most there could be real incoherence. When the argument is approached, as it was in my first chapter, as the representation of an act of teaching, then the last chapter could be regarded as a final examination, but the complications of representation and imitation, and of the prudent relations between text and practice, have made that answer inadequate. The technical language of rhetoric permits an articulation of what everyone senses is odd about chapter 26 as an ending for the text, and the question then becomes, What is the significance of Machiavelli's ending *The Prince* with an appeal outside of rhetoric, an appeal to an external topic, an *atechnos?* I think that my analysis thus far should have shown that it is not only chapter 26 but the last three chapters that "complete" a rhetorical politics by appealing to extrarhetorical resources and extradiscursive sources of stability.

In this context chapter 26 has a pair of functions. First, it both completes and destroys the project of fully subjecting prudence to art (or reinforces the destructive achievement of chapter 25 that follows on the happier, more Whiggish, ending of chapter 24). To the extent that there can be an art of prudence, we have found that the art has to rely, for its completion, on extra-artistic resources, as the prince must rely, ultimately, on luck and other conditions beyond those that can be counted as matter relative to his virtù as form. Machiavelli, by pushing to an extreme the attempt to assimilate virtue to art, has shown the limitations of that project. If Pocock is correct in describing Machiavelli's project as trying to find intelligibility within time, the ending of *The Prince* completes that project by an appeal to something outside of time, just as chapter 24 placed the new prince in timeless tradition and chapter 25 pointed to practical abilities that transcend — at the risk of becoming irrelevant to — any context and any time. Just as Aristotle finds that the moral virtues, which aim at circumstantially defined good ends, required supplement by an intellectual virtue of *phronesis* which apprehended the unified principle of those particular ends, so Machiavelli's art of being resourceful is incomplete with-

The Discourses on Livy: *Virtù Universalized*

out abilities that are independent of those circumstances and resources. But there the similarity ends, because Machiavelli's rhetorical project is far more radical than Aristotle's. If what supplements the virtues of character in Aristotle is *phronesis*, the ending of *The Prince* points to ways in which *phronesis* itself needs completion.

Second — and my placing the last three chapters of *The Prince* in the context of interparadigmatic disputes brings this "moral" to the fore — Machiavelli has represented, within the text, the relation of text and practice, but the instabilities and ambiguities of the conclusion bar a confusion of that representation with the reality it represents, and thereby prevent simple "aesthetic" satisfaction of practical urges.[1] He therefore raises the rhetorical question of how to move from the discursive to the extradiscursive (without any longer being able to give such movement its algorithmic name, "application") as well as from the extradiscursive to the discursive (the movement I have been calling domestication).

The extrarhetorical interventions of the last three chapters highlighted the complexity of interparadigmatic argument and thereby dramatized the problem of how to domesticate — make intellectually and discursively accessible — the confrontation between incompatible ends. The ambiguous conditions of resolution for interparadigmatic argument translate into the substantive impossibility of demonstrating the inadequacy of a system of action based on a single ultimate value; no partisan will be convinced that devotion to the unique ultimate good was somehow responsible, say, for the admittedly impotent situation in which Florence and other Italian cities found themselves.

The absence of such rigorous proof, though, is no reason confidently to expect the peaceful coexistence of distinct ends with distinct devotees: one cannot infer from the incommensurability of competing ultimate values to the choice among them being irrational, nor from there to a tolerance for what is beyond conclusive argument. While Machiavelli presents the prince with a radical choice between two incompatible ways of acting, it would be reading *The Prince* as the simple statement of a doctrine to infer that he similarly presents such a choice to his readers; instead, I claimed that the complexity of relations between writer, depicted characters, and readers was Machiavelli's indirect solution to the problem of plural ultimate values: prudence, for Machiavelli, took such a dramatic rather than systematic form.

Such a dramatic and literary solution is not the only way of responding to this problem; Polybian constitutionalism or Platonic and Ciceronian dialogues are other ways, besides dramatism, of seeing the problem of plural ultimate values as requiring a practical and intellectual solution more complex than a radical choice, but constitutionalism and dialogue are clearly

not Machiavelli's ways.[2] Without employing one of those methods for problematizing the choice of ends, one can have no basis for such a choice:
there must be two kinds of people in the world, and we must simply hope
for the sort of leader who can choose glory over decency (i.e., inferring
not only from incommensurability to irrationality of choice, but from there
to choice depending on personality).

If the choice of ends depends purely on the sort of person making the
decision, it cannot be called a choice. Characteristically, Machiavelli avoids
making such a simple logical point and puts it in practical terms: such
heroes, whose modes of action are so in harmony with circumstances as
to make moot the question of whether that harmony is an act of great
insight, extraordinary good fortune, or mere passivity, are very rare—
most of those Machiavelli points to are either mythical, divinely authorized, or both. (Grace and divine election are conditions to which the
categories of talent, luck, and passivity do not apply.) This cannot mean
simply that heroic characters do not come along very often: once again,
if that were the whole story, it would undercut the whole idea of character
and of history. The problem with these extra-historical and extra-human
heroes is not just that they are rare, but that heroes whose characters are
never out of joint with the times are not available as models for imitation
and in that sense are not part of an artistic solution to the problem of
prudence: the last chapters of *The Prince* move beyond prudence to the
miraculous interventions of lawgivers, sages, and heroes. Although the work
of prudence may at this point seem less exciting, proposing as it does the
role of the citizen rather than that of the lawgiver or the glorious hero,
the result is of greater analytical interest.[3]

The lack of drama, though, will make my account of the *Discourses*,
like the text itself, less formal and more diffuse than *The Prince.* I will exhibit the resources for civic virtù Machiavelli develops in the *Discourses*,
imposing my own organization on that text, much as Machiavelli himself
does on Livy's. Still, the *Discourses* are not without stylistic and performative aspects that require attention. While illustrating the good things
only heroic actors can do, Machiavelli also undercuts their practical possibility, or the possibility that their achievements offer any practical hope
for imitation, by dramatizing just what makes them heroic—that they
combine an ethically incompatible pair of talents. Such heroes cannot be
models for imitation, not because humans are not up to the task, but because there is nothing there to imitate: "He errs least and will be most
favored by fortune who suits his proceedings to the times, and always follows the impulses of his nature" (3.9). Whatever the basis for a decision
about competing ultimate values may be, it cannot simply depend on having the right character.

The Discourses on Livy: *Virtù Universalized*

When Machiavelli moves from choosing means to choosing ends, he consequently advances from offering new techniques for acquiring old ends to presenting new forms of character which embody ends. And that idea, although I think right for Machiavelli, is a highly problematic one. In particular, the choice of ends rather than means, of characters rather than techniques, cannot be a "choice" in any obvious sense, nor—and this is the point of the last paragraph—can it *fail* in any obvious sense to be a choice either. If Machiavelli does not destroy the idea of character and choice, he at least makes them less clear and stable than we are accustomed to thinking. In the Introduction, I traced the problems of practical reason that emerge in Machiavelli to their origin in the career and arguments of Socrates, and at this point those parallels become more explicit and urgent. The distinction between techniques, whose successful operation does not depend on the character of the person employing them, and virtues, which are inseparable from character, is the basis for the paradoxes Socrates poses for Polemarchus in *Republic* 1: one would go to a professional economist if one wanted to make money, but to a just man if one wanted simply to preserve it, leading to the conclusion that "in the use of each thing, justice is useless but in its uselessness useful" (334d). Similarly, the suggestion that Machiavelli's own methods, if that is what they are, are useful for acquiring states but not for maintaining them, when having the right character becomes important, and the consequent division of politics into an art of acquisition and a virtue of preservation, is a possibility that Machiavelli must refute from the beginning; it is also a possibility that keeps recurring throughout his texts.

Character stops being character when it is something external to the person, available for inspection and choice. To think otherwise is to ignore yet another Socratic paradox, this one in the *Protagoras*, where it is used to show why the choice of a way of life or of character cannot be conceived on analogy to choosing a possession or technique:

> We must take care that the sophist, in commending his wares, does not deceive us, as both merchant and dealer do in the case of our bodily food. For among these provisions, you know, in which these men deal, not only are they themselves ignorant what is good or bad for the body, since in selling they commend them all, but the people who buy from them are so too, unless one happens to be a trainer or a doctor. And in the same way, those who take their doctrines the round of our cities, hawking them about to any odd purchaser who desires them, commend everything that they sell, and there may well be some of these too who are ignorant which of their wares is good or bad for the soul; and in just the same case

are those that buy from them, unless one happens to have a doctor's knowledge here also, but of the soul. (*Protagoras* 313c–314b)[4]

Still, to call Machiavelli's—or Plato's—dramatization a *solution* seems overly sanguine unless we can specify far better what the audience is supposed to do in responding to his performance. We can say, though, that the first element in characterizing the reader's response to the dramatization of choosing competing ultimate goods must be discomfort, caused by the disappointment of the hope of treatment by a reliable and teachable technique. Developing an art or technique for politics would be one way of avoiding Machiavelli's necessary but incoherent demand that one choose a character, since techniques are ways of acting that precisely do not depend on the character of the person using them; if there were a technique for decision-making about plural ultimate ends, we would not need to have the right character in order to make the right decision. The arts, Aristotle tells us, are rational capacities for opposites: the doctor can kill or cure, and the hero of chapter 25 can be cautious or daring, and the end correlative to such generalized capacity for opposites is the unification of Italy, at the "cost" of not having a soul to lose. When Aristotle develops his conception of prudence by contrasts to *techne*, he points out that there are many arts, but only one prudence, because the employment of techniques is independent of character. There are many arts because each art has a single end that can be aimed at without having to worry about other ends; the single and all-encompassing end for prudence is the good for man which, for the reasons I have suggested, does not have the sort of unity required of an end towards which an art might aim. The acquisition of techniques is suitable for military, but not for political actions, where one needs character, practical action rather than production. This is not to deny that, as we saw in the earlier discussion of metahistory and metapolitics, military methods are sometimes perfectly adequate; their reliability is the Machiavellian parallel of Aristotle's remark that the orator will sometimes hit on scientific principles: "The happier a man is in his choice of propositions, the more he will unconsciously produce a science quite different from Dialectic and Rhetoric. For if once he hits upon first principles, it will no longer be Dialectic or Rhetoric, but that science whose principles he has arrived at" (*Rhetoric* 1.2.1358a27f).[5] The mistake consists in thinking that such techniques will be an adequate substitute for politics.

Machiavelli's rhetorical prudence makes Aristotle's treatment of practical reason more radical because it uncovers something merely implicit in Aristotle's exposition of rhetoric, ethics, and politics. Rhetoric, even for Aristotle, falls between his developed conceptions of prudence and art.

The Discourses on Livy: *Virtù Universalized*

It seems inappropriate to consider the art of rhetoric as an ability to perform self-contained activities, along the lines of the crafts. For arts other than rhetoric, one can consider how they attain their particular ends while not having to think about the relation between that specific end and the good for man in general. (People are far more hesitant to criticize a doctor for saving a murderer's life than they are to condemn a lawyer for defending him in court.) It seems similarly mistaken, though, to ignore the way the rhetorical faculty can be directed towards particular ends external to itself, in a way no virtue, including prudence, can. Unlike carpentry, rhetorical prudence possesses some internal moral values of its own; unlike justice, it can be used for the sake of external ends beyond its own consideration.[6] The problem is that while rhetoric, eloquence, and practical reason are moral activities, they are also things that can be used for further ends, and to that extent they are amoral. Practical reasoning and eloquence are activities that have a proper object, but one can employ the activity while directing it towards other objects.[7]

The Prince dramatizes the act of choice in a world of plural values by showing how someone can live with the realization that he lives in that sort of world. *The Prince* is a drama in which a single character, the new prince, acts in awareness of the multivalued nature of the world of action, while the other characters — lucky or inept hereditary rulers and usurpers, successful villains like Agathocles, or divinely ordained heroes such as Moses and Romulus — organize their actions around a single value. Machiavelli shows most people failing because of this oversimplification and demonstrates some cases — most of them semimythical — in which someone succeeds despite such a conception, or fails despite consciousness of plural final ends. *The Prince's* representation of the drama of a single character who has heard Machiavelli's declaration of this new world of multiple ultimate values suggests that its audience is to confront such a world with a combination of the discomfort mentioned above and wonder at what would happen if more than one character operated prudently. When Descartes effects a similar revolution towards theoretical self-reliance, he claims that all men guided by reason will agree in their conclusions. (Their conclusions will agree with external nature, and hence with each other.) But here there is no obvious harmony among actors who recognize that their world is constituted by plural goods: agreement on an end can lead to disputes over its possession, and disagreement over ends to partisan disputes, and in either case, increased self-reliance and virtù is not an obvious common benefit. If there were such harmony, then we could never become aware of the possible problem of the techniques of rhetorical prudence being used for external ends.

The Republic as a Community of Machiavellian Princes

The *Discourses on Livy* resolves the problems generated by the fact that *The Prince* is the representation of the problem of prudence as faced by a solitary actor and, as that representation, is watched and judged by an audience. The *Discourses* has no specified internal audience parallel to Lorenzo de' Medici; its readers are the same indeterminate public who reads *The Prince*. The literary form of the education of the new prince and the innovator permit Machiavelli to state the problems of prudence in an especially striking way, but eventually the dissonances — between the act of teaching and its representation before a wider public, between the virtù of the solitary hero and the less radical choices between equally radical ultimate ends faced by people in general — force Machiavelli's inquiry beyond the limits imposed by *The Prince* to the *Discourses*.[8]

Machiavelli slowly moves from those situations in which the new prince acting with virtù is the only self-determining and prudent agent in the world, to situations in which prudence and virtù are employed by an entire community; parallel to this movement is a gradual ascent to circumstances in which prudence is more and more obligatory. At first, the need to act in a world of plural values seems an inconvenience: it would be easier, and more enjoyable, to be a hereditary monarch than a new prince, but if you are not born a hereditary ruler, you have to accept your fate and try the harder road of seizing power. As the argument of *The Prince* proceeds, though, and even more in the *Discourses on Livy*, the simpler world of clear duties and ideological relations between rule and case becomes less and less attractive, and the demands of prudence appear less and less contingent and temporary. To discomfort and wonder must be added, in characterizing the audience's response, a gradual seduction by the attractive features of a world of plural values. Increasingly, there appear to be no alternatives to prudence, except for its corruptions and privations, no alternatives that anyone would *choose*. (Recall the argument, based on chapter 24 of *The Prince*, that while the hereditary monarch might by fortune *be* adept at Machiavelli's new politics, he could not *choose* to act in that way.)

Political attitudes towards rhetoric shift correspondingly. Initially one might regret that knowledge of social facts is not yet adequate for us to be governed by science, and thus, we temporarily have to rely on disputation; further reflection on such architectonic social science makes rhetoric more and more directly, not just provisionally, attractive. Along those lines, although republics are harder to hold than traditional monarchies, and

The Discourses on Livy: *Virtù Universalized*

despite the fact that it is easier to operate on inert matter than on people, the more difficult prospect has its own appeals: "The diversity of the genius of her citizens enables the republic better to accommodate herself to the changes of the times than can be done by a prince" (*Discourses* 3.9).[9] As prudence becomes more obligatory and attractive, the reader must, correspondingly, change his role from that of a spectator watching the prince confront his choice between incompatible ultimate values, to that of a participant in a community that will continually confront that problem. As the reader is thus gradually seduced into the world of multiple values, problems of action become *political* in the sense that they are the result of what happens when the man of virtù encounters others who operate the same way.

Consequently, I propose to turn to the *Discourses* by positing a correlation between three accounts of progress in Machiavelli's argument and the demands it makes on his readers. (1) By the end of *The Prince*, prudence has become more and more obligatory and less optional. (2) The abilities contained in virtù have developed from the selection of means for achieving a predetermined end to the articulation and choice of ends. (3) As the argument of *The Prince* advanced, prudence was transformed from a skill possessed by an individual to a mode of acting embodying a way of life whose place in the community must then be questioned.

This last account of the ascent achieved in *The Prince* is equivalent to the experience forced on the reader, who watches the education of the prince and asks, What if everyone acted like that? The question forced on us by *The Prince*, and for which the *Discourses* offers materials for resolution, is, Can there be a community of people who have learned Machiavelli's lessons and acquired Machiavellian virtù?[10] That movement of universalization, which takes us from the progress within *The Prince* to the *Discourses on Livy*, is analogous to the progress from the figure of Socrates to that of Plato as author and figure in his own right: the *Discourses* forces the reader to confront the question with which both *The Prince* and the *Apology* end, the question of universalizability of a mode of thought hitherto located in a single, unique individual. Is there a world that includes more than one Socrates? More than one new prince? In neither case can universalization mean the reproduction of a series of similar objects, because that would return us to the nonprudent sort of imitation and the nonprudent relation of principle to case that made sense only with the very strong conditions for agreement that Descartes legislates. (Socrates disowns his followers, not because he does not take money, but because they tried to learn from him by becoming "like" him.) Instead, universalization must be framed as a question of community: What are the readers then to make of such inimitable, perhaps impossible, heroes? Is there a single, coherent audience? Can the audience of *The Prince* or the *Discourses* become a community of something more than spectators, a community that at least includes Socrates or the prince as a member? The focus in *The Prince* on a single autonomous actor permitted the dramatic separation of two audiences, the internal audience of the new prince learning virtù and the wider public watching this teaching; what happens to political argument and political action when the distinction between actors and spectators is dissolved? Moreover, if the argument of *The Prince* advanced from situations in which virtù appeared optional, to circumstances in which it became obligatory, not only must we ask what a community of Machiavellian actors would be like, but must imagine a community in which Machiavellian prudence is the only way of acting. Such a community is not a Utopia; there are other modes of acting, but they will all be corruptions, privations, and perversions of Machiavellian prudence. That, rather than external ideological competition, is what causes the degeneration of the ideal states in *Republic* 8 and 9.)

Up to this point in the book, we have been considering Machiavelli's variations on the first Socratic theme of prudence I noted in the Introduction, that of flexibility and stability. At that time, I mentioned a second part of Socrates' problem of prudence that I have not yet been in a position to discuss: can there be a community of inquirers, a community of people who have learned the moral Socrates attributes to the Delphic oracle, Pursue wisdom rather than money? The problem of my last chapter concerned how to live with plural ultimate ends. The problem before us now is how to live with multiple *instantiations* of the plural goods, multiple *loci* of plural ultimate goods in distinct communities. If Machiavelli poses the first question as the clash between given Christian values and success, and locates prudence in the friction and dysfunction between the way those two map the world, he addresses the second by the dramatic shift from *The Prince* to the *Discourses on Livy*, from a drama in which a single actor recognizes plurality to one in which multiple agents each act with plural ends in view. Pocock puts the difference between a world with one virtuous prince and the republican world of nothing but virtù this way:

> In the final, Boethian, analysis, the price to be paid for a life of civic activity was vulnerability to fortune; and the republic, being that community in which each individual was defined by his activity, was the community committed by its political form to contend against that vulnerability. States and nations, like individuals, might rise and fall as ambition condemned them to mount upon the Wheel, but only the republic obliged the individual to pit his virtue

against fortune as a condition of his political being. *Virtue was the principle of republics.*[11]

This movement from conditions in which prudence is one option among several possible ways of acting to the republican world presented in the *Discourses* compounds the ancient problem of teaching virtue. The plurality of possibly conflicting values and the plurality of almost certainly conflicting loci of values requires Machiavelli to develop dramatic modes of representing prudence and its problems, and Machiavellian princes and citizens are "actors" in a much more dramatic, agonistic, competitive, and demonstrative sense than were Aristotle's *phronimoi*. As a consequence, the position of rhetoric somewhere between the virtues and the arts becomes an urgent problem for Machiavelli as it clearly was not for Aristotle, as prudent actors are able to use their practical reason in the pursuit of external ends, including, most importantly, the ends of competing with champions of alternative ultimate values and alternative communities. The arts are distinguished from the virtues not only by the criteria I mentioned earlier in this chapter but also in that they permit a separation of means and ends, and therefore a separation between the kinds of activities pursued in the name of art and the character of the person pursuing them, while it is the mark of moral actions (as opposed to amoral, not immoral, ones) that they tie what one *does* to who one *is*. If, as Pocock says, "only the republic obliged the individual to pit his virtue against fortune as a condition of his political being," then this advance to republican circumstances in which prudence becomes obligatory creates a condition in which the actors have no reserve of character or technique or doctrine outside activity; yet, at least in contrast to Aristotle's *phronimoi* and to the figure of Socrates, they still are actors.[12]

Moreover, the universalization of virtue that accompanies its dramatization means that republics recognize in their constitution the fact that the life of prudence and flexible stability *is* politics, and not one variety of politics, or one political party, among others. In *The Prince*, Machiavelli had to confront the problem Socrates delights in presenting to the Sophists: Whether virtue can be taught; he makes the problem worse by following Plato and presenting a dramatization of such teaching to his audience. The content of his teachings to the prince is contradicted by the existence of the text of the *The Prince* itself, and the public character of its teachings: the reader must ask why Machiavelli should teach the new prince to choose virtù over conventional morality, and to make that choice *in public*. In the *Discourses on Livy*, there is a corresponding tension between the praise of Roman civic virtue and the literary form of a commentary on an ancient historian. Roman civic virtue did not flourish because Roman citizens had mastered the lessons of the *Discourses on Livy;* they could not apprehend them even implicitly, since the success and stability of Rome was due to a civic virtue implanted through the variety of *indirections* Machiavelli accounts: its useful religion, the cancelling out of factional interests, and all the other devices of ruling. Readers can accept the conclusion that factions strengthened rather than weakened Rome, but drawing the practical moral that one should try to increase factional behavior is quite a different matter; one can agree that Roman religion surpassed Christianity in its promotion of courage and other masculine virtues and yet find unintelligible the practical moral that one should now reinstitute such a cult. The absurdity of such practical conclusions suggests that while Machiavelli may be offering a stark choice between competing ultimate values to the uniquely situated new prince, his teaching for the rest of us is the less exciting provision of topics around which to organize a life continually facing less dramatic decisions between principles and consequences, means and ends, customs and changing circumstances.

In what sense, though, can one claim that the *Discourses solves* the problem with which the reader of *The Prince* is left? Not, I should say at once, as a doctrine that contains a message that *The Prince* has prepared its readers for. The *Discourses* is a text with difficulties of its own that bar a straight reading and force one to regard it too as a performance, although obviously in a far different sense from *The Prince.*

I think that the way to approach the *Discourses* as further articulation of Machiavellian prudence is by looking in more detail at the consequences of Aristotle's distinction between prudence and *techne,* and to my location of Machiavellian prudence between art and Aristotelian virtue, and more generally of prudence in contrast to algorithmics and heuristics.[13] The strength of an art comes from its relative indifference to material, such that one can apply the laws of arithmetic to coins as well as cattle. That indifference to material makes it possible to formulate the precepts of art apart from any instantiations, and therefore makes the arts subjects for teaching. The relation between a rule of prudence and its material cannot be called application; virtue cannot be taught because (or to the extent that) its precepts cannot be learned apart from their instantiations.

That prudent judgment is a different sort of relation of form and matter than that found in the arts is a commonplace that I have used as a seat of arguments throughout; in the current section I have been stressing the way the arts are not only disengaged from the materials on which they operate, but also do not engage the character of the person employing them.[14] While it is difficult to do more than frame the problem of choosing ends, which seems to depend on an act of choice being both detached from and engaged with one's character, it is possible to talk about rhetoric and prudence, unlike purely artistic processes, having a more intimate relation between method and the material on which it operates. Tying action to character and tying action to its material are equivalent, in that both reject the abstraction on which the arts and sciences depend. The relation between the rule of prudence and its material is much more discursively accessible than the relation between those abstract rules and the characters in which they are embodied, and so it is the prudent relations between form and matter that will organize our examination of the *Discourses*.

Civic Virtue and Virtù Universalized

We can now see the problem that universality presents. There was something clearly wrong with imagining a community of Socrateses, or Lorenzos, and it was far from obvious what a community composed of people educated by Machiavelli or Plato could be like. Universality based on the proliferation of like characters is parallel to the abstraction from circumstances in question here: the less universal, the more technical and specialized, and therefore the more indifferent to circumstances a mode of action is. An art can ignore circumstances because it has a specific function, a specific end and value, and that specificity permits the distinction between an art's material and its circumstances, what it works *on* and what it works *within*. An art has material: the art of calculation works on discrete units; the art of sculpture works on malleable matter with a permissible range of hardness and stability. In the virtues of character, however, that distinction breaks down: the temptations of the flesh are both the circumstances in which temperance is necessary and the material on which it works. A technical definition of matter depends on distinguishing between relevant and irrelevant properties—that is, an art works on last matter—and a conception of matter appropriate to praxis must be different.

Arts are able to block questions of universalizability by separating their products from their uses; since no such distinction is possible for praxis, questions concerning the place of an action in a community are unavoidable. Aristotle is able to maintain that there are many arts but only one prudence because each art has a single end that can be aimed at without having to worry about other ends; but the single end for prudence is, for Aristotle, the good for man or, for Machiavelli, the security of the state and glory for its ruler, none of which, for the reasons I have suggested, has the sort of unity required of an end towards which an art might aim. (The kind of unity of end that an art requires is another ground for rejecting the claims of sophistic and heuristic methods to be an art. In heuristics one does find a single end — victory in argument or practical success more broadly — but such an end by itself is not a sufficient condition for sophistic itself being a single art rather than a collection of devices.) The inferences in Aristotelian prudence and art move in opposite directions: barring chance, a good product is sufficient grounds to infer the presence of artistic skill, but not conversely, while the possession of a moral virtue is sufficient grounds to infer that it will be exercised at the appropriate occasion, but not conversely. Similarly, the faculty of prudence has a unity although its end does not, while in the arts, a technical ability derives all its unity from the single kind of end it produces. Machiavelli has shown that neither of those inferences can work very well for virtù: if I possess virtù, that is no guarantee about how I will act, not only because there is no particular action associated with virtù the way not taking more than one's share is associated with justice, but also because I can possess virtù yet still *choose* not to exercise it; on the other side, tales of undeserved good and bad fortune bar any inference from success to virtù or from failure to its absence. (The recurrent Machiavellian arguments about "necessity" should be read in the context of these considerations about the direction of inference.) An artistic end can have greater unity than a prudential one because it is one among others; its exhaustiveness prevents the prudential end from having that much unity, since it cannot be thought of as this good as opposed to that one.[15] If Machiavellian virtù does not have the identity the virtues have, and the success virtù aims at does not have the unity of an artistic product, how is there any control over either practice or discourse about practice?

Given the ever-present analogies with art and Machiavelli's desire to make prudence as much as possible into an art, it would be tempting to divide prudence and its object (the good for man and security and prosperity for the state) into autonomous species, each with its own end; statecraft, for example, could be divided into departments of defense, economy, religion, and so on. But we saw in the last chapter that such strategies of evading the prudential problem of action in a world of plural ultimate goods broke down, just because the boundaries between those ends cannot be maintained the way boundaries between the ends of the arts can. Instead of achieving stability by dividing up spheres of virtue, the heart of Machiavelli's project becomes one of developing kinds of action that make further action possible, that increase, rather than constrict, the power of action belonging to both the ruling agents and the subjects and citizens acted upon. The prince becomes strong by making his subjects stronger, and republican virtue is increased in the presence of the virtues of fellow citizens.[16]

The same holds for Machiavelli himself: far from promoting the role of a counselor such that the prince would be dependent on him, his advice is designed to make the prince independent; even more to the point, the _Discourses on Livy_ is designed to take people who deserve to rule and create a situation in which they can rule. To the analogies I have drawn between Machiavelli and Socrates and Machiavelli and Aristotle, we can here add a parallel with Kant. Machiavelli's problem at this point is how to treat people — citizens and subjects — as material for action. Instead of Kant's distinction between treating people as means and as ends, or the more colloquial distinction between treating people as objects and as people, Machiavelli confronts the more pragmatic and rhetorical political problem of how to derive power from the people without that derivation "subtracting" from the people's power, how simultaneously to use and strengthen the power of the community. To take the simplest example, and the one that follows from the contrast I have been developing throughout, political security does not have the simplicity of definition that military victory does; the fact that citizens have their own desires and ends forces the ruler over citizens to rule politically. In the technical case of a simple change of ruler, time, custom, and usage work against the new prince, but in a truly republican case, as Pocock puts it, "something more than use and custom is at work."[17] Machiavelli — and his republican citizen and new prince — can succeed only if they can discover a specifically practical relation of form and matter in which the idea of matter shaping itself into form, a people becoming a community, makes sense.

Machiavelli carves out a conception of the relation of rule and case that lies between the technical conception of the relation of form and matter, in which the rules and rational structure of the art can be stated without regard for matter, and a practical conception in which nothing nonplatitudinous can be stated in abstraction, in which case virtù and prudence could not be taught at all. Finding modes of action that increase the ability to act means finding material on which to act and constructing directions for action on that material. The success of the Machiavellian project will depend on his ability to formulate such a relation between form and matter that will allow the prince, or the community as a whole, to act on something to increase the ability to act. The kind of practice Machiavelli is talking about is rhetorical, precisely because rhetoric offers the middle term between craft and virtue.

The relation between form and matter is different for making and for doing, not only because making has a number of discrete ends, its products, that can be considered separately but also because the hypothetical imperatives and clear instructions of an art must be replaced by the prudential balancing of alternatives in action, where alternatives are rooted in competing ultimate values. While these complications make impossible the reduction of prudence (even Machiavelli's rhetorical prudence) to art, they become the source for prudential acts that act on matter to increase the power to act and be acted upon. Therefore, what looked like a failure at the end of *The Prince* — the attempt to make prudence amenable to method — in the *Discourses* becomes the principle for making community, rather than individual, action fundamental. The need for community in *The Prince* was a weak one, that plural ultimate values seemed to require compromise and tolerance because of the improbability of being able to get one's own way, but here the necessity of plurovicity becomes the opportunity for the development of modes of life and methods of increasing the power of action that are essentially located in a community. The purpose of presenting the drama of the new prince facing a radical choice between ultimate goods, between kinds of character, between ways of life, and of the more complex decisions presented in the *Discourses* is to set the topics for deliberation and choice that do not avoid but honestly face problems of competing final ends. A world with a single, well-defined ultimate value would not require a practical intelligence that could adapt and respond to changing circumstances, and such a world would contain no such disjunctions between acquisition and stability, sovereignty and politics, or between past and present. But a practical intelligence facing multiple final goods must take such disjunctions seriously as the data for reasoning.

The way dysfunction opens up the field for prudence is symbolized by the way the relations between what is and what ought to be are themes in both works. The *Discourses on Livy* is dedicated to people who deserve to rule but who cannot: it starts with a gap between is and ought. In *The Prince*, the traditional ruler thinks that ought defines is; since he deserves to rule, he is the ruler, and deviations from what is right and proper "ought" not to exist. The villain, and the military agent, by contrast, live in a world in which might makes right, in which what is exhausts the possible considerations: they act in ways that take Machiavelli's opening gambit in chapter 15 of *The Prince* — "he who neglects what is being done for what should be done will learn his destruction rather than his preservation" — as the last word. The problem Machiavelli faces, then, is how to teach men "how not to be good" without losing the distinction between good and bad, is and ought. Just as Machiavelli makes room for prudence by carving out space between algorithms and heuristics, he shows that prudence functions where considerations of either is or ought, might and right, alone are inadequate.

Reading and Writing the *Discourses* as Political Acts

Machiavelli begins the second book of the *Discourses* by explicitly raising the problem of prudent judgment, contrasting its difficulties with the relative simplicity of judgments concerning artistic achievements. Not only is the evidence about practice fragmentary and designed, by deception and exaggeration, to produce epideictic admiration rather than imitation and action, but in addition, judgments about both past and present actions are clouded by hatred, apprehension, and envy: "I do not speak of matters pertaining to the arts, which shine by their intrinsic merits, which time can neither add to nor diminish; but I speak of such things as pertain to the actions and manners of men, of which we do not possess such manifest evidence."[18]

Both *The Prince* and *Discourses on Livy* try to teach prudence, and teach it by at once exhibiting it and making problematic the imitation of such exhibition. In both texts, Machiavelli recognizes that the problem of prudence demands coherently combining the demands of stability and flexibility into a way of understanding and acting that is both autonomous and responsive. Nevertheless, just how the topic of stability and flexibility is interpreted and developed differs from one text to the other according as their audiences and purposes differ. Where *The Prince* takes the literary form of showing a new prince how to seize power and then secure it, the *Discourses on Livy* is a commentary on an ancient historian, addressed to people who deserve to rule but who will not have power at any time soon. Consequently, in *The Prince*, Machiavelli makes room for prudence by employing as his principal topic acquisition and keeping, comparing the characters and circumstances of seizing a state and of staying in power, while the *Discourses on Livy*'s variant on the theme of flexibility and stability comes from the more historiographical topic of greater or less distance between past and present, the intermixture of the permanence of human nature and the shifting perspectives on such constant realities that prevent it from being directly accessible either in knowledge or action. Constant human nature cannot be directly manipulated but must be understood in its particular embodiments, because the people's superstitions and attachments to possessions define their nature in the only form in which it is accessible to manipulation. (Once again, if human nature were directly accessible to the prince, then the method of the fox could be the basis for a political science.)

If Machiavelli is successful, he will achieve the emotional impact of presenting the new dimensions of choice in radical terms, while also offering some account — still short of a method — of how to deal with the complexities to be encountered in this new world. Machiavelli is not only presenting the shocking news that we now must live in a world of competing final ends, and not only seducing his audience into giving up nostalgia for the false comforts of a simpler moral world; he is also supplying some equipment for living in the new world. This latter project, although less spectacular, and less Machiavellian, than the one dramatized in *The Prince*,

The Discourses on Livy: *Virtù Universalized*

has practical value of its own. Early in the analysis of *The Prince,* I appealed to Cicero's classification of kinds of cases in terms of the kinds of difficulties they presented; here we can say that the movement to the *Discourses* turns to a different kind of difficulty: no longer indifference of the audience (the rhetorical equivalent of prime matter) but rather hostility (the condition of matter that, left alone, will produce results opposite to those desired, which is what corruption means). It is possible to be technical or artistic towards prime matter, but one has to be practical towards citizen matter.

It is not too difficult to see *The Prince* as directed towards a pair of effects on a pair of audiences, nor do I think it difficult to see the connection between its performative structure and its substantive purpose, the kind of politics and political argument it advocates. There is an evident fit between method and matter: Machiavelli uses a rhetorical method, and more particularly a rhetorical method in which invention is the leading office, for handling a practical situation of great instability and indetermination. The method, a rhetoric of invention, and the substantive purpose, showing how to acquire and preserve one's rule in a world of instability, combine to yield the politics of invention. But when we turn from *The Prince* to the *Discourses,* we find a text that has none of the obvious marks of a performance. The *Discourses* is not *staged* and presented as a drama of teacher and student, because Machiavelli collapses the two audiences of *The Prince,* the prince learning his lessons and the public overhearing Machiavelli teaching the prince. Instead of playing on the distinction between those two audiences, Machiavelli dedicates the *Discourses* to people who deserve to rule but are in fact practically impotent, preparing them for some indefinitely remote time so that they can "imitate the virtues of [former times] whenever fortune presents them the occasion" (*Discourses,* Intro. to book 2). The method and matter do not fit as obviously in the *Discourses on Livy,* which is neither obviously rhetorical nor obviously political; it is difficult to see what kind of performance it is and how to characterize the uptake appropriate to its indefinitely specified audience, and it is equally difficult to see any sense in which it too transforms practice from ideological application to rhetorical deliberation and judgment, makes politics into essentially contested argument: how is writing a commentary, not on Roman history but on a Roman historian, a political act?

The *Discourses* has at least this much in common with *The Prince:* it cannot be read literally and nonrhetorically for long; its instabilities — the tensions between expanding the scope of talk about action while constricting the possibilities for action — are even easier to see than those of *The Prince.* The audience to whom the *Discourses* is dedicated are people who cannot act, and reading the *Discourses* will not make them suddenly able to seize power and become political actors. Yet Machiavelli begins the *Dis-*

courses by promising a reorientation of our attitudes towards the past: the Italian public thinks practical action impossible and so takes an epideictic attitude, passively distributing praise and blame — "this practice of praising and decrying" — without a thought that the present, like the past, is a time when great things are possible.

The dissonance between audience and purpose might be superable if Machiavelli can change the audience's attitude in accordance with his purpose, but there is a more serious dissonance between his purpose and what the reader finds in the narrative. An algorithmic attitude towards history and its lessons makes Machiavelli's purpose into exhortation, convincing his audience that they too are capable of action, since the present is no different from the past, but that reading cannot withstand the presentation of the way the putative uniformity of human nature produces such a diversity of effects. Worse still, the actual narrative he offers seems at odds with any purpose of empowering his audience: if anything, he *increases* the distance between past and present. His accounts of Lycurgus and Romulus, to take just one example, present them as erecting permanent structures, starting with an empty stage; the more past actions are described as *original*, as creating *ex nihilo*, the more acts of foundation, and the qualities required for them, appear different from acts of preservation and restoration and what they require, and so the less does history teach us that great things are possible today. Just as in *The Prince*, the narrative seems to constrict, not expand, the range of the practical and political; a stable straight reading seems impossible when Machiavelli says he will expand the range of the practical while his actual narrative appears to do just the opposite.

In fact, I think the dissonance between Machiavelli's purpose and content greater still. Machiavelli accuses his audience of taking an impractical attitude towards both past and present, but he himself seems to use, or imitate, rhetorical school exercises which make discourse inconsequential: chapter titles like "To whom can the guardianship of liberty more safely be confided, to the nobles or to the people?" suggest the schoolroom and not the assembly, and so do Machiavelli's answers, giving the argument on both sides, and then offering a split decision — under these circumstances to the nobles, and under those circumstances to the people. (While *The Prince* was a dramatic representation of the act of teaching, the *Discourses* seem to be an especially undramatic representation of an academic disputation, which is itself an undramatic representation of actual political argument.) Asking whether a new state should be set up in rich or poor soil makes the past look like the time for action and the present a time for idle speculation — who, after all, could ever have such a choice except some legendary figures of antiquity?[19]

Such a judicious disposition of the question destroys the essentially contested character of politics: an essentially contested concept is not just a subject on which argument currently can be found on both sides because the arguments, and the concept under dispute, might still be "disambiguated," shown to apply in perfectly unambiguous and uncontested fashion to the right circumstances, and Machiavelli seems to avoid permanent ambiguity in favor of pairs of categorical judgments with restricted ranges of application.[20] All the evasion strategies of chapter 4 are ways of destroying the essentially contested character of politics by segregating the range of application of distinct ultimate values. Deliberation, not the distanced objectivity of theoretical judgment or the phony scholastic resolutions of the set piece, is the only way of resolving disputes over essentially contested concepts, but Machiavelli's exposition seems completely at odds with that political sense of argument.

Earlier I said that advance made by the *Discourses* was that prudence becomes obligatory in the sense that its only alternatives are corruptions, privations, and perversions defined as fallings away from prudence, rather than modes of action with their own competing principles. Rhetorically, we can say that the alternatives to deliberation are uses of discourse and force, either distinct from rhetoric altogether or—what constitute in the long run a more serious threat—forms of judicial and epideictic rhetoric that occlude the problematic relations between principle and case that deliberation brings to the foreground. Machiavelli's presentation of examples of deliberation and resources for deliberation will be the *Discourses'* solution to how to live in a world of plural ultimate values, complicated by the postulation of plural loci of ultimate values. Deliberation and practical judgment are the only resources for accurately estimating the distance between past and present that Machiavelli has made puzzling.[21] In the next section I will show in detail the way Machiavelli distinguishes between for instance, productive, deliberative relations among factions and enervating, judicial relations, or between adherence to religious values as productive of public virtue and the empty celebration of impotent values. That taxonomy and exemplification of the forms of corruption, the ways of failing to deliberate, become important in proportion as prudence and deliberation themselves are not capable of direct formulation.

The *Discourses* as a Work of Rhetoric

There are, however, two prior matters to attend to. I have to say something about how the rhetorical or essentially contested nature of political argument is transformed as one moves from *The Prince* to the *Discourses;* what comes to the same thing, I have to explore the less apparent performative dimensions of the *Discourses,* showing the relation between its content and conceivable political effect. The primary effect of *The Prince* was the development of a new rhetorical politics, and the secondary thrust, which became focal in the last three chapters, was directed toward the creation of a framework in which the old and new politics can compete for the allegiance of princes, subjects, and citizens, shifting from an individual attempt at effective practical discourse to an examination of the conditions of effective practical discourse. In one sense Machiavelli's problem in the *Discourses* is the same, because here too he has to make politics rhetorical. It would be too easy to make politics rhetorical to his own satisfaction; that, after all, might be done *in* the saying, by being one of those illocutionary acts whose successful accomplishment occurs in discourse in the literal-minded sense that Searle gives to promising as an illocutionary act. To "prove" that politics is rhetorical might also be something that Machiavelli could accomplish within the *Discourses,* but his ambitions are higher. He wants to make politics rhetorical in an appropriately efficacious sense, not only in this text, but in a continuing discourse which this text initiates.

But the differences between *The Prince* and the *Discourses* are no less important. In *The Prince,* Machiavelli initiated debate by taking a position and upholding it, but his tactics of invention and origination must differ in the *Discourses,* because the intended result is not prudential innovation by the new prince but practice in a much more general and indeterminate sense. Here the prudential and rhetorical problem of plural ends is no longer the ethical problem of how to choose ends and characters; it has become the political problem of how to construct a community composed of citizens whose ultimate ends may be at variance.

Commensurate to that purpose, Machiavelli's argument initiates debate not by stating a position but by making room for argument, arguing both sides of questions, making practical action seem both impossible and dependent on prudence, judgment, and self-reflection. Successful practice is possible only when it is action *in and against* the framework of ancient and contemporary history — otherwise it is private and capricious — and so Machiavelli's reliance on Livy, and his distance from Livy, together create the space in which practical argument and action is possible.[22] The relation between principle and case, between general formulation and individual case, which distinguishes ideological from rhetorical politics, here is brought to a head in the relations between history as account, *historia narrans, historiam rerum gestarum,* and history as event, *historia narrata, res gestae.* Machiavelli will break the hold ideology has on his audience by collapsing the distinction between history as account and history as event.[23]

Saying how a commentary on an ancient historian can be practical, how to resolve the dissonance between specified audience, intended effect, and the actual content of the narrative, means showing what the proper uptake, response, or *imitatio* to the *Discourses* could be. While in *The Prince*, for the hereditary monarch to enter the field of rhetorical argument is for him to lose, in the *Discourses*, Machiavelli's argument that contemporary Italians are impotent invites a counterargument which by itself could be an instance of prudential action, and so a refutation of the charge of impotence, and thus an initiation of both political debate and political action. Lest Machiavelli's task of initiating political discourse seem too easy, such that answering back was a performative which in the act of counter-assertion produced political discourse, we have to raise two questions: What could such counterargument look like? and, What could make it into a political act, rather than just an intellectual substitute for action?

How can Machiavelli's virtuosity in argument invite practical counter-argument—not just the schoolroom exercise of assembling reasons on both sides? How can his virtuosity fail to *reduce* the room for maneuver by his audience, in the way that seeing what had been accomplished by past heroes may diminish current capacities for action? Deliberation about how to respond to Machiavelli's text encounters a problem parallel to figuring out how to act in the uncertain and ambiguous world Machiavelli has described. Machiavelli invites a series of experiments, and performs most of them himself, inviting as uptake more of the same. Machiavelli offers a series of arguments and examples, and often adds his own counterarguments and counterexamples; the reader should counter Machiavelli's arguments, offering considerations leading to the opposite conclusion. (Machiavelli's own participation in the activity of counterargument shows the reader that a merely refutative stance is inadequate.)[24] Rhetorical argument traditionally depends on being able to see and argue both sides of a question; here, facing Machiavelli involves seeing that each of a pair of opposed stratagems may be successful, depending on some things which are and some things which are not under one's control. Machiavelli and his audience conspire together to create the space in which political argument can go on, as argument and counterargument establish the boundaries of that space: the reader can argue topically for the malleability, rather than the fixity, of human character, for the power of choice rather than fortune, but *cannot* argue topically in favor of unreflective morality (whether Christian, patriotic, or "Machiavellian"), cannot argue for traditional obedience or for depending on fortresses, because, as we saw in examining *The Prince*, such things are destroyed by being argued for.[25] Politics, at least rhetorical politics, consists in the discursively defensible, while ideology, blind obedience, and depending on fortresses cannot be argued for: they are serious cases of illocutionary suicide. Machiavelli is aware that not all politics is in that sense rhetorical; occasionally argument hits on a principle that makes further argument pointless. For example, he indicates that counterargument is not a possible response to his discussion of fortresses in the Discourses on Livy by dropping his usually balanced treatment of a subject and his usual, argumentatively distanced stance towards his audience and addressing them directly, or, as he puts it, "in a more familiar manner," decreasing the distance between himself and audience by increasing the distance between himself and Livy. Here Machiavelli uses an apostrophe: "Prince or republic, you would either keep the people of your own city in check by means of fortresses, or you wish to hold a city that has been taken in war. I shall turn to the prince, and say to him that 'nothing can be more useless than such a fortress for keeping your own citizens in check. . . .'" Machiavelli considers the various possibilities in turn and concludes that "to hold one's own country fortresses are injurious, and to hold conquered territory they are useless" (Discourses 2.24; cf. also The Prince, ch. 20).

The proper response to the Discourses is counterargument, because it is only through experiments in rebuttal that one learns the limits of practical action: the field of praxis is that on which one can argue both sides of a question. But what could make such a response into political discourse, and not just discourse about politics? As I have argued before, the mere production of such counterarguments cannot automatically be a political act, with the respondent accepting responsibility for his actions and consenting to being an agent rather than a spectator to history; our one certainty in following Machiavelli's plottings is that if political discourse and action are possible, they will not be easy achievements. Such "acceptance of responsibility" and "consent" are not performatives achieved by saying so, but must reflect the demand that practical, as opposed to technical, actions must engage the character of the actor. The degeneration from political argument to its academic shadow cannot be reversed by a simple intellectual act.[26]

It would be a mistake to underestimate the difficulty of the cooperative enterprise of rhetorical politics that Machiavelli proposes. Rhetorical argument constitutes a community because it is essentially contested argument, and hence requires that one regard one's opponents as not simply wrong, stupid, lazy, or venal (although they can be all those things too); rhetorical argument needs an adversary, while other kinds of discourse and thinking, and other forms of politics and community, find adversaries an inconvenience, maybe an inevitable one, but nothing essential to one's own thinking. Machiavelli must refute the old politics, but that refutation will not simply convict the old politics of error; Machiavelli's refutation will initiate permanent debate, although not an unchanging one. This is a difficult relation to one's opponent to conceive, making heavy intellectual and, as we shall see, moral demands; one has to aim at defeating one's opponents in each debate but not at removing them from debate altogether; one has to be able to distinguish dissent from treason, heresy, and schism. Such a conception of debate is difficult because it seems to require a standpoint distinct from the position from which one engages in argument, a difficulty that has already emerged in the complications of the final chapters of *The Prince*, where Machiavelli tried to create a discursive representation of standing outside the realm of discourse. We have been trying to make sense out of the dissonance between Machiavelli's expanding the scope of debate and his constricting the scope of action, but the resolution comes, surprisingly, by inverting both sides of that proportion. Thus, when he teaches the prince to be mistrustful, Machiavelli is in fact crediting the people with greater powers of action than the traditional ruler does or than Machiavelli himself would do if he were to counsel the prince to be confident in his manipulations and treat his subjects like things, not men. In attempting to overcome the powers of the people, Machiavelli endows the people with power, just as, in attempting to overcome the power of the traditional politics, impotent as its practitioners are in accomplishing anything in action, Machiavelli endows the old politics with practical power, reviving it at the same time that he strips it of its superhuman dignity.

One consequence of the difference between principalities and republics — another respect in which the *Discourses on Livy* represents an advance over *The Prince* — is in what happens to essentially contested concepts as Machiavelli teaches this more difficult attitude toward one's opponents, an attitude to be considered in more detail in the next chapter. In *The Prince*, the new politics needs the old because it is by nature polemical; the prudent relation between principles and cases defines itself in opposition to explicit algorithmic and covert heuristic relations. The new prince, unlike the audience of the *Discourses*, does try to eliminate his opponents rather than accept them as a permanent part of the scene. One must wonder — and this is just another version of the instability in the project of *The Prince* that I have pointed to all along — what happens to a politics that defines itself in opposition to the old politics once that old politics disappears.

In its easier form, this is just the usual question of what happens when revolutionaries become the establishment; Machiavelli resolved that problem in *The Prince* by constructing proportions between the acts of acquiring and keeping states. There is a more difficult, and indeed more philosophical, form of the problem, though, that becomes urgent in the

The Discourses on Livy: *Virtù Universalized*

Discourses. If the real "victory" of the new, prudential politics comes in the *Discourses* rather than *The Prince,* because it is there that one asks what a world would be like in which everyone acted prudently, then the problem of universalization in the *Discourses on Livy* becomes, What happens to this essentially polemical politics when it "wins," when it now exists in a world in which it is the only politics, or where the only alternatives are kinds of acts that try to be political and fail? (In the Kuhnian language of paradigms and normal science whose analogies to the old politics I exploited in the preceding chapter, the revolutionary rhetoric of a paradigm shift must be replaced by a new normal science that excludes rhetoric. That narrative frame would make revolutionary rhetoric essential to the overthrow of the old paradigm but only accidental to the new science itself. Machiavelli, on the contrary, follows a permanently problematizing strategy.) Part of the answer is that the alternative to a Machiavellian politics is not now a different kind of politics with its own integrity, which only happens to be inappropriate for these times and unavailable to the aspiring new prince, but, as I have already suggested, instead the alternative now is corruption in the sense of a falling away from, a perversion of, the Machiavellian politics. It is by its nature liable to corruption and impermanence not just because it has powerful enemies, but because of its own inevitable particularity, which it cannot overcome except by imitating the Roman republic and trying to conquer the world, thereby becoming *per accidens* the only exemplar of its politics. The essentially contested argument of Machiavellian politics thenceforth has internal enemies, especially its own matter, in the form of armies, religion, and factions, the three principal kinds of matter and sources of power in the *Discourses,* whose detailed examination occupies my next chapter. Here then is how Machiavelli's expansion of argument also expands the ability to act—except that in the first instance, the ability to act that is expanded turns out to be that of one's opponent! Victory in argument consists in successful deliberation, the formulation of desirable and effective policy, instead of silencing one's opponent through irrefutable demonstration.[27]

6

CIVIC VIRTUE AND

THE NEW RHETORICAL VIRTUES

Materials for Civic Virtue

I claim, then, that the philosophical formulation of the problem Machiavelli faces in the *Discourses* is one of the proper relation between form and matter, recognizing, of course, that this is far from the way Machiavelli himself would formulate it. That relations between is and ought, between means and end, between appearance and reality, are not smooth is precisely what makes form and matter into a *problem* demanding Machiavelli's intellectual resources. A successful resolution of the problem requires finding the appropriate sorts of material on which to operate and appropriate ways of organizing it into stable structures. The assimilation of politics to rhetoric means that form for Machiavelli consists in the discursively accessible, the discursively defensible and articulable, rather than other sorts of form, such as virtuous activity and stable institutions in Aristotle, constitutional forms for material interests and factions in the *Federalist*, or the rule of wisdom for the material of the passions in Plato. Since Machiavelli is not interested in constitutional arrangements, and does not read the history of the Roman Republic the way Madison and Adams did, the criterion for judging any institution is its ability to make that transition from matter to form, from potent energy to secure strength. The optimum would be for the uniformity of human nature to lead to the permanence of republics. (Once again, that would be a scientific rather than a prudential resolution of the problem of form and matter, a resolution that depends on the matter of human nature reliably and dependably producing the desired form. In the terms from the *Rhetoric* that I have cited before, one would then have hit on a first principle and would no longer need rhetoric.) Short of that, Machiavelli tries to find arrangements that allow the channeling of energy into strength rather than enervation; politics then consists in the permanent task of adjusting to independent and unpredictable changes in the matter, rather than the Lycurgan task of setting up laws and forms that will permanently organize material.

If rhetorical form consists in the discursively accessible, the corresponding matter consists in rhetorically structured places and resources for in-

Civic Virtue and the New Rhetorical Virtues

creased prudent action. While in *The Prince* Machiavelli employed the idea of example both in its rhetorical sense as a kind of argument and in its pedagogical sense as a model to be imitated, in the *Discourses*, he similarly appeals to what can be seen as another transformation, this time not of the example but of the enthymeme into a piece of factuality embedded into history and action as well as a form of rhetorical argument. The focus of the *Discourses on Livy* is on deliberative rhetoric and practical judgment about what to do, as opposed to the inventive stress on judicial rhetoric in *the Prince*. Hence its examples and reasoning are more substantive, and as is appropriate to deliberative rhetoric as opposed to judicial, the overall verbal and intellectual structure of the *Discourses* exercises less tight control over the individual arguments than one sees in *the Prince*. Whereas *The Prince* presents a number of great examples, the *Discourses* presents only one example, the history of the Roman Republic. Therefore the order of argument goes in opposite directions: *The Prince* moves from contradictory examples and contradictions within examples to stable structures, while the *Discourses on Livy* finds contradictory lessons and argues *in utramque partem* concerning the internal constitution of Rome in book 1 and its external relations in book 2, in order to clear ground for the actions of great men in book 3.

Machiavelli's interest — and the interest of his audience — is therefore in locating efficient causes that can take matter and produce form. Machiavelli wants to endow republics with the dependability associated with *techne* along with the energy and adaptability associated with praxis. Therefore his attention is directed to phenomena that lie between Aristotle's moral virtues and technical productions. Prudence and political wisdom in Aristotle are similarly located, but are more closely allied to moral virtue than in Machiavelli because of the impossibility of separating their *logoi* from circumstances the way technical *logoi* can be, while Machiavelli employs rhetoric in order to make the forms of good action more discursively accessible. Therefore the material for Machiavelli consists in things that, left by themselves, become *atechnoi*, substitutes for argument, ways of achieving stability or success that make action unnecessary. Consequently, in this section I will explore the *Discourses'* treatment of powerful material, and in the final section turn to the abilities necessary to use those materials to strengthen the state.

Among the kinds of material, factions are the most important because they permit the discovery of material as political potential, matter relative to the new public form, but already existing in the form of private interest and direction of action. In addition to factions, and to be considered later, military force and religious authority are further alternatives to argument, must as torture, contracts, and the like are in Aristotle's *Rhetoric* alternatives to debate that dictate a judgment. In all cases, Machiavelli's rhetorical task is to convert alternatives to argument into material for argument. (In this sense, Machiavelli's rhetoric is more Roman than Greek. In Roman rhetoric, Aristotle's *atechnoi* become "external topics," sources for argument [topics] that lie outside the subject under consideration. That is the move that Machiavelli attempts to replicate here.) Machiavelli gives depth to this project by treating these different sources of material differently, making religion subject to the epideictic celebration of values, and armies to forensic disputes over possession, and factions' attachments to distinct values bearing on the newly expanded sense of deliberation.

The dysfunction that provides the field for prudence takes its most practical form in the discussions of factions, and it is factions that will provide Machiavelli with his clearest example of acting on matter to increase the power of action. The *Discourses on Livy* starts by claiming that civic strife between nobles and people is the cause of Rome's freedom, stability, and power. Nevertheless, one cannot draw an algorithmic lesson from Roman history by inferring that if you want to be free, you should aim at factions. The notoriously Machiavellian side of Machiavelli bars an algorithmic substitute for prudence by refusing to infer from the fact that factions lead to good results to the conclusion that factions are good and should be chosen: while sometimes they should be chosen because they lead to desired results, they are not on that account good. Even worse, not only are factions bad in themselves and sometimes bad in what they lead to, but they are also an impossible object of choice for one's policies, because part of their nature is to exist apart from their political organization and domestication. Factions do not act for the common good, although that may be their effect; they do not think they are pressing the claims of one ultimate value against another that ought also to be heard. Rather, they think they are defending the good against evil, and so "advocating factions" is an impossible stance. This impossibility is the converse of the difficult relation mentioned earlier, of advocating one position while acknowledging that one's opponents are taking the part of another side of an essentially contested concept. All along, I have pointed to the difficulties of imitating the past as Machiavelli presents it; here those difficulties take an especially acute specific form as the difficulty of aiming at something bad to accomplish something good. It is one thing to acknowledge, as he does in *The Prince*, that good results may sometimes require bad acts, and even therefore to advocate those bad actions, but the "Machiavellianism" of *The Prince* is not adequate for this more political problem, because here the republican citizen must aim at allowing someone else's evil to persist rather than try to destroy it. The tolerance and self-restraint required to see value in factions, while they have a more liberal sound to them than the blunt recommendations of The Prince, may be even more upsetting than those more notorious precepts. It is for this reason that the form/matter relations explored in the Discourses will require the new rhetorical virtues to be considered next.

Machiavelli has found material for substantive rhetorical argument because sometimes factions lead to freedom and sometimes lead to the destruction of the state:

> The enmities that at the outset existed in Rome between the people and the nobles were ended by debating, those in Florence by fighting; those in Rome were terminated in law, those in Florence by the exile and death of many citizens. . . . The people of Rome wished to enjoy supreme honors along with the nobles; the people of Florence fought to be alone in the government, without any participation in it by the nobles. Because the Roman people's desire was more reasonable, their injuries to the noble were more endurable, so that the nobility yielded easily and without coming to arms. . . . On the other hand, the Florentine people's desire was harmful and unjust, so that the nobility with greater forces prepared to defend themselves, and therefore the result was blood and the exile of citizens, and the laws then made were planned not for the common profit but altogether in favor of the conqueror.[1]

The problem for the prudent politician is to learn to use such material.

The search for "lessons in history" uncovers in factions a most important and most frustrating case. Factions, "the cries of the people furious against the Senate, and of a Senate declaiming against the people," may seem "strange means" to attain "public liberty" (Discourses 1.4), and indeed, two chapters later Machiavelli bars one easy generalization from the discovery of how factions led to health in Rome by finding other "republics that have maintained their liberties without such enmities and disturbances" (1.6). He finds that the circumstances in these other republics, Venice and Sparta, that permitted freedom without factions are nearly impossible conditions to duplicate, more like boundary conditions for practical judgment, while the Roman example more nearly fits the only real practical situation, starting from current difficulties rather than a tabula rasa. Still, he cannot draw a practical conclusion—let a thousand factions bloom—from a discovery that reverses the requisite form/matter relation: one cannot say that one's form, a free and disciplined state, requires a certain kind of matter, namely factions, and then go out and create the factions; instead one has to take matter as given and learn how to organize it into the desired form.

Pitkin neatly captures the prudent difficulty at turning a lesson from Roman history into a prescription when she says:

> For Machiavelli, at his best, the real point is not some unified harmony at which politics theoretically aims, but the activity of struggling toward agreement with and against each other, in which citizens take active charge of the historical processes that would otherwise direct their lives in hidden ways. And that activity is not mere courtly dialogue, but a genuine conflict, in which needs and important interests are at stake. Without passion and struggle there can be no liberty, but only reification, habit, and drift. Yet political conflict must also always be kept within limits; politics is not civil war. The struggle must be kept open and public, rather than clandestine and private. It must involve a genuine appeal to principle, to what is reasonable and what is just; the public and principled aspect of politics must be kept lively in it. And citizens must be kept aware of their interdependence, their shared stake in fair rules and right principles, the civil limits (*i termini civili*) that forbid wiping out their opponents. These requirements are both prerequisites for and products of a healthy politics (which is one reason why the initial founding of a *vivere civile* is such a puzzle). . . . Instilling this capacity for mutuality within difference is a crucial part of Machiavelli's effort at the political education of his factional fellow Florentines.[2]

Pitkin's observations on the treatment of factions show how rhetorical Machiavelli's prudence has become. The "openness" she describes corresponds to my earlier remarks on Machiavelli's domestication of evil and of the difficulties of aligning rule and case by making them all open and discursively accessible.[3]

Factions are domesticated, then, and become participants in a rhetorical argument, not when they agree to live peacefully and moderately alongside each other—once again Machiavelli has no interest in the tempting, modern inference from the absence of a perfect resolution for disputes to the spirit of liberal compromise and toleration—but when their disputes are framed in civil, open, and therefore negotiable language, language that can lead, not to compromise, but to rhetorical judgment and decision. Machiavelli makes this point by once again comparing the civil, and energizing, factions of Rome with the enervating disputes in Florence. In Florence, the constitutions varied "not between liberty and slavery, as many believe, but between slavery and license. The promoters of license, who are the people, and the promoters of slavery, who are the nobles, praise the mere name of liberty, for neither of these classes is willing to be subject either to the laws or to men" (*Florentine Histories* 4.1; Gilbert ed., p. 1187).

Moreover, the civil limits "that forbid wiping out their opponents" are rhetorical in that they are what we have been looking for all along—limits to virtuous action that come not from some external "moral" restraint but from the nature of the actions themselves:

> That is the reason, also, why Machiavelli places so much stress on the Roman institution of accusations. It allowed charges to be brought lawfully against even the rich and powerful who engaged in abuses; where the charges were found valid, the abuses were countered 'with public forces and means, which have their definite limits' and therefore 'do not go on to something that may destroy the republic.' Hidden antagonisms seek private modes of expression which divide the community into factions that prefer vengeance to the public good, that consequently may even call in foreign forces to assist their private aims, and that fail to recognize the essential civic or civil limits (*i termini civili*) distinguishing political conflict from civil war.[4]

Machiavelli shows, both in *The Prince* and in the *Discourses*, that external moral limits on action no longer restrain, and so he has to search for limits built into the nature of practice itself; what were earlier seen as the surprising constraints on the range of practical efficacy will be seen in the next section as Machiavelli's new rhetorical virtues, the answer to the question of how to take the materials we are now isolating and use them as the potency for stable, autonomous action.[5]

This contrast between uses of factions that increase the power of the community and those uses that destroy community enables Machiavelli to do two further things that complete his investigation of the sources of political power. First, it allows him to lay out a taxonomy of the kinds of corruption. At the beginning of this chapter I said that once Machiavelli's argument had advanced from *The Prince* to the *Discourses*, there were no longer any alternatives to prudence, except for ways of failing to be prudent. Those ways of failing can be described as ways of either trying to avoid a rhetorical relation to the material that is the potential for action, and trying instead to make such material a substitute for action— as, for example, by making action into production and subject to art—or they can be ways of substituting judicial or epideitic rhetoric for deliberation.[6] Just as it is especially tempting for a prince to try to replace deliberation by a ceremonial rhetoric that masks clandestine decisions, it is an especially common temptation for republican citizens to turn toward past insults and injuries rather than plans for the future.[7]

That central case of factions suggests a couple of different relations between matter and form, satisfied by other kinds of human potential as well. While the correct way to make factions contribute to the health of the state is to recognize them as alternative objects of allegiance, alternative and exclusive formulations of values that require negotiation, discipline, and limitation to become part of the public life of republics rather than a source of enervation and corruption, religion and military valor are kinds of material that have different relations to the form of the state. They both differ from factions in that neither should be treated as an independent source of values that merely has to be organized by the state, as factions are; instead, both have to be made by the state, and must not be allowed to be independent sources of value. But while religion requires specialists to preach and interpret, armies require as many citizens and subjects as possible to be subjected to military discipline and participate in military activity.[8] Consequently, these three primary sources of power for the stable republic — factions, armies, and religion — represent different approaches to the problem of universalization, ranging from universal participation, desirable for armies, to permitting the existence of specialists, as religions do. Factions fall in between those extremes because their relation to the community as a whole is more problematic owing to the *direct* disjunction between means and ends. Factions, armies, and religions make more complex the problem of universality as applied to republics; Aristotle's assumption that the moral life is a life that can be lived in common here becomes a new field for political argument: "Which mode of life is the more desirable, the life of active citizenship and participation in politics, or rather the life of an alien and that of detachment from the political partnership; next, what constitution and what organization of a state is to be deemed the best,— either on the assumption that to take an active part in the state is desirable for everybody, or that it is undesirable for some men although desirable for most" (*Politics* 7.2.1324a13–19).

Factions are useful, and crucial to them is that they have an independent existence prior to and to some extent opposed to their organization in the state. Machiavelli seems to deny such status to religion, and suggests instead that only state religion, such as the Roman religion instituted by Numa and praised in *Discourses* 1.11, is beneficial. Factions and religions, both seem to take a single ultimate value and make it into an overriding one; why, then, should they be differently treated? The damage done to Italy by Christianity Machiavelli imputes not to Christian principles but to a failure of prudence properly to apply those principles in practice, and so religion need not differ from factions on this count: "If the Christian religion had from the beginning been maintained according to the principles of its founder, the Christian states and republics would have been much more united and happy than what they are. . . . And whoever examines the principles on which that religion is founded, and sees how widely different from those principles its present practice and application are, will judge that her ruin or chastisement is near at hand" (*Discourses* 1.12). But factions and religions require distinct treatment because factions are organized by the state through political devices of negotiation that makes their disputes manageable, and finite; the religious equivalent of political negotiation, the principal forms of religious rhetoric, are preaching and, for written scriptures, interpretation. Religious activity, then, offers essentially contested concepts without being able to provide a structure in which it is evident that they are essentially contested concepts.[9] Consequently their political value is less, and their political danger higher, than other sorts of factions and parties.

Machiavelli's New Rhetorical Virtues

This overview of the *Discourses* is only half complete. In addition to indicating the available material a republican community can use to strengthen itself, we must say something about the abilities Machiavelli teaches for using such material prudently. In the fully rhetorical world that Machiavelli lays out, the admirable moral and intellectual qualities we look for in the persuasive speaker and the prudent republican citizen are not expressions of (or masks of) some more fundamental and real qualities possessed by the person speaking and acting: the relevant moral and intellectual qualities are dimensions of rhetorical excellence. Moderation, restraint, prudence, and respect for one's fellow man, in particular, are values fully defined by the demands of successful rhetorical performance.

While these rhetorically redefined virtues will not always manifest themselves in instances that will commend general approval, the rhetorical connection between these qualities and action, through discursive accessibility and defensibility, insures the practical potency of virtues whose admirability at times seems inversely proportional to their efficacy. As the new rhetorical virtues become harder to identify because of the more problematic connection between principle and case, they become more inextricably bound up with their particular circumstantial embodiment. Such qualities are therefore always open to the charge that they have purchased practical power with the coin of protean hypocrisy, that their practical power comes from their lack of integrity; calling them rhetorical *virtues* means showing that their intrinsic limitations supply an adequate substitute for moral restraint. We saw at the end of the last section, for example, that the essentially contested argument that characterizes rhetorical politics requires loyalty to something one shares with one's opponents, whether hope for a united Italy or respect for the ancient glories of the Roman republic; rhetorical politics requires something beyond victory at which one can aim. Defining, or redefining, one's ends as functions of what one can do tempers one's attitude towards opponents by making one aim at the adoption of a particular policy and not at the destruction of the enemy.

When moderation and restraint are qualities of rhetorical activity, they can be specified further in terms of the three principal kinds of material Machiavelli explores in the *Discourses*. With respect to armies, these virtues will subordinate military action to political ends and criteria instead of encouraging overreaching attitudes that put military victory above everything else. With respect to religion, moderation comes from focusing on the acts of interpretation and preaching instead of occluding their nature as actions and looking only at the content of what they say. We saw earlier how Machiavelli taught the prince to read, and part of the lesson was learning how to avoid taking *The Prince* as doctrine by making explicit the acts and agents of reading and writing involved; Machiavelli invites us to treat religious discourse in the same way. As to factions, finally, restraint means simply keeping on the point and not making appeals — whether to one's own character or that of one's opponent, whether to the feelings of the audience or the exigencies of the subject matter — that are broader than necessary for the decision at issue. Rhetorical restraint thereby dictates a sort of pragmatic narrowing of judgment to deliberative considerations of what is to be done, pushing as far as possible into the background forensic issues about who is right and who has been wronged and epideictic topics of what values are being upheld in the proposed course of action. While Aristotle's *Ethics* and *Politics* began with good ends of action and transformed them into good activities — virtues and constitutions — that are their own end, Machiavelli's rhetorical praxis, in these three cases, employs the new rhetorical virtues of moderation and restraint to recognize the performative dimensions of argument in ways that neither algorithmic nor heuristic politics do, making argument and what argument is about into the primary objects of attention and valuation. Moderation and restraint in argument thus become not extra-argumentative ethical demands but part of understanding politics as rhetoric. Machiavelli's achievement, more generally, is to embody the ethical virtues in the rhetorical character of the effective speaker.

To articulate the requisite prudent abilities, and to show why they can be called virtues and not just technical abilities, I think we should turn to the considerations with which Aristotle begins *Rhetoric* 2, slightly amended for our purposes by the *Politics*. Machiavelli has forced his readers to participate in performative arguments and not rest content with a doctrinal,

Civic Virtue and the New Rhetorical Virtues

constative, "straight" reading, and so he forces us to move from the sorts of considerations Aristotle advances in the first book of the *Rhetoric*—proofs and their materials—to the ethical qualities the speaker and the rhetorical politician must possess, and teach, to carry conviction and produce uptake. In *Rhetoric* 2 Aristotle points to three ethical qualities, aside from knowing what he is talking about, that make a speaker credible: virtue, prudence, and *philia*, or loyalty to the existing constitution, or, in more modern language, patriotism. A slightly different list appears in the *Politics* (5.7.1309a33f); loyalty, virtue and justice, and competence (*dynamis*), i.e., the sort of skills covered in the first book of the *Rhetoric*. Competence drops out in the *Rhetoric* because the subjects of rhetorical deliberation are things that require no special ability or knowledge: recall that as soon as a knowledge of some subject gets too technical, too much the province of special abilities, it ceases to be fit for rhetorical treatment. But in the more indeterminate world of Machiavellian politics, one cannot presume that the requisite abilities either do or do not require specialized skills and knowledge. (Military ability is an essential quality in both the prince and the republican citizen, and we have seen how it alternatively appears both rhetorical and extrarhetorical, admitting of specialized knowledge and performance and then requiring integration into more general civic abilities.) Consequently, our survey of Machiavellian prudence will be complete if we can indicate what happens to competence, to loyalty, and to prudence itself when they become rhetorical abilities. While other taxonomies are obviously possible, this trio of virtues is a convenient way of specifying further the overwhelming prudential virtue of bringing intelligence to bear in action.

Each of these virtues, moreover, contributes a dimension to the second Socratic problem of prudence that I claimed impelled Machiavelli to move from *The Prince* to the *Discourses*: the problem of the universalization of intelligence. In my Introduction, I noted that a history of prudence had a complication not found in the history of scientific reason because the functioning of practical reason is embodied in different practical agents and thinkers—the partisan, the sage, the historian, the critic, and others. The argument of *The Prince* forced us to turn to the *Discourses* to ask, What if everyone learned Machiavelli's lessons? or, in more neutral terms, Can Machiavelli's new rhetorical politics be not only a way of acting but also a way of living? Part of the force and direction of Machiavelli's redefinition of prudence comes from powerful acts of abstraction that formulate a kind of practical intelligence whose ties to particular political and social rules are not clear, precisely because of the scope of the abstraction. The following new rhetorical virtues serve, in different ways, to situate this new mode of practical intelligence in a community.

COMPETENCE

For the old politics, competence is simply knowing one's resources, alternative courses of action, and possible opponents — nothing too different from what Aristotle meant by *ability* in the first book of the *Rhetoric*. As easy as this sounds, Machiavelli repeatedly shows that the current rulers are incompetent even in these terms: they constantly think that gold, rather than soldiers, will win wars, and that good laws, rather than good arms, will support states. Once again, we see a parallel between Machiavelli's own practices and those he recommends to the prince as he tells the prince not to put his faith in gold and fortresses, and shows his readers how not to rely on doctrine and ideology but on performance and intellectual arts. Competence is nothing harder than knowing what one's resources are, but the current rulers wrongly identify the sources of their power, taking epiphenoma for malleable material. On an ideological reading of *The Prince* and the *Discourses*, the new politicians's competence comes from knowing the past, learning about great actions and stable institutions in the past. His resources consist not in money, or even arms, but in a repertoire of actions he can imitate and an ability to read the past and present. The use of knowledge in action can here well be called application.

We saw, though, that that reading would not stand still. Parallel to our first performative reading is a performative sense of competence consisting in following Machiavelli's argument; the object of *imitatio* is not just history as past events but history as narrative argument. Competence consists not in possessing the past as a *copia* of resources but in being able to *use* the narrated past in rhetorical deliberation and judgment.

But even that, as we saw, is not enough. The competence Machiavelli teaches consists in possessing *public* knowledge of the past: the prince must not only learn from the past but appear to, and the reader of the *Discourses on Livy* not only learns Roman history but learns Livy's history of Rome. While the old prince inherits the throne from a father, the new prince inherits his right to rule from the heroes whose actions he imitates and brings to life. The competence the rhetorical politician must have is not just possessing some knowledge; a fully rhetorical quality can be completely actualized in the rhetorical act; even more, it must be the ability to display and appeal in argument to such knowledge.[10] (As in Aristotle, displaying one's knowledge does not prevent deception from having a role in persuasion or intelligent action. For the difference between acting reflectively and acting explicitly, see the virtue of prudence below.) Thus when Aristotle treats historical examples in *Rhetoric* 2.20, contrasting them with parables and fables, he takes for granted that those historical examples will be drawn from a common fund of customary knowledge; such com-

Civic Virtue and the New Rhetorical Virtues

petence is the presumed common possession of all citizens. Machiavelli's rhetorical politician draws his examples from books, from a written record of great achievements, and so competence to learn from history and construct historical arguments becomes a more erudite, and specialized, ability. Many scholars of rhetoric have concerned themselves with the adaptation of rhetorical production from the generation of oral to written language. Machiavelli is here engaged in something analogous, shifting the resources which the rhetorician must draw upon and interpret from common to erudite knowledge.

While this more robust sense of competence makes greater demands on the agent, at the same time Machiavelli imposes a progressively diminished role on expert knowledge, something that the rhetorical politician could delegate. The ideological politician can farm out the collection of the facts and thereby depend on others for his competence. For the prudent agent who tries to make everything a function of his own powers, competence consists in the ability to use available materials, and not in the encyclopedic collection of data. The tension between autonomy and community here surfaces as the conflicting demands of a competence demanding erudition and specialization but not capable of delegation. The rhetorically prudent agent must not only use available material but make that use manifest. Competence consists in the ability to make the judgment about where to draw a line between those things that are and are not within one's own power — the fundamental topic, recall, of *The Prince*. As such, this new rhetorical virtue is the ability to manipulate the topic of the internal and the external, to invent resources governed by the scope of his own art, and to use ready-made *atechnical* resources whose origin falls outside the art.

LOYALTY

As political knowledge becomes rhetoricized, *philia* receives modifications parallel to the required changes in the meaning of competence. For the ideological politician, philia consists in obedience to hereditary rulers and traditional values; Machiavelli points out that such respect becomes daily more difficult as the rulers are more and more obviously undeserving of honor. For the rhetorical politician, on a straight reading, loyalty and patriotism consist in learning from and allying oneself with the past, not only Florence's recent past, and thereby becoming able to accomplish things everyone admits are good things: expelling the barbarians and unifying Italy. But Machiavelli's readers are supposed not only to learn from the past but also to become its evident heirs; history is not only material for learning but also the standard of rightness and glory. The new prince displays philia when he appears as old as the traditional ruler, and the citizen of sixteenth-century Florence displays philia by being a citizen loyal to the Roman republic Livy describes. If history is nothing but material to be mastered, then that learning can be distinct from the exhibited character of the rhetorical politician, but if history is the stage on which that politician must appear, the scene in relation to which he acquires legitimacy and honor, then he must master not only history as *res gestae* but history as *historia rerum gestarum* — every prince, and every citizen, his own historian!

But even that is not enough. Such a connection between politician and history requires an audience: Machiavelli usurps history that the prince may usurp power. Just as in the case of the new rhetorical virtue of competence, so here, the extension of the range of materials on which the republican citizen and the new prince's actions and virtù can work requires a transformed conception of philia. The new prince can exhibit philia just because *The Prince* is publicly circulated, and not just sent privately to Lorenzo: every prince has to be his own historian, but so does everyone the prince persuades or argues against. The new prince will expect his subjects to be obedient, and citizens can expect equivalent loyalty to the republic, but that obedience will be the allegiance of political actors. Those people can exhibit philia who can imitate and becomes heirs to Machiavelli the historian, where being an heir means acting and arguing in the space and format that Machiavelli opens up through his act of publicity and public history. As patriotism becomes a rhetorical quality, it must be tied to more effective motives; what Pocock says of Guicciardini is equally true for Machiavelli: "Republican and patriotic values are being expressed in the form of ego-serving ideals like honor, reputation, and generosity, rather than in the distributive, social, and far more traditional ideal of justice."[11] Moreover, as philia becomes rhetorical, it (as well as the other new Machiavellian rhetorical virtues) not only becomes more ascriptive and more tied to these supposedly more powerful motives, but it also becomes more competitive and more dependent on display before a public. If prudence is to be taken as flexible practical rationality, then Machiavelli is showing how the principal manifestation of practical intelligence is necessarily tied to competitive glory. (The inherently competitive aspect of Machiavellian virtù is one of the clear differences between even his republican virtue and the civic virtues of other authors in that tradition, especially Guicciardini.)

The friendship required in Machiavellian politics is the ability to treat oppositions as disputes within a community. We saw above that the critical material of factions depended for its successful management on such an attitude; such an attitude can be embodied in a method to the extent that this new virtue is a way of addressing what I called the second So-cratic problem, that of the universalization of virtue into a community. The use of intelligence in action is a use of multiple intelligences; this vir-tue depends on successfully seeing oneself both as a participant in a debate and as part of a larger whole in which that debate takes place. Later think-ers will address this problem by constitutional devices of representation and mixed government; Pocock has explored the way the thought of Ma-chiavelli and Guicciardini led to, without being identical with, such ini-tiatives. For example, he points out that "it is [Guicciardini's] use of that key term (_virtù_) that distinguishes his thought from schematic Polybian-ism. He does not attribute a separate virtue to each of the three forms [of government], because he uses the word in such a way as to define it as a quality of the elite or few."[12] For Machiavelli, though, loyalty and the relation between one's own actions and the values of the community con-stituted a new problematic dimension for action, one of figuring out proper roles for specialized intelligence. As we saw in the last section, the mili-tary, the clergy, and the prince's advisers all raise questions of whether values can be upheld and goods acquired by delegation and representa-tion. Loyalty, then, must rhetorically take into account the shifting demands of universality and particularity, using part and whole, citizen and state, as a topic for rhetorical invention and understanding.

PRUDENCE

Prudence undergoes shifts analogous to the variations on competence and philia. For the ideological politician, virtue and prudence consisted in up-holding the values authorized by one's ideology. As easy as that may sound, Machiavelli finds instead hypocrisy and corruption. On a straight reading of Machiavelli, prudence and virtue are reduced to the amoral skills of mere cleverness and effectiveness, argumentative virtuosity, the ability to rationalize any decision and persuade any audience. When Machiavelli's texts are read as performances, though, and when politics consists in essen-tially contested argument, every putative act of virtue and prudence is at the same time an act of taking a stand in favor of one conception of value, more or less self-consciously adopted, and adopted in opposition to com-peting conceptions and rejected possibilities. When, finally, reading and understanding Machiavelli's texts become public performances, virtue and prudence are no longer instrumental; instead, they are directed towards and embody ends: the purpose of prudent action is participation in the political debate Machiavelli has begun and maintenance of that debate, preserving it and keeping it from degenerating into ideology or force.

The topic that organized the new rhetorical virtue of competence was the internal and the external, one's own resources and things outside one's power, the central topic of *The Prince*. Philia was organized around the fundamental topic of the *Discourses*, part and whole, citizen and state. Rhetorical prudence, finally, consists in the ability topically to use appearance and reality, rule and case. As an intellectual virtue concerned with analysis of people and resources and with effective communication, it requires, among other things, an ability to be abstract and concrete. In Chapter 4 I explored one variant of this prudential problem in the strategies of making things explicit that made negotiable the relations between an individual ruler and the kind of politics he represents; prudence there consisted in the ability to calculate the methods and benefits of making clear the foundations of one's rule. In the first chapter, I quoted Pocock when he points out the abstract character of Machiavelli's analysis:

> Machiavelli conducts his analysis neither in the specific context of Florence nor with regard to the specific problem of citizenship; his concern is solely with the relations between the innovator and fortune. . . . [While Guicciardini, Vettori, and Alamanni] specified, in varying degrees of detail, the exact historical changes that had constituted [the Medicean] innovation, Machiavelli in *Il Principe* starts from innovation as an abstract principle, and the specific case that most closely resembles that of the Medicean ruler — the case of a citizen who becomes a prince by the support of a party of his fellow citizens — is considered in chapter ix carefully, it is true, but without special emphasis, as one among a gallery of types of 'new prince.'"[13]

This relation to and abstraction from circumstances is something Machiavelli's readers must learn to imitate; throughout this chapter I have noted the way rhetorical prudence and rhetorical politics fall between the arts that can comfortably abstract from circumstances and a traditional prudence whose right rules cannot be stated abstractly at all. The new virtue of prudence consists in imitating Machiavelli's strategies in finding the right amount of specificity for his propositions.

Throughout, I have pointed to examples of Machiavelli exercising this kind of rhetorical judgment. Most notably in *The Prince*, he uses rhetorical topics to formalize situations into the rhetorical equivalent of kinds, types of cases whose identity consists in the sort of argument appropriate to them. The particular emotions treated in chapters 15–21 are selected from the whole field of possible emotions because only they permit consistent argumentative treatment, consistency being supplied by the topics that organize the text. These emotions permit Machiavelli the right amount of specificity to avoid both the moralizing he rejects in chapter 15 and the great examples whose edifying value he has questioned in the first eleven chapters. In a different way, the *Discourses* notably identifies kinds or species of material, and the principle of differentiation of these species is the different relations each can bear to the community as a whole, and the different kinds of abilities and judgments required to actualize those materials into the form of a stable, dynamic state. Prudence is a virtue that resists a methodical substitute because species are not given and labelled in advance: it is a misleading image to suppose that propositions are laid out on a scale that ranges from the fully abstract, "Do your best," to the fully individualized, "Pericles succeeded by making this decision about this issue in these circumstances," and to suppose, further, that prudence consists in selecting the right intermediate amount of generality from a list of given, or generable, propositions. It is an open question whether the traditional rhetorical topics can uncover in chapters 15–21 of *The Prince* particular emotions that will have the requisite combination of stability and flexibility, and an equally open question whether the argument of the *Discourses* will lead to the identification of kinds of material with the requisite structural powers to qualify as material on which prudence and the other rhetorical virtues can work. In circumstances of greater intellectual and practical stability, Aristotle could without much difficulty identify the particular moral virtues as species of the genus moral virtue, but Machiavelli has an analogous task to perform in much less favorable circumstances.

The difficulty in making this rhetorical judgment about the right amount of abstraction from circumstances is marked by the fact that it provides one of the rare occasions for Machiavelli to disagree explicitly with and mark his distance from Livy. Machiavelli claims that practical judgment on particulars is more reliable than that on generalities because generalities can be used to cover and justify anything. In our examination of *The Prince* we have seen this latter judgment, that the moral universals and analogous eternal truths about human nature were either empty or were filled only surreptitiously. In the *Discourses* (1.47) he constructs a narrative around that topic by telling the story of the people first demanding the right to elect tribunes, and then electing patricians. He relates Livy's moral: "The result of this election teaches us how different minds are during the contentions for liberty and for honors, from what they are when they have to give an impartial judgment after the contest is over." Machiavelli, however, draws a different moral, saying that "this difference arises . . . from this, that men are apt to deceive themselves upon general matters, but not so much so when they come to particulars."[14] As the *Discourses* proceeds, Machiavelli returns to the topic of universal and particular judgment and develops that contrast further. The comparison of princes and publics in the chapter called "The People Are Wiser and More Constant than Princes" (1.58) allows Machiavelli, after there comparing princes and peoples, to the latter's advantage, to say: "As regards prudence and stability, I say that the people are more prudent and stable, and have better judgment than a prince. . . . it is exceedingly rare that, when they hear two orators of equal talents advocate different measures, they do not decide in favor of the best of the two; which proves their ability to discern the truth of what they hear." Next, the prince's passion is greater, and so more likely to mislead. Because the people judge particulars, "a licentious and mutinous people may easily be brought back to good conduct by the influence and persuasion of a good man, but an evil-minded prince is not amenable to such influences." This argument culminates in the claim that as a consequence republics are less subject to the vicissitudes of fortune than an individual: "Rome was a republic that produced citizens of various character and dispositions, such as Fabius, who was excellent at the time when it was desirable to protract the war, and Scipio, when it became necessary to terminate it. It is this which assures to republics greater vitality and more enduring success than monarchies have; for the diversity of the genius of her citizens enables the republic better to accommodate herself to the changes of the times than can be done by a prince" (3.9). The prudent power to judge particulars is Machiavelli's best solution to the problem of the intelligibility of changing particulars, and consequently to the problem of stability in a world of change.

Since the principal topics of the new virtue of prudence are rule and case, appearance and reality, prudence is the ability to confront problems of the practical uses of intelligence reflexively, and in particular, to make judgments about the efficacy of knowledge. Like the other problems of prudence encountered throughout the book, this one can also be characterized as a Socratic problem. While Socrates notoriously proclaims that the unexamined life is not worth living, the narrative of his career of examining in the *Apology* reveals more fine-grained distinctions. The force of Socrates' exposure of ignorance varies, depending on whether the person he is examining is a maker or an actor. First he visited politicians, and found that while they thought they were wise, they actually knew nothing. The poets did not know anything either, since they could not speak well about their compositions. Yet in that case, unlike the first one, their ignorance did not invalidate their products: their poems were fine, although they could not explain them. But the politician who did not act through knowledge could not have done well through some other source, such as prophecy, and so his ignorance *did* invalidate his actions. Socrates does not conclude that the unexamined life of the poets is exempt from the charge of being not worth living, but for a quite different reason: "The good artisans had the same failing as the poets; because of practising his art well, each one thought he was very wise in the other most important matters, and this folly of theirs obscured their wisdom" (*Apology* 22d). In the same way, there are complications with the idea that the truth shall automatically or necessarily make you free, complications that demand consideration if one tries to make Socrates' maxim into a counsel of prudence.

We have seen all along that Socrates' maxim cannot be taken as an algorithmic principle. The kinds of knowledge that Machiavelli offered his readers were not automatically liberating, and Machiavelli was careful to show ways in which reflection led to constrained possibilities for action rather than to liberation.[15]

Machiavelli forces us to reject any claims that an inference from knowledge to improved action can be apodeictic, and he does so in such a way that it is clear that no additional premises could be supplied to tighten sufficiently the connections between thought and action. The shifting images he uses for opposing fortune point to such instability: fortune as a river must be treated differently from fortune as a woman, and different uses of intelligence are required in preventing floods, preparing for bad weather, and knowing how much of one's capital to gamble. Not only does knowledge sometimes not lead very smoothly to better action, but it sometimes seems even to inhibit good action. Bernard Williams frames this latter possibility in these terms: "If we accept that there can be knowledge at the hypertraditional or unreflective level; if we accept the obvious truth that reflection characteristically disturbs, unseats, or replaces those traditional concepts; and if we agree that, at least as things are, the reflective level is not in a position to give us knowledge we did not have before— then we reach the notably un-Socratic conclusion that, in ethics, *reflection can destroy knowledge.*"[16]

If that possibility were not bad enough, one can make it more sobering still by asking about whether the very conditions that make such reflective knowledge possible do not at the same time make it ineffectual, that is, whether just what makes thought efficacious at producing knowledge is not what makes thought ineffective in praxis. Vico's warning is apposite here: "So long as the peoples keep to good customs, they do them instinctively, not from reflection. But when they are corrupted and ruined, then, because within themselves they ill endure their sense of lacking such things, they speak of nothing but decency and justice, just as it comes naturally for a man to talk of nothing but what he affected to be and is not."[17]

Socrates' treatment of the supposedly wise men of Athens suggests how we might confront that ultimately dysfunctional possibility of the relation of thought and action, although Machiavelli will not permit us to take as very stable Socrates' distinction between the praxis of the politicians and the making of the craftsmen. The politician who does things, but cannot explain what he does, presents the specific formulation of the problem of the role of intelligence in action as the problem of the disclosure of the principles of action. We saw earlier that a rhetorical conception of the critique of ideology, or of established common beliefs, did not lead to an unclouded view of reality. To quote Williams again, "It is one aspiration, that social and ethical relations should not essentially rest on ignorance and misunderstanding of what they are, and quite another that all the beliefs and principles involved in them should be explicitly stated. That these are two different things is obvious in personal relations, where to hope that they do not rest on deceit and error is merely decent, but to think that their basis can be made totally explicit is idiocy."[18]

While the ideological politician stands convicted of basing his regime and allegiance to it on ignorance and deception, it does not follow that the rhetorical politician must abandon rhetoric for the direct and plain statement of the truth. He can still rely on all the methods of the fox, the methods of indirection, without having to depend, as a traditional ruler does, on "ignorance and misunderstanding." For the rhetorical politician, the deceptive methods of the fox do not stand in contrast to some algorithmic sense of telling the truth, because he must construe deception in terms of the relations among discussants and their purposes.[19] Ideological conceptions of rhetoric as flattery, deception, or mere style divert attention away from the serious problem of prudence, a problem at once philosophical and rhetorical. The deep problem here is one of the place of reflection — and the disclosures allied with it — within a practical world, that is, a system of values, attitudes, and related practices. The anti-Socratic possibility that the examined life cannot be lived, that one cannot both think about and be a part of a form of practical life is well expressed by Lovibond:

> It might now be argued that we could never, on pain of surrendering all our dignity as autonomous moral subjects, consent to take our place in what we consciously recognized as a structure of relationships of material control and submission. In that case, the argument would continue, the likely outcome of our historicist insight would be a perpetual ironic standing-off from the social practices to which, before we gained that insight, we were able to bring a naive conviction; or if we found the ironic pose too hard to sustain, we might be tempted just to reimmerse ourselves sentimentally in forms of behavior which seemed to us to have offered a meaningful life to earlier generations — people who understood less than we do about the matters under consideration here.[20]

Civic Virtue and the New Rhetorical Virtues

Lovibond rejects that unprudential interpretation of, and rejection of, Socrates' interpretation of the oracle and instead frames the problem as one of establishing

> a language-game in which we could participate ingenuously, while retaining our awareness of it as a specific historic formation. A community in which such a language-game was played would be one which had succeeded in integrating the "outer" conception of human subjectivity (that of the philosopher, standing "outside" the language-game and reflecting upon it) with the "inner" conception (that of the "trusting" participant). That is to say, it would be a community whose members understod their own form of life and yet were not embarrassed by it.[21]

Framed this way, the problem is not simply an intellectual one, one of figuring out the "right" relation between reflection and action. Whether an intelligent and practical relation between thought and action is possible depends not only on our intellectual resources, but on the community and the modes of action in question.[22]

The possibility of being a part of and yet apart from a society, of recognizing that one cannot stand outside society yet can still be critical, depends on the ability of a system to recognize its own incompleteness. That is, it is impossible rationally to criticize some societies without ceasing to be a member of them and becoming a schismatic. This is another form of the problem of prudence Machiavelli recognized above when he asked why factions contributed to the strength of Rome but the impotence of Florence; here we are asking why reflection is a value sometimes so at odds with the other values of a community that the examined life can have no place there, while other communities can accommodate the Socratic life.

The "practical" problem posed by the preface of *The Prince* returns with a vengeance: in what sort of community could the persona of Machiavelli the counsellor have a function, a role that was neither ceremonial nor usurpatious? In what sort of community could the explicit practical purpose of the *Discourses*—making rulers out of people who deserve to rule—be possible? Machiavellian advice and Machiavellian history are obviously not the only kinds of prudent reflection possible, but they are subject to the general prudent problem of the relation of examining and living.

Socrates' treatment of the poets and artisans reveals the other side of what happens when one tries to make the life of inquiry into a principle of prudence. Socrates could not claim that products suffered when their authors lacked reflective knowledge, but he pointed to the *political* problem that such ignorance engendered, the problem that success in one realm made people think they were, or could be, successful in living in general, since they made a simple universalization of their activity instead of asking how that activity could be part of a community. Problems of prudence require for their management a specific form of rhetorical philia, one that is even more urgent in more technological societies than in Machiavelli's: the problem of factions that are based not on "interests," the erecting of an ultimate good into an overriding good, but on competences, on the fallacy of supposing that one sort of knowledge extends beyond itself to constitute the wisdom meet for ruling a community. Whereas the earlier problem of factions depended for its solution on an acknowledgment and placement of the multiple ultimate goods, this new problem of factions depends on knowledge recognizing its own limits—the prudent interpretation of the Socratic wisdom that consists in knowledge of its own ignorance —as Socrates' Delphic oracle is replaced by the no less enigmatic pronouncements of fortuna.

Once again, I find this problem of prudence usefully articulated in another dialogue of Plato's, in the Prometheus myth told by Protagoras. Particular crafts, particular kinds of science and technology, were stolen from Hephaestus and Athena by Prometheus and distributed among men in a pattern modeled after Epimetheus' distribution of specialized modes of life among the animal species, since "one man possessing medical art is able to treat many ordinary men, and so with the other craftsmen" (*Protagoras* 322c). But when Zeus saw that these experts could not live together, he ordered Hermes to give each man a share in justice and eloquence: these could not be subjects for specialization. Technical questions remain subjects for a few experts, while questions of justice and politics are within everyone's ken. According to this myth, mankind's initial endowment was technological, and it was only the inadequacy of those arts that forced Zeus to intervene and send Hermes down with the gift of justice. I read that temporal priority as an allegory for the way our conception of being reasonable is typically generated with the image of scientific thinking in mind, and consequently the way the challenge to prudence must always be framed by the expectations set by algorithmic reasoning and an ethics of principles: when we discover that technical reason alone cannot resolve political problems or hold communities together, we then have to reform our expectations of what being reasonable in practical affairs means.

I have been claiming throughout that the *Discourses* raised the Machiavellian equivalent of the Platonic question of Socratic universality: what would happen if everyone joined in Socrates', or Machiavelli's, pursuits? I want to recall a distinction from Sidney's *Apology* that I quoted in the first chapter, between "mak[ing] a Cyrus, which had been but a particular excellency, as Nature might have done, [and] bestow[ing] a Cyrus upon the world, to make many Cyruses if they will learn aright, why, and how

Civic Virtue and the New Rhetorical Virtues

that maker made him."[23] This latest problem of prudence — the problem that any knowledge, including political understanding, must recognize its own limits — reveals what has happened to the question of universality. It is one thing for an individual, such as Socrates, to question the basis of ordinary beliefs and behavior or, like Machiavelli, to show the absence of nondiscursive constraints on knowledge, discourse, and action, and quite another for a community to institutionalize such questioning and exposure. The prudent ability to negotiate between the extreme claims of the automatic practicality of knowledge and its opposite, automatic ineffectuality, has a practical and political interest, in addition to its being a continuing intellectual problem for an individual. A community of many Machiavellis is as likely as a community of many Socrateses or one of many Cyruses.

But there is one positive contribution that we have seen knowledge make all along to action: by setting the limits to what intelligence can do in action, prudence also sets limits on what action itself can do. Whereas modesty as a matter of social decorum was something that Machiavelli had to dissociate from prudence, a prudent understanding of the use of intelligence in action entails a different sort of modesty, a restriction of good actions, actions worth doing for their own sakes, to things that can be accomplished *in* the doing of those actions, a restriction that follows from Machiavelli's discovery, noted earlier, of constraints within the operation of virtù. The heart of Machiavellian prudent practice is in actions that have their own value, not as Aristotle's good actions as their own end, but here rhetoricized into glorious and competitive actions that the prince can accomplish precisely by limiting himself to the practicable, that which can be accomplished *in* the doing. Like Aristotle, Machiavelli eschews the Socratic or Stoic interpretation of acts possessing intrinsic value, the interpretation that makes them invulnerable to fortune, but instead embraces the more complicated relations to fortune, to what cannot be controlled by either method or action more broadly.

Machiavellian prudence uncovers, as a permanent field for inquiry and deliberation, the ambivalent relations between reflection and action that flexible continuity depends on. Parallel to the appropriate, and prudent, ambivalence about the relation between reflection and action is a similar ambivalence we have encountered all along about constraint; and it is that simultaneously liberating and confining sense that the prince, and republican citizen, must act within his own power, while trying to increase that power, which supplies the rationale for Machiavellian prudence and replaces the ineffectual moralizing symbolized by other conceptions of prudence. One example of such prudent, as opposed to moralistic, restraint is given in the *Discourses* 2.27: "The use of insulting language towards an enemy arises generally from the insolence of victory, or from the false hope of victory, which latter misleads men as often in their actions as in their words; for when this false hope takes possession of the mind, it makes men go beyond the mark, and causes them often to sacrifice a certain good for an uncertain better."

But it is important to note that this prudence, as opposed to its algorithmic cousin, emphasizes a practicability that does not necessarily mean that one aims at *less* than one would otherwise, that the function of prudence is to help men avoid "going beyond the mark." Sometimes the equivalence of rhetoric and politics leads to an expansion of ambition, as when one treats people as people and not as things. As Pitkin notes, "The point is never just getting others to do what you want, but changing them, introducing new patterns of action and of relationship. Such redirection of human affairs is the most challenging task a man can undertake, for nothing is 'more difficult to plan or more uncertain of success or more dangerous to carry out than an attempt to introduce new institutions.'"[24] The distinction between treating people as people and as things has, of course, a rich history; embodied in the popular understanding is Kant's distinction between legal and ethical duties, since ethical duties are duties to pursue certain ends rather than to perform certain acts.[25] Just as I earlier showed the way Machiavelli bars the easy inference from plural ultimate ends to liberalism, tolerance, and compromise, so here he bars the easy inference that it is always "better" to treat people as persons rather than as things.

Prudence, and its transformation of moderation, then, is ultimately the formulation of the ethical and political problem of the permanently problematic and hence rhetorically debatable relation between knowledge and action. The idea that knowledge is automatically practical posits a direct connection between knowing and acting by ignoring questions of the place of this knowledge and this action, and of this knower and agent, in a community; consequently, knowledge that is automatically practical must be, as Machiavelli is often accused of being, usurpatious. While the Sophists were as a matter of historical fact outsiders, because they came to Athens from other Greek cities, the example of Machiavelli shows that the kind of practical knowledge that can be defined independently of its place in a community must always be essentially seditious. On the other hand, I suggested above that the opposite extreme — ineffectual knowledge and ceremonial rhetoric — is equally knowledge without a role and hence without a function. Prudence therefore involves locating practical knowledge between the two most common bad images of rhetoric from the time of the first Sophists, between the presumptive claims that give rise to sedition and the despair that consoles itself with mere ornament.

CONCLUSION

In the Introduction I raised the question of what it could mean to claim that prudence had a history to which this book was designed to be a contribution. At that point, though, I concentrated on prudence, and asked whether it was the sort of thing that could have a history, an intelligible course of change through time. Now I want to end by shifting attention to the other side of that question, and ask what sort of *history* a history of prudence could be. I can indicate what a history of prudence should look like, and the role of the present work in such a history, by comparing my argument with the texts of Machiavelli and Aristotle that have figured centrally in it. One kind of history of prudence, to which the present work contributes almost nothing, is an account of paradigmatic prudent acts, and the sorts of character and circumstances that made them possible. We have just been looking at one outstanding example of that genre before us, Machiavelli's own *Discourses on Livy*. That kind of history could be as useful today as in Machiavelli's time, and as difficult to write; it is that circumstantially compelled reflection that makes works like Machiavelli's *Discourses* more interesting than a Herodotean series of memorials to great and noble deeds. But this book is not an instance of that kind of history.

Aristotle's *Ethics, Politics,* and *Rhetoric,* as I have used them, lay out a conceptual framework that relates the development and use of prudent abilities to other abilities and to other forms of education. That conceptual framework, however, is not in any evident way a contribution to the history of prudence. While individual states have histories, Aristotle would not be receptive to the proposal that *phronesis* or political wisdom has a history. I have found prudence in the Socratic paradoxes of flexibility and stability, individual and community, but have defined practical reason by relying on Aristotle's articulation of its interrelations and contrasts to other abilities, namely, art, science, and experience. At the center of my analysis has been the different possible relations between rule and case laid out in algorithmic, prudential, and heuristic methods. Prudence is articulated in the explorations of the themes of education, imitation, representation—all of them specifications of relations of rule and case that I have used to contrast prudence to its competitors. The sort of imitation required in the acquisition of prudence, and the sort of uses of history available in the practice of prudence, are fundamental dimensions in prudence's career, and in fact constitute the first set of evidence to the claim that prudence can have a history. Prudence is articulated by the topics that characterize Machiavelli's texts—form and matter in *The Prince*, past and present in the *Discourses*—and the topics that characterize the new rhetorical virtues and the resources they exploit.

In the process of laying out Aristotelian conceptual analysis and using it to analyze Machiavelli's texts, I have tried to show how prudence has an external history because the names of its heroes change—as does the relation of heroic to prudent action—and because its enemies, the tempting alternatives to prudence, have a history. More important, those relatively external and contingent factors give rise to an internal history of practical reason because as the kinds of tactics people rely on to evade prudential reasoning shift through time, the tactics and resources available to prudence vary correspondingly. Despite the model of the history of degenerating states in *Republic* 8 and 9, the case of Machiavelli suggests that this history of resources, tactics, and methods has a strong element of contingency and unpredictability about it, so that the history of prudence cannot be generated from a philosophical study of it. Consequently, the study of prudence requires a study of its history: no theory alone could get beyond Aristotle's laying out of the terrain or my abstract account of three kinds of rules. Just as no theory of logic can generate all significant argumentative tactics, and no theory of style can generate all beauties of language, so for practical reasons no theory alone could anticipate the resources and strategies called for.

The history of prudence, then, has been generated by the interrelation between Aristotle's framework and Machiavelli's textual performances. It follows that we also know something about what sort of history prudence has. It has a history in a way science and art do not because of the shifting relations of form and matter that characterize the *orthoi logoi* embodied in prudence. The basic narrative frame for histories of theoretical reason has been the gradual enlightenment of mankind and the progressive removal of prejudices, although more finely grained histories reveal complexities that embellish that framework. But there is no parallel narrative frame given in advance for histories of prudence because the autonomy of practical reason and the autonomy of practical action whose stories would be told in such a history are more contestable phenomena.

Although a history of prudence traces the career of a character called practical reason, practical reason, as I pointed out in the Introduction, is in turn embodied in several characters that can have different relations to each other, so that the history of practical reason, as opposed to a history of an idea of practical reason, is a story with some complexity that histories of scientific reason have not found necessary. The complexity—

Conclusion

especially a complexity relative to the perhaps mythical but certainly compelling picture of simple scientific progress—does not come simply from the ambivalent connections between intention and result that characterize all practical action. The complexity, and the drama, of a history of prudence, comes from the flexible relations of rule and case that are essential to prudent action and its species, such as education and deliberation, and also from a further dimension of that relation of form and matter, rule and case—the relation between practical reason and its embodiments. While the history of practical reason is a history of the practical uses of intelligence, it will often take the dramatic form of the story of the practical functions of intelligent agents taking specific roles. Machiavelli occupies a central place in such a history as he carves out a specific place for reasoning, for discourse, and for people adept at thinking and speaking. One of the dimensions of the history of prudence, which we saw emerging in the last chapter, is the extent to which practical reason, or some parts of it, can be delegated and specialized. There is always something recognizably called "the problem of the experts," but that problem varies in form as well as in content and urgency.

The permanently defeasible and essentially contested nature of any history of prudence, and the way the history of prudence must be a history of the embodiment of practical intelligence in specific roles and characters, appear most critically in the way shifts in practical autonomy are connected to the changing relations between ethics and politics. My account has shifted between Aristotle's practical science and Machiavelli's strategic teachings, and the relationship between those two authors generates the history of prudence, as what is implicit in Aristotle becomes explicit in Machiavelli, or what is unproblematic becomes questionable or difficult. (That relation suggests that there can be no final event in the history of prudence, with all problems solved and all dimensions in comfortable and stable equilibrium.) In particular, Machiavelli helps to make the relations between ethics and politics problematic. If one conceives of practical autonomy such that its possibility is indifferent to circumstances—the good man is happy on the rack—then that mode of autonomy has no history, because its manifestations are everywhere the same and its achievement is always equally available to everyone. On the other hand, if autonomy is awarded by the state (or by any other superhuman agency, from God to the forces of production) to the individual—a most paradoxical form of autonomy that can be given rather than achieved—then it has a history only in a derivative sense, since its history is then a consequence of the history of rights and freedoms. The problematic relations between ethics and politics have been symbolized in the question of the universalizability of virtue and virtù, in the question of whether a community of followers of either Socrates or Machiavelli is possible.

Yet it must be stressed that the history of prudence of which this book represents a start—unlike Machiavelli's own contribution to the history of prudence in the *Discourses* and his other works—is a history of texts, rather than a history of heroic deeds, seminal ideas, or stable institutions. Machiavelli's discursive strategies, in writing and in reading, are themselves part of the history of prudence because he brings attention to the connections, and the distance, between verbal and practical efficacy, virtuosity, adaptability, and propriety. A further dimension in a history of prudence, consequently, is the functional, and occasionally dysfunctional, prudent use of prudent language, in education and in action. While other histories of prudence could well center on any number of other authors or actors, a history in which prudence provides the multiple connections, and barriers, between language and action cannot have a better hero than Machiavelli.

NOTES

BIBLIOGRAPHY

INDEX

NOTES

Introduction

1. The lack of a history of practical reason parallel to a standard history of theoretical reason is suggested by J. B. Schneewind, "Divine Corporation," p. 173: "It is widely held that modern philosophy begins with Descartes and is essentially defined by its epistemological concerns. . . . So when we teach a course called 'the history of modern philosophy,' we usually teach the history of epistemology and metaphysics, and we do not ordinarily offer a comparable course, held to be of equal importance, on the history of modern ethics." Machiavelli's place in such an unwritten history of practice is universally acknowledged, however. See, e.g., Felix Raab, *The English Face of Machiavelli*, p. 1: "As far as the modern world is concerned, Machiavelli invented politics. Nowhere in medieval thought is there a consciousness of political activity as an autonomous, self-justifying sphere."

   There is, though, no necessary reason why the history of theoretical reason has been written the way it has (or has taken the course it has). A fuller history of prudence would have to take into account the conflict between the kind of narrative I offer, in which Machiavelli occupies a central place, and the competing narratives, in which his place would be taken by Hobbes, or in which there are no turning points or no heroes or villains. It is at least plausible to argue that the parallel history of theoretical reason too could have competing heroes, and hence conflicting narratives, if Bacon stood to Descartes as Machiavelli does to Hobbes, the first member of each pair generating a history of one sort of reason as "self-assertion," and the other as "self-grounding." The relations between theoretical and practical reason would then also have to be transformed, and possibly even dissolved. Richard Rorty suggests the possibility of such an alternative history for scientific reason: "Had Bacon — the prophet of self-assertion, as opposed to [Descartes's] self-grounding — been taken more seriously, we might not have been stuck with a canon of 'great modern philosophers' who took 'subjectivity' as their theme. We might, as J. B. Schneewind puts it, have been less inclined to assume that epistemology (i.e., reflection on the nature and status of natural science) was the 'independent variable' in philosophical thought and moral and social philosophy the 'dependent variable.' We might thereby see what Blumenberg calls 'self-assertion' — the willingness to center our hopes on the future of the race, on the unpredictable successes of our descendants — as the 'principle of the modern.'" Rorty, "Habermas and Lyotard," p. 170.

2. For one version of the difference between the histories of theoretical and practical reason, see Alasdair MacIntyre, "Objectivity," p. 21: "The philosophy of science is now recapitulating the history of ethics and politics." For some of the details of that recapitulation, see ibid., p. 23: "Ethics has shown a striking tendency

to anticipate the philosophy of science in its commission of error, so that contemporary philosophers of science often remind us of nineteenth-century moralists. Consider, for example, Kuhn's reincarnation of Kierkegaard, and Feyerabend's revival of Emerson — to mention the counterpart to them all, in which the eighteenth century outbids the nineteenth, Polanyi's version of Burke." Ibid., p. 27: "What went wrong? How did subjectivism and relativism achieve these victories first in ethics and the philosophy of religion and then in the philosophy of science? . . . Since rules can no longer be vindicated by objective, impersonal reason, and since experience no longer seems to provide a neutral court of appeals, two and only two relationships between the individual and the rules seem to be possible. Either I accept or reject the rules by my own free, unconditioned, criterionless choice; or the rules can be imposed upon me by some external power of influence." MacIntyre shows how early in its history it became clear that practical autonomy could be a mixed blessing; but that the same might be true for physics has only recently been faced. Therefore we have only recently seen explorations of the covert ways such autonomy is restricted, not by the rule of reason but by tradition, paradigms, the tacit dimension, and all the varieties of force and fraud Feyerabend delights in exposing.

For one simple reason to expect theoretical and practical autonomy to differ, see Bernard Williams, *Ethics and the Limits of Philosophy*, p. 111: "The scientific understanding of the world is not only entirely consistent with recognizing that we occupy no special position in it, but also incorporates, now, that recognition. The aim of ethical thought, however, is to help us to construct a world that will be our world, one in which we have a social, cultural, and personal life."

3. J.G.A. Pocock, "'The Onely Politician,'" pp. 265-95, esp. 276: "Machiavelli's works constitute a series of enquiries into how the political intelligence in various forms — the legislator, the legitimate prince, the non-legitimised 'new prince,' the republic, even the commander in war — may best attempt to understand events and restore stability."

4. As Socrates develops this conception of identity in the *Apology*, the alternative to identity is not mutability in general, since one does not become someone else by any change, but yielding unjustly to anyone, being passive in that quite specific sense. In this sameness, he opposes himself to the poet who is transported (*Ion* 541e), the rhapsode who is like Proteus, always changing into different things (*Ion* 541e), the sophist who cannot be pinned down (*Prot.* 320c), and the priest whose words will not stand still like the statues of Daedalus (*Euth.* 11b-c). (For several of these references, see Gerald Bruns, *Inventions*, p. 98.) In addition to these aspects of "mutability", see Alcibiades' description of Socrates in the *Symposium* as someone who could abstain from food and drink and could also take the greatest pleasure in it. For the Socratic interpretation of practical autonomy as immutability, see Bernard Williams, *Moral Luck*, p. 20: "There has been a strain of philosophical thought which identifies the end of life as happiness, happiness as reflective tranquillity, and tranquillity as the product of self-sufficiency — what is not in the domain of the self is not in its control, and so is subject to luck and the contingent enemies of tranquillity. The most extreme versions of this outlook are certain doctrines of classical antiquity, though it is a notable fact about them

that while the good man, the sage, was immune to the impact of incident luck, it was a matter of what may be called constitutive luck that one was a sage or capable of becoming one: for the many and vulgar this was not (on the prevailing view) an available course."

5. Pocock, "'The Onely Politician,'" p. 276: "Where neither scholastic reason, institutionalized tradition nor apocalyptic prophecy — Savonarola being dead and rejected — seemed capable of coping with the flow of events, Fortune reigned: Fortune who, we see more and more clearly, symbolizes precisely the flow of events neither intelligible, justifiable nor controllable; the savage woman, the river in flood, '*senza pietà, senza legge o ragione*'. Humanism, the intelligence applied to the relevant data, offers the sole hope of taming her." In a certain sense, that is always the problem of prudence, as the story of Socrates indicates: Socrates refuses to rest content with Athenian custom (or whim), or with the eternal *nous* posited by Anaxagoras, and rejects the temptation of interpreting the accusation the oracle levels at him as an intervention that puts him outside human judgment. For an example of the ambivalent evaluation of flexibility drawn from a different area, see Boyle's account of the place of the figure of Proteus in the dispute between Luther and Erasmus. According to Erasmus, Boyle says, "the *scopus* of true theology is Christ. To achieve it, accommodation is necessary. When Luther called Erasmus a Proteus for his mutability, he meant it pejoratively. Erasmus rejected that connotation, reassigning it to Luther. But he affirmatively and readily called his own theology Proteus, for he understood accommodation, not only as a requirement of the classical orator whom he wished to imitate, but also as the mission of Christ himself. Christ was Proteus, Erasmus taught, in the variety of his teaching and his life: testifying now to his divinity, now to his humanity; summoning some men while rejecting others; granting or refusing miracles; exacting silence, demanding witness; fleeing from the crowd, embracing it. . . . The disciples of Christ imitated their master in this virtue. The aspostle Paul especially was a chameleon and a polypus, like the sea creature which could mutate its coloring at will to deceive fishermen." Marjorie O'Rourke Boyle, *Rhetoric and Reform*, pp. 105–6. See also p. 79: "The Protean epithet derives not only from the classical topic of mutability but also from its Christian application in polemics against Skepticism. For Augustine, Proteus personified verisimilitude. In disputing the Skeptics, he remarked that in poetry Proteus 'portrays and personates the truth, which no one can lay hold on, if he is deceived by false images, and loosens or loses his hold on the nodes of understanding' (*Contra academicus*, 3.6.13)." Boyle's entire book, with its account of the debate between Luther and Erasmus, is an exhibition of the different interpretations of the activity of adaptation to circumstances.

6. When philosophy and rhetoric are conceived of as opponents, one of the dimensions of that opposition lies in the way the act of knowing is supposed to be identical with its object (so that a good method for acquiring knowledge should not inject its own coloring), while there is something disreputable when discourse becomes "like" its audience, a fair definition of flattery.

7. Richard Bernstein, *Beyond Objectivism and Relativism*, p. 230: "When Aristotle sought to clarify what he meant by *phronesis* and the *phronimos*, he could still call upon the vivid memory of Pericles as the concrete exemplar of the in-

dividual who possessed the faculty of discriminating what was good for himself and for the *polis*. But today, when we seek for concrete exemplars of the types of dialogical communities in which practical rationality flourishes, we are at a much greater loss."

8. J.G.A. Pocock, *Machiavellian Moment*, pp. 166–67: "Machiavelli enters the realm of moral ambiguity by the single step of defining *virtù* as an innovative force. It is not merely that by which men control their fortunes in a delegitimized world; it may also be that by which men innovate and so delegitimize their worlds, and . . . it may even be that which imposes legitimacy on a world which has never known it. The only constant semantic association is now that between *virtù* and innovation, the latter being considered rather as an act than as a previously accomplished fact, and *virtù* is preeminently that by which the individual is rendered outstanding in the context of innovation and in the role of innovator. Since innovation continues to raise ethical problems, this use of the word *virtù* does not deny its association with ethics, but it employs the word to define the situations within which the ethical problems arise." That "constant semantic association" also means that we will not be able to trace the history of prudence by tracing the history of the word *prudence* and its translations, but will have to look at the variety of uses of practical intelligence and their connection to character in Machiavelli. For a subtle treatment of the relations of *virtù, prudenzia*, and related terms in Machiavelli, see Paul Renucci, "Machiavel."

9. In this case the parallel to Aristotle may obscure more than it illuminates. Aristotle, too, initially avoids defining virtue, and turns instead, at the beginning of book 2 of the *Nicomachean Ethics*, to the question of how it is acquired. But Aristotle's point in so doing is that virtue is the kind of thing that is in part defined by how it is acquired; more precisely, the genus of virtue, habits or "dispositions," *hexeis*, are powers of action acquired through performing acts of the same kind.

10. Alasdair MacIntyre, "How Virtues Become Vices," pp. 97–111. MacIntyre lists four conditions under which virtues become vices, two of which are apposite here: when "a disposition valuable for its own sake, and valued for its own sake, as any genuine virtue must be (it may of course also be valued for further ends that it serves) comes to be valued only or primarily for its employment as part of a technique," and "when a quality valued for its own sake is made available for sale" (pp. 105–6).

11. I here follow Aristotle in attaching to Plato's name one important antiprudential move, that of replacing prudential regard for the contingent with something better, a wisdom whose objects are eternal and necessary. Such arguments can, of course, be found in Plato, but they must not be taken outside this context as an adequate account of Plato's understanding of prudence. One evidence of the necessity Plato presents for dealing with the contingencies of human choice is the conversation between Socrates and Glaucon in *Republic* 2: Socrates had described, Glaucon says, a city of pigs; although Socrates notes its peaceful and stable character, he is easily persuaded to give it up for the construction of a fevered city ruled by desire. The ideal state constructed to solve the fevered state's problems and limit those desires is, relative to the city of pigs, one whose complexity does

restore a place for prudence, albeit a Platonic place as detached as possible from contingencies by such devices as the elimination of property for the guardians and an absence of coercive laws. Such an ideal state inevitably declines just because contingencies cannot be permanently eliminated — recall that the decline of the ideal state comes from the error introduced in calculating the nuptial number. Still, a guardian must be prudent in distinguishing friends and foes. Guardians are therefore called *phronomoi* at *Rep.* 412a4–7, b8–13, 428a11–29a7, 440e8–441b1.

12. An ethics of principles is captured in Butler's formulation in *Fifteen Sermons*, 3.4, quoted by Alan Donagan, *Theory of Morality*, pp. 18–19: "Let any plain honest man before he engages in any course of action ask himself, Is this I am going about right, or is it wrong? Is it good, or is it evil? I do not in the least doubt but that this question would be answered agreeably to truth and virtue, by almost any fair man in almost any circumstance." The ethics of principles can also be conceived of as "politics as the application of moral principles." Richard J. Burke, "Politics as Rhetoric," *Ethics* 93 (1982): 46.

13. Because of the alliances I shall explore between prudence and rhetoric, it is no accident that, just as prudence seems to have no method, it is a traditional accusation against rhetoric that it has no method. See, for example, Sextus Empiricus, *Against the Professors* 1.187–96: "Since every art has an end which is fixed and stable, like philosophy or grammar, rhetoric too, if it is an art, will have to profess one or the other of these. But it has not an end which is always stable . . . and therefore it is not an art." See also Cicero, *De oratore* 1.3.12.

14. See Bernard Williams' reflections on this contrast, interpreted as a conflict of accounts of justice: "Is a just outcome to be understood as one reached by a just method, or is a just method, more fundamentally, one that leads to just outcomes? At a first glance, there seem to be examples which tell either way. Aristotle's own preferred examples tend to be ones in which the relevant merit or desert of the recipients is understood (at least by the distributor) beforehand, so that the basic idea is of a just outcome, namely that in which each recipient benefits in proportion to his desert, and a just method will be, derivatively, a method which brings about that outcome. On the other hand, it seems different if one takes a case in which some indivisible good has to be allocated among persons who have equal claims to it, and they agree to draw lots. . . . Here the justice is not worn in its own right by the outcome of, say, Robinson's getting it, nor is it the fact that it has that outcome that makes the method just; it is rather the other way round." Williams, *Moral Luck*, p. 88. Just as I want to complicate that distinction by finding a *tertium quid*, so Williams too finds that "this distinction is more fragile than it first looks, and is sensitive to the ways in which the outcome and the method are described. Thus if the method is itself described as that of allocating say, the food to the hungry, the 'desert' can come to characterize the method itself, and not merely the outcome. . . . There is [nevertheless] a class of cases in which the justice very specially rests in the method rather than in the particular outcome. . . . Under such a theory, the process by which someone receives something is constitutive of the justice of his holding, and there is no independent assessment of the justice of the outcome at all."

15. For one controversial example of a heuristic method, justified only by suc-

cess, see Williams' account of Gauguin, quoted in the text at p. 15. The distinction I am drawing between algorithmic and heuristic methods is a familiar one, although often expressed in different terms. For that reason a short compilation of other ways of expressing this distinction places my exposition in a variety of contemporary contexts. For an account of algorithmic methods, see Imre Lakatos, "Infinite Regress," p. 4: "The basic definitional characteristic of a (not necessarily formal) deductive system is the *principle of retransmission of falsity* from the 'bottom' to the 'top', from the conclusions to the premises: a counterexample to a conclusion will be a counterexample to at least one of the premises. If the principle of retransmission of falsity applies, so does the *principle of transmission of truth* from the premises to the conclusions. We do not demand, however, from a deductive system that it should transmit falsehood or retransmit truth." On p. 7 Lakatos contrasts this initiative with what I am calling heuristics: "some dogmatists tried to save Knowledge from the sceptics by a non-Euclidean method. Defeated at the top, reason sought refuge and anchor at the bottom. But truth at the bottom does not have the power of truth at the top. Induction was expected to restore the symmetry. The Inductivist Programme was a desperate effort to build a channel through which truth flows *upwards* from the basic statements, thus establishing an additional logical principle, the *principle of retransmission of truth*. Such a principle would enable the inductivist to inundate the whole system with truth from below." The contrast between algorithmic and heuristic methods corresponds to Hirsch's distinction between general and local hermeneutics: "Local hermeneutics consist of rules of thumb rather than rules. . . . Local hermeneutics can . . . provide models and methods that are reliable most of the time. General hermeneutics lays claim to principles that hold true all of the time. . . . That is why general hermeneutics is, so far, the only aspect of interpretation that has earned the right to be named a 'theory,'" E. D. Hirsch, *Aims of Interpretation,* p. 18. Hirsch, of course, intends his distinction to be exhaustive. The meaning I am giving to algorithmic methods is also what Heidegger means by method generally: "'Method,' as a kind of 'procedure' . . . requires a 'fixed ground plan,' the 'essence of technology.'" Martin Heidegger, "Age of the World Picture," p. 118.

16. Bruns, *Inventions,* p. 94.

17. My use of the topic of three kinds of rules represents a departure from most treatments of Machiavelli. Still, that Machiavelli is in some sense concerned with the relations between principles and consequences has often been noted. Here are some attempts to approach Machiavelli with such a problem in mind; they should situate my analysis of Machiavellian prudence in the contemporary discussion, and highlight some of the differences. Mark Hulliung, *Citizen Machiavelli,* p. 203: "Contemporary scholars have placed Greek values under the concept of a 'results-culture.' To the Greeks good intentions were never good enough, not just in politics but everywhere, because in the virtuous man's unending competition for honor and glory there could be no acceptable alternative to success. Courage, honesty, or any other value was valuable — the Greeks believed — only so long as it led to success. . . . In Greek culture, it follows, there was no need for a Machiavelli; at Athens or Sparta his rhetorical powers would have been nil, and his notoriously

shocking words would have been so ordinary as to make him a bore." For a different use of the same *topos* on the originality of Machiavelli, see Joseph Anthony Mazzeo, *Renaissance and Seventeenth-Century Studies*, p. 143: "It is perhaps the greatest strength of Machiavelli that, while he is acutely aware of the limitations of an ethic of good intentions or of absolute ends, he is also aware of the limitations of an ethic of results or responsibility. The ethic of result has its own dilemma in that it introduces the dimension of time into an act of ethical judgment so that judgment becomes ambiguous simply because he cannot always determine the farther consequences of any particular result." See, finally, R. N. Berki, "Machiavellianism," p. 111: "Instead of saying that Machiavelli is mindful of the limitations of morality by expediency, I would like to argue that he has a rudimentary conception of the *self-limitation of morality*, or, to make my meaning clearer, of the curious and inevitable tendency of moral rules to be contradicted, or qualified, by their being put to practice. . . . Machiavelli's teaching, and the practice of Machiavellianism in politics, etc., is nothing but the conscious recognition of the heightened relevance of this tendency to certain areas, and its subsequent elevation to the status of an essential principle of political policy making. Machiavellianism is the visible tip of an iceberg whose base is hidden deeply in the waters of everyday life."

18. The three kinds of ethics, with three kinds of rules, structure the argument of Cicero's *De officiis*: my triad—algorithmic, heuristic, and prudent ethics—corresponds to its three books, which exhibit an ethics of principles under the heading of *honestum*, an ethics of consequences under the title *utile*, and a reconciliation of the two in the prudential considerations of the third book. For ways in which Machiavelli follows and then diverges from Cicero's prudent adjustments of the *honestum* and the *utile*, see Marcia L. Colish, "Cicero's *De officiis* and Machiavelli's *Prince*," pp. 81–93. Cicero does not, as Colish puts it, "assert that the *honestum*, being intrinsically good and an end in itself, should be the changeless criterion by which the admissibility of the *utile* should be judged" (p. 86). Again, "his first step toward reconciling the *honestum* and the *utile* therefore has been to reformulate the *honestum* itself as a mode of the *utile*" (p. 88). Also see p. 89: "He has assimilated the *honestum* to the *utile* by recasting the traditional meaning of the terms. Yet, the *De officiis* cannot be seen as an exercise in unadulterated pragmatism. For Cicero, the *honestum*, or the common good, and the *utile*, or individual interest, cannot conflict because man is part of a larger social and moral whole, which makes radical individualism unacceptable as a basis for ethical action." And again: "It is true that he removes the conflict between the *honestum* and the *utile* by treating them both as forms of the *utile*. . . . But it is also true that the harmony between public and private goods which he envisions is predicated in turn on a political and ethical ideal of his own, a good society in which the individual and the public good would truly be reciprocal if not identical" (p. 90). The three kinds of rule also correspond to the three sources of premises for syllogisms in Aristotle's organon: the demonstrative syllogisms set out in the *Posterior Analytics* exhibit a kind of necessity like that of modern algorithmic methods, despite other important differences, while his equivalent of heuristics is pre-

sented in the *De sophisticis elenchis*. The *Topics* and the *Rhetoric* occupy the room between necessary and fallacious inferences, and those dialectical and rhetorical syllogisms set forth his prudential methods.

19. David Perkins, "Reasoning as Imagination," contrasts formal and informal reasoning in ways parallel to my distinction between algorithmics and prudential methods. Among the differences he notes, "Good informal arguments almost always have to address both sides of a case; a good formal argument never does, assuming consistent axioms, because formal arguments on both sides would amount to an outright inconsistency" (p. 21).

20. Hence the other contrasts Perkins draws: "Informal arguments can incorporate data from all sorts of unexpected sources forbidden to formal argument, which must work only with the givens. . . . Good informal arguments usually need to be hedged; the strict deduction of formal argument makes this unnecessary. . . . An informal argument typically needs many lines of reasoning since no single line has perfect reliability; a formal argument needs only one, which settles the matter" (ibid.). For similar observations, see Newman, *Grammar of Assent*, p. 223: "'All men have their price; Fabricius is a man; he has his price'; but he had not his price; how is this? Because he is more than a universal; because he falls under other universals; because universals are ever at war with each other; because what is called a universal is only a general." See also Bruns, *Inventions*, p. 74. "To look on the world mathematically is to regard it problematically as a universe wherein to be insoluble (that is, resistant to systematic assimilation) is to be unthinkable, perhaps even mysterious, or full of mystification and deceit; but method conspires to reduce or resolve the insoluble, and to absolve the universe of our doubts about it. . . . A system is almost by definition that which contains no secrets, because it allows nothing to be set apart."

21. "Thinking will remain controversial until it can be made single-minded—which, as it happens, is the whole point of turning ideas into systems. A system is, in principle, incapable of existing in the form of versions: that is the whole difference between a system and a story, which can only exist in the telling of it, and which can never get told the same way twice. Systems presuppose the operation of method, which is to say the power of duplication wherein the production of a different version of anything is either an accident or an error." Bruns, *Inventions*, p. 85.

22. Victoria Kahn, *Rhetoric, Prudence, and Skepticism*, p. 51: "While the will was the faculty which enabled man to respond freely to the contingencies of everyday life, it also proved to be a source of contingency itself. . . . Like the arguments of Academic *and* Pyrronist skepticism, the concept of the will proved to be divided and to function *in utramque partem* within the humanist tradition." Skepticism is divided because the lack of algorithmic certainty either creates room for action and the opportunity for prudence, or it removes all criteria of better and worse apart from success, and eventually even any means of determining success. The presumption that principles and consequences are exclusive and exhaustive alternatives also gives rise to the rhetorical debate about whether the good orator is one who speaks the truth or wins cases. See, e.g., Quintilian, *Institutes*, 2.14.5–2, 2.15.38, 2.17.23.

23. John Rawls, *Theory of Justice*, pp. 422-23.

24. Williams, *Moral Luck*, p. 23. Many of Polya's problem-solving techniques for mathematics are tactics with no merit apart from their productivity. There is no reason why they should work, but they often do. The idea that prudence depends on flexible rules, rather than heuristics justified purely by success, has its own history in rhetorical texts. See, e.g., Cicero, *De oratore* 21.71, 35.12, and Quintilian, *Institutes* 12.10.2, 2.13.8.

25. I show the alliance between conclusions that are always open to further dispute and classical rhetoric in "Rhetoric and Essentially Contested Arguments" (1978). See also Henry Johnstone, *Philosophy and Argument*, p. 30: "A refutation is absolute when it proves beyond any question that the proposition it attacks is false. The propounder of a proposition that has been absolutely refuted cannot claim that there is any sense in which the proposition is still true. As Passmore says, 'No evasion is possible.' Now the only area in which propositions are conclusively shown to be false and no evasions are possible is that of formal deductive reasoning. Here evasions are not possible because evasions are not to the point. . . . But conclusions in nonformal reasoning can always be evaded, and nonformal premises can always be questioned." Lakatos has exhibited techniques such as monster-barring, perhaps the clearest examples of evasion strategies functioning even in the most august domain of formal reasoning, mathematics.

26. After Peirce attempts to turn scientific reasoning from algorithmic to prudential standards, he then criticizes moral systems that are based on algorithmic, rather than prudential, methods. See, e.g., C. S. Peirce, *Collected Papers*, 1.61 (p. 26): "One of the worse effects of the influence of moral and religious reasonings upon science lies in this, that the distinctions upon which both insist as fundamental are dual distinctions, and that their tendency is toward an ignoring of all distinctions that are not dual and especially of the conception of continuity. Religion recognizes the saints and the damned. It will not readily admit any third fate. Morality insists that a motive is either good or bad. That the gulf between them is bridged over and that most motives are somewhere near the middle of the bridge, is quite contrary to the teachings of any moral system which ever lived in the hearts and conscience of a people. . . . It is not necessary to read far in almost any work of philosophy written by a man whose training is that of a theologian, in order to see how helpless such minds are in attempting to deal with continuity. But continuity, it is not too much to say, is the leading conception of science." For applications to Machiavelli, see John O'Neill, *Sociology as a Skin Trade*, p. 109: "Machiavelli is a difficult thinker because he forces upon us the ambiguity of virtue from which self-styled humanists so often shrink, preferring the history of principles to the history of men. Between Montaigne, Machiavelli, and Marx, on the other hand, there is common effort to consider the nature of history and politics within the boundaries that men set for themselves. That is to say, human action always achieves something more and something less than it envisages and yet political man must assume the consequences. Far from being a fatal flaw in the nature of action this essential ambiguity is what makes human actions neither blindly impulsive nor divinely efficacious. At the same time, the ambiguity of political action is not a justification for the lack of political conviction or fidelity. For what

introduces ambiguity into political action is precisely the metamorphoses of truth and justice experienced in putting them into practice without any absolute guarantee that this project will not be attacked, sabotaged, and even undermined from within. It is, in short, the denial of political innocence even at the birth of freedom." As Richard Burke points out, in rhetorical politics "pluralism is accepted as normal, whereas in the other two models there is a tendency toward a monolithic structure, either of values or of power" ("Politics as Rhetoric," p. 48); the examples he cites are Plato and Hobbes.

27. Contrast the Sophistic conception of the irrelevance of such detailed knowledge of particulars with Aristotle's *Topic*, book 1, where, unlike more "formal" logics, the first *organon* of invention is knowing the facts about the problem in question. When philosophy and rhetoric are seen in conflict, a further dimension of that battle is that such concessions to circumstances are seen as a philosophical vice, while respect for particularity is a rhetorical virtue. See Kant, *Fundamental Principles of the Metaphysics of Morals*, p. 5: "All trades, arts, and handiworks have gained by division of labor. . . . Does [not] the nature of science require that we should always carefully separate the empirical from the rational?" Again (pp. 12–13): "Even if it should happen that, owing to special disfavor of fortune, or the niggardly provision of a step-motherly nature, this [good] will should wholly lack power to accomplish its purpose, if with its greatest efforts it should yet achieve nothing . . . then, like a jewel, it would still shine by its own light, as a thing which has its whole value in itself. Its usefulness or fruitfulness can neither add to nor take away anything from this value. It would be, as it were, only the setting to enable us to handle it the more conveniently in common commerce, or to attract to it the attention of those who are not yet connoisseurs, but not to recommend it to true connoisseurs, or to determine its value."

28. Bernard Williams, *Descartes*, p. 46. "A typical situation is that the truth-ratio would be somewhat improved without giving up any classes of beliefs altogether, but that the cost of doing so would be too high, relative to other activities (including other activities of enquiry). A might be able fruitfully to enquire further into the reliability of a given method, or whether its application on a given occasion was appropriate, but such activities take time and effort, which it may not be sensible to spend in any given case; while it is impossible to spend them in every case. In actual life, investment of effort into enquiry turns importantly on what is at stake: we check the petrol more thoroughly before a drive across the Sahara than before a drive across town. Moreover, there is the important point for both practical and for more theoretical enquiries, that each of us is one enquirer among others, and there is a division of epistemic labour, so that what it is rational (in this economic or decision-theoretical sense) for Y to investigate in detail, it is rational for Z to take on Y's say-so.

"All these are reasons why A in his everyday circumstances either cannot increase his truth-ratio or should not regard it as rational to try. *But for Descartes' enquiry none of these conditions applies.*"

29. Francesco Guicciardini, *Ricordi*, p. 57: "How much luckier astrologers are than other men! By telling one truth among a hundred lies, they acquire the confidence of men, and their falsehoods are believed. Other men, by telling one lie

among many true statements, lose the confidence of others, and no one believes them even when they speak the truth. This comes about because of the curiosity of men. Desirous of knowing the future, and having no other way to do it, they go running after anyone who promises to reveal it to them."

30. For a subtle recent treatment, see Onora O'Neill, "The Power of Example."

31. For a characteristically antinomian interpretation of "staking the character of the speaker," see Thoreau, *Civil Disobedience:* "All voting is a sort of gaming, like checkers or backgammon, with a slight moral tinge to it, a playing with right and wrong, with moral questions; and betting naturally accompanies it. The character of the voters is not staked. I cast my vote perchance as I think right; but I am not vitally concerned that the right should prevail. I am willing to leave it to the majority. Its obligation, therefore, never exceeds that of expediency. Even voting for the right is doing nothing for it. It is only expressing to men feebly your desire that it should prevail. A wise man will not leave the right to the mercy of chance, nor wish it to prevail through the power of the majority." For complications in the relation of moral and intellectual virtues, and hence of the relation of prudence to good action, see the minor intellectual virtues at the end of *Ethics* 6, which seem to be about practical matters but which are not a function of character.

1. *The Prince*

1. See, for example, Hannah Gray, "Renaissance Humanism"; Jerrold Seigel, "Civil Humanism or Ciceronian Rhetoric?"; Eugenio Garin, *Italian Humanism;* Ernesto Grassi, "Can Rhetoric Provide a New Basis for Philosophizing?"; Terence Cave, *The Cornucopian Text.*

2. The way treatments of Renaissance rhetoric would be deepened by considerations of Machiavelli has been noted. See Nancy Struever's review of Jerrold E. Seigel's *Rhetoric and Philosophy in Renaissance Humanism,* p. 71: "Some of the longstanding confusions about the nature of rhetoric disappear when one grasps that for certain intellectual elites rhetoric was everything, not simply stylistics, that it functioned on many of the levels of inquiry now distinguished and separated." See also Donald Wilcox, *Development of Florentine Humanist Historiography* p. 22: "The humanist concern for elegance, which the fifteenth century tended to see as a narrow problem of style, appeared to Machiavelli a broader one of form and order."

3. Nancy Struever, review of *Rhetoric and Philosophy,* p. 67: "Would it not be possible . . . to construct a schematic model of the internal relationships in such a knotty and seminal work as Niccolo Machiavelli's *The Prince?*" Ibid., p. 69: "To the rhetorician the *topoi* or *figurae* are codes, universally applicable, used to draw significance from and enhance the persuasive value of concrete events and expression."

4. For a full discussion of the genre into which Machiavelli places *The Prince,* see Allan H. Gilbert, *Machiavelli's "Prince" and Its Forerunners.* The rhetorical roots of the genre are suggested by the fact that Isocrates is regarded as its author.

5. Pocock, *Machiavellian Moment,* and "Custom and Grace," esp. p. 156. Brayton Polka, commenting on Pocock's "Custom and Grace," is wrong when he says

that "it was quite impossible for Machiavelli to have a coherent theory of innovation [because] the Christian-Aristotelean framework" was one of eternal entities
and therefore could not deal with change. Polka, "Machiavelli's Concept of Innovation," p. 177. Polka follows Pocock and ignores the fact that rhetoric, which contained a "coherent theory of innovation," was part of that framework.

    6. Pocock, "Custom and Grace," p. 156: "Such means as [late scholastic thought]
did possess for rendering the particular intelligible were also the means available
to it of understanding the sequence of events in time and of rendering political
actions viable and political structures stable in time."

    7. For a detailed study of the difference between examples serving as the basis
for imitation and for reflection, see Karlheinz Stierle, "L'Histoire comme exemple."
Stierle's contrast between examples calling for imitation and those which provoke
reflection constitutes, for him, Boccaccio's advance over the Middle Ages. Stierle
claims, moreover, what I am claiming for Machiavelli, that this more reflective
use of examples is a way of confronting the ambiguities of the Renaissance moral
world. Lawrence Manley also points to the connections between the dialectical
and the political side of this rhetorical treatment of examples. E.g., *Convention*,
p. 209: In "'politic' history, the function was still the provision of examples, but
examples that were no longer understood as practical demonstrations of philosophic norms and precepts: instead, they were themselves treated as the source
of precepts. Specific rather than general in its conclusions, 'politic' history increasingly removed normative discourse from the influence of the abiding natural principles inculcated by moral philosophy. In keeping with this transformation, the
formerly 'logical' art of history was frequently reclassified among the practical arts
of statecraft. Taking as its 'principle and proper work' the instructing of men 'by
the knowledge of actions past, to bear themselves prudently in the present and
providently towards the future' (Hobbes, Preface to Thucydides), history increasingly replaced the language of wisdom and virtue with the language of prudence
and success, and the abiding integrity of natural norms with a variety of particular
choices." See also Daniel Javitch, *Poetry and Courtliness*, p. 100: "Examples allow
the poet to so disguise moral truth that its discovery depends on the reader's exercise of his ethical awareness. The use of precepts entails moral assault; that of examples invites moral participation of a sort kindred to esthetic involvement." Cf.
Marion Trousdale, "Renaissance View of Form," and John Wallace, "Examples Are
Best Precepts."

    8. Francis Bacon, *Advancement of Learning*, in *Works*, 3:403: "The most real
diversity of method is of method referred to Use, and method referred to Progres-
sion; whereof the one may be termed Magistral, and the other of Probation.

    "The later whereof seemeth to be *via deserta et interclusa* [a way that is aban-
doned and stopped up]. For as knowledges are now delivered, there is a kind of
contract of error between the deliverer and the receiver: for he that delivereth
knowledge desireth to deliver it in such form as may be best believed, and not
as may be best examined; and he that receiveth knowledge desireth rather present
satisfaction than expectant inquiry; and so rather not to doubt than not to err:
glory making the author not to lay open his weakness, and sloth making the dis-
ciple not to know his strength.

"But knowledge that is delivered as a thread to be spun on, ought to be delivered and intimated, if it were possible, *in the same method wherein it was invented;* and so is it possible of knowledge induced. . . . For it is in knowledge as it is in plants: if you mean to use the plant, it is no matter for the roots; but if you mean to remove it to grow, then it is more assured to rest upon roots than slips. So the delivery of knowledge (as it is now used) is as of fair bodies of trees without the roots; good for the carpenter, but not for the planter; but if you will have sciences grow, it is less matter for the shaft or body of the tree, so you look well to the taking up of the roots."

Bacon's distinction resembles, in important ways, Aristotle's distinction in the *Poetics*, ch. 3, between the two manners of imitation, dramatic and narrative.

9. Sir Philip Sidney, *Apologie*, ed. Sheperd, p. 22; Rosalie Colie, *Resources of Kind*, p. 4.

10. Cicero, *Topics* 2.8, defines a topic as a region (*sedes*) of argument, a place from which arguments are drawn. The topics are the fundamental resource for rhetorical invention, and consequently the literature on topics is enormous, but at this point it is sufficient to say that a topic is a formal device which makes invention possible by giving an inquiry structure without predetermining its result.

11. Cf. *Discourses* 3.5, where the hereditary monarch can lose his throne only if he systematically disregards the ancient customs of his people. These two kinds of states are related to the first two kinds of cases in Cicero, the honorable and the difficult: "An honorable case is one which wins favor in the mind of the auditor at once without any speech of ours: the difficult [or *admirable*, a translation of the Greek *paradoxos*] is one which has alienated the sympathy of those who are about to listen to the speech." Cicero, *De inventione* 1.10. Each kind of case on Cicero's list — the difficult, the obscure, the ambiguous, and the honorable — sets its own strategic problems of how to begin a speech and how to win over an initially indifferent or hostile audience. The honorable case, where the audience is already on the speaker's side, is the one kind of speech where an introduction is unnecessary. The Machiavellian parallel is the hereditary monarchy, where there are no problems of acquisition. For another Renaissance classification of "cases" similar to Cicero's, showing the practical significance of this technical distinction, see Boyle's examination of the dispute between Erasmus and Luther, in *Rhetoric and Reform*, p. 11: "In *Diatriba* [Erasmus] classifies freedom of choice among the *adiaphora*, those issues which are in Epictetus' definition 'independent of the moral purpose.' Of the divine intention he writes, 'Certain matters he wished us to know exceptionally well; this class comprises the precepts for good living.'" See also p. 12: Erasmus classifies questions into those "about which God has wished man to be ignorant, such as the last day, and concerning which it is irreligious, therefore, to dispute. There are those with which he has wished men to be very well acquainted, and even to commit to heart. These concern moral conduct. Furthermore, there are some questions which it is possible to examine, but only within limits, for what surpasses the human intellect is reserved for eschatological revelation. . . . Last of all Erasmus numbers those questions which, although they may be true, ought to be prudently restricted, as their public discussion may endanger piety and peace."

12. Pocock, *Machiavellian Moment*, p. 167: "The only constant semantic association is now that between *virtù* and innovation, the latter being considered rather
as an act than as a previously accomplished fact, and *virtù* is preeminently that
by which the individual is rendered outstanding in the context of innovation and
in the role of innovator." Mazzeo, *Renaissance and Seventeenth-Century Studies*,
p. 92, says that Machiavelli, "along with his contemporaries and Renaissance predecessors, revived the old deities of *fortuna* and *virtus* because their very indefinite-
ness permitted greater fidelity to the problematic character of both personal and
political affairs."

13. Pocock, "Custom and Grace," p. 169.

14. Pocock, *Machiavellian Moment*, p. 160: "Machiavelli conducts his analysis
neither in the specific context of Florence nor with regard to the specific problem
of citizenship; his concern is solely with the relations between the innovator and
fortune. . . . [While Guicciardini, Vettori, and Alamanni] specified, in varying degrees of detail, the exact historical changes that had constituted [the Medicean]
innovation, Machiavelli in *Il Principe* starts from innovation as an abstract principle, and the specific case that most closely resembles that of the Medicean ruler —
the case of a citizen who becomes a prince by the support of a party of his fellow
citizens — is considered in chapter ix carefully, it is true, but without special emphasis, as one among a gallery of types of 'new prince.'"

15. Pocock, *Machiavellian Moment*, pp. 173–74, notes the formality of the relation of virtù to Cesare Borgia as a counterexample; if the cases considered in Machiavelli's argument did not have such formal relations, a counterexample would
refute the prior thesis: "In Cesare [Borgia] we see combined the maximum *virtù*
with the maximum dependence on fortune. He is presented as a man of extraordinary ability who got his chance only because his father happened to become
pope, and whose virtue was displayed in the efforts he made to establish his power
in the Romagna on an independent basis before his father should happen to die.
. . . Cesare's position differs formally from that of the legislator in that his *virtù*
and his *fortuna* are not in a simple inverse relation. Because the legislator's *virtù*
is superhuman, *fortuna* has no power over him; Cesare's *virtù* is only human — he
is related to the legislator somewhat as the Aristotelian 'man of practical wisdom' is
to the Platonic philosopher-king — and is seen in his struggle to escape the power
which *fortuna* exercises." I claimed above that chapter 6 presents the case of interest to Machiavelli and his readers, the state that is difficult to acquire but easy
to maintain. Quentin Skinner, *Machiavelli*, p. 24, thinks that the prince who has
come to power through fortune is the center of interest: "Although [Machiavelli]
has taken care to present his argument as a sequence of neutral typologies, he has
cunningly organised the discussion in such a way as to highlight one particular
type of case, and has done so because of its local and personal significance. The
situation in which the need for expert advice is said to be especially urgent is where
a ruler has come to power by Fortune and foreign arms. No contemporary reader
of *The Prince* could have failed to reflect that, at the point when Machiavelli was
advancing this claim, the Medici had just regained their former ascendancy in
Florence as the result of an astonishing stroke of good fortune, combined with the
unstoppable force of foreign arms supplied by Ferdinand of Spain." Skinner is right

if Machiavelli is trying to make himself useful by providing advice of a rather un-reflective sort; instead, I find Machiavelli undercutting the possibility of that sort of advice.

16. On my reading, the contrast between Cesare Borgia as an instance of virtù and Agathocles and others as villains is a contrast necessary to develop a formal meaning of virtù. On other readings of *The Prince* the contrast is a sign that even Machiavelli is hesitant to equate virtù with success. E.g., Jerrold Seigel, "*Virtù* In and Since the Renaissance," p. 483: "It would seem that Machiavelli was himself somewhat awed by his own conclusions about the true nature of virtue." For a different approach, see Peter E. Bondanella, '*Machiavelli and the Art of Renaissance History*, p. 138: "Modern readers have a concept of character in narrative which has been aptly described as 'hopelessly novel-centered.' Consequently, the reader's first impression of Machiavelli's nonfictional characters is their relative psychological simplicity. None of these figures is the kind of complex individual the modern reader has come to expect from long exposures to the novel, a genre that commonly stresses both character development and varying degrees of introspective analysis. . . . Machiavelli's remarks that Lorenzo de' Medici seemed to be composed of 'two different persons' reveals his reluctance or inability to deal with complex, and therefore conflicting, personality traits in his nonfictional characters." See, finally, Hannah F. Pitkin, *Fortune Is a Woman*, p. 5: "Some have suggested that the tensions and ambiguities in [Machiavelli's] thought simply indicate the carelessness of a second-rate mind. Others regard them as evidence of duplicity, of an effort to convey simultaneously an esoteric and an exoteric message. The initial suggestion of this book will be that the apparent contradictions in Machiavelli's thought arise neither from ineptitude nor from manipulative cleverness, but from ambivalence — intense but incompatible feelings that can be neither given up nor reconciled. The focus of ambivalence in Machiavelli's texts, as I shall suggest, is manhood: anxiety about being sufficiently masculine and concern over what it means to be a man."

17. Pitkin notes the way Machiavelli's treatment of villainy and the civic principality are means for giving a meaning to the formal conception of virtù without begging crucial questions: "Machiavelli complicates things by talking not only about prudence and boldness, rival aspects or ways of *virtù*, but also about a number of other qualities opposed to fortune's power: ingenuity, sagacity, judgment, intelligence, wisdom, even self-knowledge. But perhaps these are all aspects or ways of *virtù*. In addition, in *The Prince*, ch. 8, he mentions two alternatives to the fortune-*virtù* dyad. One is conduct so effective as to succeed without or in spite of fortune, yet so thoroughly evil that it cannot be considered *virtù*. His prime example is Agathocles the Sicilian, who rose from a lowly *fortuna* to become king of Syracuse. Nothing or very little in his career was due to fortune, yet it wasn't due to *virtù* either, for 'It cannot . . . be called virtue (*virtù*) to kill one's fellow-citizens, to betray friends, to be without fidelity, without mercy, without religion; such proceedings enable one to gain sovereignty (*imperio*), but not fame.' A second exception is the man who becomes prince through popular support among his fellow citizens, creating what Machiavelli calls a 'civil princedom (*principato civile*).' It is achieved neither by *virtù* alone, nor by fortune alone but rather by 'a fortunate

shrewdness (*una astuzia fortunata*).' Neither of these alternatives is explored further, nor do they recur in Machiavelli's other writings." Pitkin, *Fortune Is a Woman*, pp. 155–56, n. 90.

18. The secondary literature about Machiavelli's use of virtù is of course huge; one especially apposite piece is Seigel, "*Virtù* In and Since the Renaissance." He recommends that we keep distinct two "different facets of Machiavelli's approach to *virtù*: (1) the confrontation between traditional moral virtue and the non-moral sense of virtue as capacity for action; (2) the development of a theory of human action through the analysis of *virtù* in the second sense" (p. 479). The argument of *The Prince* from chapter 6 on is such a development. The interconnections between virtù and *prudenzia* are explored in Renucci, "Machiavel."

19. Pocock, in "'The Onely Politician,'" a review of Raab, *The English Face of Machiavelli*, says, "Machiavelli . . . wished to transcend the search for stability altogether. Throughout the introductory chapters of the *Discourses*, we find a series of decisions against studying the closed, aristocratic, defensive state — Sparta or Venice — which makes stability its only goal, and in favor of studying the dynamic, popular, warlike state — Livian Rome — which opts for liberty, expansion, and dominion, even if this choice condemns it to ultimate decline and even tyranny. Since Machiavelli did not believe that the world of cities could be rendered finally proof against Fortune, he chose to embrace the goddess rather than wall himself off from her" (p. 277). I think it is more useful and accurate to say that Machiavelli is changing the definition of security from rest to the continuing ability to act than to say that he is abandoning the search for security. The new sense of stability is indeed one which embraces Fortune rather than walls itself off from her.

20. "Mi resta ora a discorrere generalmente le offese e difese che in chiscuno de' prenominati possono accadere." I claim that this refers to the whole following section, chapters 12–23, and not just, as the words could be taken to mean, only to the next three chapters on military offense and defense.

21. If chapters 12–23 offer these general methods, chapter 24 echoes my claim that innovation becomes the paradigm case of stability: "The suggestions made above, if acted upon, will make a new prince seem one well established and will set him up more firmly and securely in his state than if he had had it for years."

22. To anticipate my final chapter, Machiavelli's search for material on which to exercise virtù ranges over the three qualities of a good ruler, and orator, which I draw from Aristotle's *Rhetoric* and *Politics*: chapters 12–14 concern the prince's competence (*dynamis*), 15–21 deal in a perverted or inventive way with *philia* or the goodwill shown by the prince towards his subjects, and 22 and 23 are concerned with *phronesis*, prudence as it is shown in the relations of the prince to his counselors.

23. Pocock, *Machiavellian Moment*, p. 157: "What Machiavelli is doing, in the most notorious passages of *Il Principe*, is reverting to the formal implementation of the Roman definition [of *virtus* as that by which the good man imposed form on *fortuna*] and asking whether there is any *virtù* by which the innovator, self-isolated from moral society, can impose form upon his *fortuna* and whether there will be any moral quality in such a *virtù* or in the political consequences which can be imagined as flowing from its exercise. Since the problem only exists as the

result of innovation, which is a political act, its exploration must be conducted in terms of further political action."

24. In the same way, Aristotle, in the *Rhetoric* 1.1.1355b12ff., redefines the end of rhetoric by making it into an activity that is a function of an art. The function of rhetoric "is not so much to persuade, as to find out in each case the existing means of persuasion. The same holds good in respect to all the other arts. For instance, it is not the function of medicine to restore a patient to health, but only to promote this end as far as possible; for even those whose recovery is impossible may be properly treated." For further elaboration of the way Aristotle's practical sciences and methods make ends a function of activities, see my "Aristotle's Genealogy of Morals." That distinction between the given and redefined end of rhetoric should remove the misunderstanding present, for example, in Pocock's accepting Hexter's claim that the purpose of the new prince is "to maintain himself in the position of power and insecurity which innovation has brought him. . . . *Stato* means that one's eye is always upon immediate dangers; *virtù* is that by which one resists them, not that by which one is emancipated from the need to fear them." *Machiavellian Moment*, pp. 175–76. There is an important truth here: security is never freedom from the problems of fortune. But Hexter accepts as a factual and exhaustive distinction the contrast between innovation and the world of becoming on the one hand, and security and eternity on the other.

25. The parallel in Aristotle's *Rhetoric* is 1.4; unlike the rest of the sources of argument, talk about legislation and the resources of government is talk based on knowledge of a subject, and not just knowledge of what people believe. Therefore the rhetorician must in that case draw on *scientific knowledge* of politics, and not merely on the opinions and arguments of men. Hence the initial plausibility of McCanles's reconstruction of the organization of *The Prince*, with chapter 12 marking a turning point from rhetorical production to rhetorical interpretation; the military virtues Machiavelli discusses in these chapters are fundamentally virtues of interpretation. See Michael McCanles, "Machiavelli's 'Principe,'" p. 8: "It is appropriate to divide the central concerns of *Il Principe*'s two halves into text production and text interpretation respectively. The first half (chapters One to Thirteen) illustrates how the prince's discourse generates political events, and is limited to the effect of the prince's text on the actions he initiates and suffers. The second half (chapters Fourteen to Twenty-five) expands this relation to take in the prince's actions themselves as a kind of text that requires and invites transcoding into verbal discourse." But it is important to note that it is not the prince's actions that are a "kind of text" here, but the past of military history and the present of strategic opportunities.

26. I follow Machiavelli's own analytic procedure here in the following sense. Machiavelli differs from Guicciardini and other contemporary Florentines in appealing to more general categories of analysis, most crucially "the innovator" as opposed to more empirically tied terms (see n. 14 above). In the same way, I find the distinction between ideology and prudence, although not one that Machiavelli would express in these terms, more useful in capturing his mode of practical thinking than experience-near concepts such as the hereditary ruler and the usurper. I think that the ultimate justification for my language of prudence and ideology

comes from the affinities I propose to establish between Machiavelli's problematizing strategies in opposing traditional rulers and traditional politics on the one hand and the distance between two conceptions of practical reason, which I call ideological and prudential. For some preliminary justification for this terminology, see Bernard Crick, "On Theory and Practice," p. 31: "A doctrine is doctrinaire and likely to prove impractical less by the character of its intentions, than by whether or not it claims that its set of principles or its set of intended results must entail a unique and specific set of actions-as-means. For political theory would lead us to believe, both on empirical and moral grounds, that the means must vary according to circumstances. . . . When policies cannot be changed without undermining the authority of the doctrine, then the doctrine must have been formulated in terms over-specific and insufficiently generalized."

27. Once again I think it worth displaying some of the parallels between my discussion of Machiavellian prudence and some other dimensions of current thinking, and here Pocock, Pitkin, Fumaroli, and Manley are apposite. Pocock, *Machiavellian Moment*, p. 49: "It can be argued that the ideal of the citizen implied a totally different conceptualization of the modes of political knowledge and action from that implicit in the scholastic-customary framework which we have so far studied. Within the limits of that framework, the individual employed reason, which disclosed to him the eternal hierarchies of unchanging nature and enjoined him to maintain the cosmic order by maintaining his place in that social and spiritual category to which his individual nature assigned him; he employed experience, which disclosed to him immemorial continuities of traditional behavior and could only counsel him to maintain them; and he employed a blend of prudence and faith on those occasions when the stream of contingent and particular events faced him with a problem so individual that neither reason nor syllogism, experience nor tradition, provided a ready-made answer to it. Only on these occasions, it might be contended, did he behave like a decision-making animal (and even then, not infrequently, more like an apocalyptically guided true believer); for the rest his behavior was that of the inhabitant of what some theorists call a traditional society." See also Pitkin, *Fortune Is a Woman*, p. 276: "One should construe the forgetfulness that gradually corrupts a composite body as reification: a coming to take for granted as 'given' and inevitable what in fact is the product of human action. Thus people may come to consider their civic order beyond their choice or control and, therefore, beyond their responsibility, secure without any special effort on their part. Then each may feel free to poach on the public spirit—or the public-serving habits—of others, behaving as if someone else were in charge and losing touch with his own stake in public life. When the polity is 'left to heirs,' it soon reverts to *rovina* (ruin) for 'heirs quickly degenerated from their ancestors.'" The traditional rule Machiavelli attacks fits Marc Fumaroli's description, in his "Rhetoric, Politics, and Society," p. 254, of Baron's "aulic humanism": "Hans Baron distinguished between a Florentine civic humanism and the aulic humanism of the Italian courts, the one linked to a republican political ideal, the other to a monarchic ideal. In the first case, eloquence and the orator, taking as paradigm the senatorial eloquence of the Roman republic, take on a heroic dimension; the spoken word, fed by wisdom and sustained by virtue, makes itself the responsible guide of the

city. In the second case, the only hero is the prince, and public speech has no other function than the celebration of the prince; it is the festive link between him and the people; politics retires into the secret of the court and into the deliberation between the prince and his counsellors." For the way in which the old politics has a restricted range for rhetoric, see also Manley, *Convention*, p. 113: "Where humanist ideals gave way to more purely courtly ones, where the conditions of civic freedom or learned exile gave way to courtly service and diplomacy, this element of *pathos* became the basis for a highly rhetorical conception of human personality. Not only did this conception shift the framework for discussion of human morality from universal nature and the hierarchical stability of ethos to the flux of pathos, but it did so in explicitly rhetorical terms."

28. "Even if the multitude is utterly deceived, subsequently it hates those who have led it to do something ignoble." Aristotle, *Constitution of Athens* 28.3–4.

29. Compare Aristotle's contrast in *De sophisticis elenchis* 184a1–6 between earlier rhetorician's ready-made precepts and his own art (quoted in the Introduction, p. 22).

30. The overtly formal mode of presentation of *The Prince* has often been noted, although not, as I have tried to do, in connection with its substantive purpose. In addition to McCanles, "Machiavelli's 'Principe,'" (see n. 25 above), see Pocock, *Machiavellian Moment*, pp. 162–63: "The analysis of innovation is carried out in the first third of *Il Principe* and supplies a key to the pattern of at least part of the book. Chapters iii to v deal with the relation between the new prince's power and the customary structure of the society over which he has acquired it; chapters vi to ix with the degree to which innovation renders him dependent on fortune. To complete the conspectus which this approach to *Il Principe* suggests, we may observe that chapters xii to xiv deal with the prince's military strength and xv to xxi with his personal conduct in relation to his subjects; this is the section chiefly concerned with what came to be known as Machiavellian morality. In xxiv and xxv Machiavelli returns to his main theme and confronts the new prince once again with the hereditary prince and with *fortuna,* and the concluding chapter xxvi is the famous and problematic 'exhortation to liberate Italy from the barbarians.' *Il Principe* does not take the form of a systematic exhaustion of categories, but there are patterns discernible in it, of which this is one." I would claim that the "pattern" I have identified is a pattern of argument and, hence, that the text I am explicating is coherent in a sense in which Pocock's is not.

Two more analyses of the formal structure of *The Prince* may be found in Mazzeo. First he quotes Butterfield's version: "Although the formal structure of *The Prince* is not at first immediately apparent, it is an organized work. Its chapters can be classified into three groups, a first on the form of the state and the acquisition and maintenance of power, a second on military problems and foreign affairs, a third on the problems of relations within the state such as the relations of rulers and ruled, rulers and their advisors." Mazzeo, *Renaissance and Seventeeth-Century Studies*, pp. 129–30, n. 4. He then offers his own analysis: "A more detailed structural analysis could be made as follows: chapters one to four are concerned with the problems facing new princely governments in the territories they have just acquired; chapters five to nine deal with the necessary variations in the methods of administering such territories according to whether they were gained by force, favourable circumstances, tricks, or the favour of the citizens; chapters ten to fourteen deal with the ruler's problem of possessing sufficient power to defend himself whether with his own or foreign forces, or by 'divine protection.' This problem leads to a consideration of different types of armies, mercenary, national and auxiliary: chapters fifteen to eighteen deal with the ruler's relations with subjects and friends, and further methods of keeping and increasing power, in particular the covert or 'fraudulent' ones such as clever liberality, wise parsimony, cruelty, dissimulation, bad faith as may be required by circumstances or a 'higher' political objective: chapters nineteen to twenty-three are concerned with how the ruler can save his reputation by avoiding contempt and hatred, how he may maintain his reputation by recourse to armament, resoluteness, prudence in alliances, generous support of artists and men of talent and ability, and by exercising caution in choosing his ministers and in relating himself to his courtiers. The final chapter is an exhortation to free Italy from the barbarians."

31. The first paragraph of chapter 24 "is not a declaration that the new prince can found a system more durably institutionalized and legitimized than by use and tradition, so much as a declaration that men in the world of innovation live in the present." Pocock, *Machiavellian Moment*, p. 178.

32. Consequently, I find Machiavelli's treatment of fortuna here tightly subordinated to his argument; it is one of the functions of rhetorical invention to convert commonplaces or clichés into commonplaces, sources of invention. Pitkin, by contrast, sees as incoherent that shift from fortune as an external cause to fortune as material; chapter 25 "opens with the question of whether to apply any metaphors at all, that is, whether there is any such agency as 'fortune,' other than a mere name for the consequences of what we do. And the chapter may be read as a meditation on the choice between the two metaphors introduced in the previous chapter: between fortune as a rival and fortune as a woman. For though both metaphors suggest human activism, they have conflicting implications for conduct. Bad weather cannot be prevented, but it can be foreseen and prepared for. But instead of proceeding then to explain how a prince might prepare for bad weather, the passage instead distinguishes two policies available to those caught *unprepared:* flight with a fantasy of being loved and recalled, or autonomy in 'defending oneself.' But how is one to defend oneself against a storm for which one has neglected to prepare?" Pitkin, *Fortune Is a Woman*, p. 148. Her conclusion, though, is too hasty: "The confrontation between *virtus* and *Fortuna*, indeed, became so frequent in Roman literature even before Cicero as to be commonplace, 'even so banal, that it could sink to the level of a pedagogical device for rhetorical exercises'" (p. 139; Pitkin here quotes Klaus Heitman, *Fortuna and Virtus: Eine Studie zu Petrarcas Lebensweisheit* [Cologne, 1958], pp. 18–19).

33. A test can be difficult in two different senses. First, it can be difficult because the material is already formed in the opposite way, and hence one must destroy that original form and replace it with another, as the orator in the difficult case — which is also called the admirable or paradoxical case — must destroy the prejudices of the audience and replace them with judgments favorable to him. The test here is difficult in a second sense: it is the kind of case that Cicero calls ambiguous

(*anceps*): "The ambiguous case is one in which the point for decision is obscure, or the case is partly honorable and partly discreditable so that it engenders both good-will and ill-will" (*De inventione* 1.15). Earlier I showed the way Machiavelli adapts Cicero's classification of cases to his initial taxonomy of kinds of states.

2. Discursive Virtuosity and Practical Virtù

1. Pocock, "Custom and Grace," p. 156.

2. Gray, "Renaissance Humanism," p. 506: "The terms *decorum* and *imitatio*, for example, are central in both rhetoric and moral philosophy, and the humanists often appear to fuse their meanings whatever the context. Thus, the imitation of stylistic and ethical models are spoken of in identical terms; or the idea of always speaking appropriately, of suiting style and manner to subject, aim and audience is treated as the exact analogue of behaving with *decorum*, of choosing the actions and responses which are best in harmony with and most appropriate to individual character and principles on the one hand, the nature of circumstances on the other."

3. When a commentator ignores the difficulty of prudent imitation, he makes Machiavelli's project seem easy and consequently implausible. "Most of the mirror-for-princes writers continue to endorse the familiar humanist assumption that, since the right kind of education is of crucial importance to shaping the character of the *vir virtutis*, there must be a close connection between the provision of the best educational and the best political advice. Machiavelli constitutes something of an exception to this rule, since he only glancingly mentions the question of the ruler's intellectual training—perhaps because he genuinely believed (as he sometimes seems to imply) that the best education for a prince would simply consist of memorizing." Skinner, *Machiavelli*, p. 122.

4. This, I take it, lies behind Struever's doubt that there is anything at all to imitate in Machiavelli. "There is very little the Prince as receptor can imitate in a normal or classical transparent sense: the prince is constrained by the counsellor within a domain of artifice, quite like Castiglione's court, which requires technical virtuosity, illocutionary ability, not nobility of mind." Nancy Struever, "Machiavelli and the Available Languages of Morality," p. 14. The image of the archer is also apposite to Struever's further comment: "Just because Machiavelli claims in the Preface to *The Discourses* to prefer imitation to admiration as response, does not mean that the text provides for, enjoins imitation: what is not only enjoined but constrained by the text is judgment of a peculiar distancing sort" (p. 13). See also Thomas Greene, *The Light in Troy*, p. 75, with quotations from Seneca's Epistle 84: "The preference for the filial over the painterly relationship seems to rest on the former's organicity; the organic can be controlled but not programmed. There is also in this filial analogy, as the context makes clear, an understood element of *un*likeness. The painting is contrived to reproduce its subject as faithfully as possible, but the son is allowed to recall his father's features with only a vague 'family resemblance.' . . . I think that sometimes it is impossible for it to be seen who is being imitated, if the copy is a true one; for a true copy stamps its own form upon all the features which it has drawn from what we may call the original,

in such a way that they are combined into a unity. Do you not see how many voices there are in a chorus? Yet out of the many only one voice results.'"

5. *Advancement of Learning*, in *Works*, 3:453. After making that distinction, Bacon praises Machiavelli for following the second use of examples: "The form of writing which of all others is fittest for this variable argument of negotiation and occasions is that which Machiavelli chose wisely and aptly for government; namely *discourse upon histories or examples*. [Note that Bacon situates histories and examples next to fables, parables, and aphorisms, following the classification given in Aristotle's *Rhetoric*; later we will have to examine the transformation of rhetorical "examples" and history in particular in Machiavelli's hands.] For knowledge drawn freshly and in our view out of particulars, knoweth the way best to particulars again. And it hath much greater life for practice when the discourse attendeth upon the example, than when the example attendeth upon the discourse. For this is not point of order, as it seemeth at first, but of substance. For when the example is the ground, being set down in an history at large, it is set down with all circumstances, which may sometimes control the discourse thereupon made and sometimes supply it, as a very pattern for action; whereas the examples alleged for the discourse's sake are cited succinctly and without particularity, and carry a servile aspect toward the discourse which they are brought in to make good" (ibid.). Even the best of contemporary critics find it easy to fall prey to the temptation to use such an easy contrast. Stierle's distinction between examples used for imitation and for reflection, and Manley's contrast between the language of wisdom and its alternative, politic history, thus reduce prudence to an ethics of consequences based on examples without rules (see chapter 1, n.7).

6. G.W.F. Hegel, *Vorlesungen über die Philosophie der Geschichte*, p. 83: "Moral truths learned as precepts from authority are perhaps more quickly and completely reduced to platitude than any other kind of statement. Our own desire for comfort drives us to it; for to understand the teachings of our moral tradition as real truths would limit our freedom and reduce our self-importance."

7. John. J. Richetti, *Philosophical Writing*, p. 7: "A profound transformation of what might be called the dominant literary genres of philosophy marks the emergence of modern thought, as the autobiographical meditation, the essay and the treatise succeed older forms such as the medieval commentary with its catechetical and interrogatory structure that is a form of dialogue. In the process the rhetorical and polemical features of philosophy are transformed, as a new dramatic scene for thought is developed and enforced by those genres. The modern philosopher-writer is a man alone, a sort of voluntary Robinson Crusoe or self-appointed philosophical Adam whose thought tends to represent itself as a new beginning rather than a continuation and modification of older thought. This philosopher often claims not simply to have thought but to have established conditions that make authentic thought possible and truth available at last. The dialogue, polemic, commentary, and disputation of ancient and medieval thought have a communal context. They require, continually add to, and redefine a preexisting philosophy. Such thought has visible social location as well as overt ethical and political concerns. The radical epistemologizing of thought after, say, Descartes requires the denial or at least the functional dismissal of context. Society and its

concerns become effects of consciousness rather than its cause or its accompaniment." Machiavelli would fall on the medieval side of Richetti's dichotomy. For a quite different version of this history, see Terence Cave, cited in the following note.

8. Richetti, *Philosophical Writing*, p. 15: "Style thus rivals the static formulations of truth to which philosophy, at least implicitly, aspires. Style is a property of the text as it is experienced, something that cannot be adequately represented by paraphrase or summary, a performance that argues the presence of an enacting self in a dramatic situation. Style belongs to what Richard Lanham calls *homo rhetoricus*, who is necessarily skeptical and drawn to the play and pleasure of language, an actor whose identity 'depends on the reassurance of daily histrionic reenactment' and who is 'thus centered in time and concrete local event.' Lanham contrasts rhetorical man with *homo seriosus*, who thinks of himself as 'central' rather than social or dramatic and who views language as an imperfect means of expressing ontological stability." The reference is to Lanham's *Motives of Eloquence*, pp. 4, 6–8. This performative dimension in Machiavelli is, similarly, closely connected to what Cave calls "plural": "The notion of 'plurality' is used to denote the character of a discourse which resists interpretive integration, not because it is obscure, or because it has several levels of meaning, but because it is set up in such a way as to block normal interpretive procedures." Cave, *Cornucopian Text*, p. xx. See also Dominick LaCapra, *Rethinking Intellectual History*, p. 32: "A documentary approach to the reading of texts has predominated in general historiography and, in important respects, it has also characterized intellectual history. If the dominance of this approach is open to question in other areas of historiography, it is perhaps even more questionable in intellectual history, given the texts it addresses. For certain texts themselves explore the interaction of various uses of language such as the documentary and the worklike and they do so in ways that raise the issue of the various possibilities in language use attendant upon this interaction. . . . The issue may be raised in relation to any text in a manner that both opens it to an investigation of its functioning as discourse and opens the reader to the need for interpretation in his or her dialogue with it. Indeed there would seem to be something intrinsically wrong-headed in the idea of a purely or even predominantly documentary approach to a markedly worklike and internally 'dialogized' text making claims on its readers that are not met by documentary understanding alone."

9. Pitkin, *Fortune Is a Woman*, p. 9: "The finding, interpretation, and application of the community's law and custom are the work of particular ranks in the social hierarchy. Every rank is understood as bound by obligations and subordinated to a still higher rank—a hierarchy culminating in God. There may be wicked rulers who misapply the law, but there is no right of rebellion against them." These common nonprudential, nonrhetorical readings of Machiavelli are what LaCapra calls "reductive": "A discipline may constitute itself in part through reductive readings of its important texts—readings that are contested by the 'founding' texts themselves in significant ways. These readers render the texts less multifaceted and perhaps less critical but more operational for organized research. Here the decisive role of certain disciples and practitioners lies not in the fine-tuning of a

paradigm enunciated in 'founding' texts but in the active reduction of those texts to their paradigmatic level." LaCapra, *Rethinking Intellectual History*, p. 60. For this, see also Cave, *Cornucopian Text*, pp. 94–95, who notes a French translation of Erasmus's *Praise of Folly*, published in 1520, which "puts to the test of transcription a mode of writing developed in order to resist schematic interpretation. . . . The sixteenth-century French translator, responding no doubt to the pressure of a moralizing tradition embedded in fifteenth-century French scholarship, attempts to eliminate this plurality by glossing (or glossing over) the text as he translates, systematically restricting the production of meaning and turning the piece into a didactic tract. . . . The model of interpretation . . . moves towards the articulation of a 'hidden sense' not simply in the margins of the original text but in its place: Erasmus, Ovid, and Jean de Meun are systematically displaced by their allegorizers, while at the same time the range of their signification is trapped in what is essentially a monologic discourse."

10. Nancy Struever, "Historical Rhetoric," p. 12: "The self-consciousness of the Renaissance historians about history as *writing* seems to entail a certain consciousness of history as *reading*, as a matter of readers' as well as writers' competence. . . . For historical discourse, the relevant frames [of discourse] are the rules of debate, the constraints placed on the author/reader in discussion. Machiavelli changed not so much the subject matter as the results for discussion of political history; the virtue of his discourse demonstrates the increase in range of discussable issues, liberation from irrelevant obligations for all participants in the discussion."

11. My claim that the shift from hereditary monarchy's reliance on epideictic rhetoric to Machiavelli's prudential dependence on deliberation has its parallel in Fumaroli, "Rhetoric, Politics, and Society," pp. 258–59: "Like Montaigne, Muret sees [that] to exercise the authoritative power of *eloquentia cum sapientia conjungenda*, he [must have] recourse to the deliberative only through the epideictic. In other words he can counsel the prince, act for the best on his mind, only by taking the detour of praise. Epistolary art and its oral counterpart, the art of conversation, sum up the eloquence at court. Both suppose an art of pleasing whose essential values are clarity, elegance, urbanity (in French, *honnêteté*), polite and ingratiating pleasantness, wit (*ingenium*). The model of this eloquence can be found not in the *Orationes* but in the *Epistolae* of Cicero." Above I cited LaCapra's notion of reductive readings of canonical texts (see n. 8). The alternative he posits is "performative" readings. See p. 62 of his *Rethinking Intellectual History*: "With specific reference to intellectual history, I would argue for a more 'performative' notion of reading and interpretation in which an attempt is made to 'take on' the great texts and to attain a level of understanding and perhaps of language use that contends with them."

12. Aristotle recognizes the need for properly dividing dialectical labors: "It is not within the power of one party only to ensure the proper accomplishment of the common task." *Topics* 8.11.161a20.) See also J.G.A. Pocock, *Politics, Language and Time*, p. 33: "Communication rests upon ambiguity. From the premise of institutionalization [of language], it follows both that we can never fully understand one another (or even ourselves) and that we can always answer one another (and in soliloquy, we can answer ourselves). There is a certain refraction and recalci-

trance in the medium which ensures that the language I bend to perform my own acts can be bent back in the performance of others' acts against me, without ceasing to be available for my counter-replication. Language gives me power, but power which I cannot fully control or prevent others from sharing. In performing a verbalized act of power, I enter upon a polity of shared power." See also Pitkin, *Fortune Is a Woman*, pp. 68–69: "In the very structure of [*The Art of War*], lies an even greater puzzle. Its substantive message is, as we have seen, activist, military, militant, and republican. Yet the form and style in which these themes are presented convey a very different message: they are ritualized and stylized to the point of representing a romantic idyll free of all conflict, and they constantly suggest hierarchy, authority, discipline, and self-denial. The form of *The Art of War,* one might say, is altogether at odds with its manifest content. We should imitate ancient warfare, the book tells us, rather than ancient forms of art; yet it is itself an imitation of ancient literary form in the best humanist tradition. . . . Though in form dialogical, the book is in no sense a true dialogue but a mannered monologue, a courtly dance of deference and decorum."

13. Bernstein, *Beyond Objectivism and Relativism*, p. 157: "As Aristotle stresses, and Gadamer realizes, *phronesis* presupposes the existence of *nomoi* (funded laws) in the *polis* or community. This is what keeps *phronesis* from degenerating into the mere cleverness or calculation that characterizes the *deinos* (the clever person). Given a community in which there is a living, shared acceptance of ethical principles and norms, then *phronesis* as the mediation of such universals in particular situations makes good sense."

14. Thomas Greene, "The End of Discourse," p. 58: "*The Prince* signals its willed estrangement from the cultural processes it claims to analyze. It will not enjoy the ritual comforts of the products of high culture, including the factitious ending, the dialogue that fabricates consensus, the generous unrealities and bland conclusions of fiction that passes for description."

15. Therefore speech act theory, with its distinction between illocutionary act and perlocutionary effect, will take us only so far, because it fails to overcome antinomies that Machiavelli overthrows. Speech act theory offers goals easy to achieve—illocutionary success and uptake—and because of this ease, a writer, especially in Machiavelli's circumstances, must be tempted to adopt them as purposes of writing. Achieving such illocutionary success would then offer justification and rationalization for failing to achieve—even to attempt—more serious political goals. On the other hand, going beyond mere illocutionary success and trying to specify perlocutionary goals would be a usurpation on Machiavelli's part of his readers' job, and so of his readers' autonomy. Speech act theory has a value, because it rejects the distinction between language which states facts and action which does things, by reminding us how people do things with words. But its subsequent distinction between the linguistic (illocutionary) and extralinguistic (perlocutionary) brings back in the distinction it was designed to overturn. (In the same way, Austin wants to overcome the priority of referential language, of constatives, so that by the end of *How To Do Things with Words* constatives are just one kind of speech act among others, but he reintroduces their centrality in the form of the locutionary act contained in any complete speech act.) Speech act theory thus has no means

of distinguishing political discourse from mere talk about politics, and its appeal to conventions is too limited to help.

16. Pitkin, *Fortune Is a Woman*, p. 93.

17. This passage continues with a most impractical-sounding consolation: "But men should never despair on that account; for, not knowing the aims of Fortune, which she pursues by dark and devious ways, men should always be hopeful, and never yield to despair, whatever troubles or ill fortune may befall them."

18. Struever, "Machiavelli and the Available Language of Morality," p. 5: "The whole semantic field of *telos* is short-changed: the use of ethological metaphors of lions and foxes sharpens and narrows capacity, and does not expand, but constricts, goals." See also McCanles, "Machiavelli's 'Principe,'" pp. 16–17: "Machiavelli equates political difficulties that lie in the future with a disease that is already present but difficult to recognize. This implies that the future is always already present, buried as a potentiality within what is currently visible. . . . The true nature of a situation may well be that negation of itself which it excludes and (therefore) implies."

3. The Politics of Rhetorical Invention

1. John O. Ward, "Rhetoric and the Writing of History," p. 41.

2. Hayden White, "Contemporary Philosophy of History," p. 43.

3. Along the same lines, it is instructive to contrast Descartes's list of sources of secure truth with Quintilian's rhetorical set: "We may regard as certainties, first, those things which we perceive by the senses . . . ; secondly, those things about which there is general agreement, such as the existence of the gods or the duty of loving one's parents; thirdly, those things which are established by law or have passed into current usage; finally, there are the things which are admitted by either party, and whatever has already been proved or is not disputed by our adversary." *Institutes* 5.10.12–14. For a subtle treatment of the relation between accessible and technical language in the social sciences today, see Ely Devons and Max Gluckman, *Closed Systems and Open Minds*. See also the comments on that book by Dorothy Emmet, *Rules*, p. 141, n. 1: "Ely Devons and Max Gluckman have discussed the 'limits of naivety in Social Anthropology,' i.e. what line should a social anthropologist adopt when his research raises questions dealt with by other disciplines such as economics or depth psychology. The authors suggest ways of distinguishing where 'naive' assumptions about questions in these disciplines will not in fact affect the social anthropologist's analysis of his own problem, and where it will be necessary to relegate the question as one requiring the techniques of an expert in the other disciplines."

4. White, "Contemporary Philosophy of History," pp. 44 and 48. Nancy Struever, "Topics," p. 79: "A topical reading of Machiavelli would define his innovation as a change in the rules, a new stipulation of the range of civic event and behavior which is worthy of discussion, a change which augmented historical inquiry, made useful demands on the historical readers."

5. The conflict between conservative history and metahistory is thus a revision of the ancient quarrel between rhetoric and philosophy, between common and eso-

teric wisdom. Struever, "Topics," p. 78: "Aristotle's *Topics*, and particularly the section on definition, represents a rejection of the inequitable, and therefore of the
initiative we now call 'professionalisation.' For any attempt to professionalise, that
is, to exclude amateurs, to limit to experts, is fraught with danger to the historical
enterprise, may issue in a 'loss of problems,' to cite Wittgenstein. Topical discipline
resists elitism, reduction. Unlike the immediate gratification conveyed by the self-
conscious application of sophistical systematic methods, such as the tropology [of
Hayden White], the use of topical analysis purveys discomfort: it is therapeutic
only in an unsettling way; it adds nothing, but takes away a great deal." The conflict between arcane knowledge and rhetoric is also expressed by Petrarch: "Let
others engage in speculation and prove those things with torturous and intricate
reasons, if those things are provable which can neither be grasped by the intellect
nor maintained against the force of a subtler mind; [such] things, after they are
known, neither make men more moral or more prudent in human affairs." *Ep.*
2.295, cited in Kahn, *Rhetoric, Prudence, and Skepticism*, p. 203, n. 31. See also
Bruns, *Inventions*, p. 40: "From Socrates to Derrida the philosophers have always
defined themselves by their opposition to what can be put publicly into words.
Philosophy is secretive, whereas rhetoric is full of public exclamation. Rhetoric,
to be sure, is the art of concealing motives, designs or ulterior purposes — but not
doctrines or meanings; rather one should say that rhetoric uses meanings for the
concealment of practical objectives, whereas philosophy is secretive precisely in
respect of what it knows (or what it seeks), as was Socrates, who made it part
of his self-definition, part of the whole justification of his life, that he never spoke
in public, and who left the world ignorant of what it was that came to him in those
periods of philosophical enchantment when he would stand for hours motionless
and alone (*Symp.* 220c-d)." While philosophy and rhetoric need not always be
conceived in opposition, the conflict between esoteric and public knowledge is one
of the bases for the periodic struggles between them. Both philosophy and rhetoric, as I shall soon show for rhetoric, contain resources for dealing with both learned
and general audiences, accessible and erudite truths.

Parallel to White's distinction between conservative history and metahistory is
the opposition Richard Rorty develops between Habermas and Lyotard. For example: "Anything that Habermas will count as retaining a 'theoretical approach'
will be counted by an incredulous Lyotard as a 'metanarrative.' Anything that
abandons such an approach will be counted by Habermas as 'neoconservative,'
because it drops the notions which have been used to justify the various reforms
which have marked the history of the Western democracies since the Enlightenment, and which are still being used to criticize the socioeconomic institutions of
both the Free and the Communist worlds. Abandoning a standpoint which is, if
not transcendental, at least 'universalistic,' seems to Habermas to betray the social
hopes which have been central to liberal politics.

"So we find French critics of Habermas ready to abandon liberal politics in order to avoid universalistic philosophy, and Habermas trying to hang on to universalistic philosophy, with all its problems, in order to support liberal politics." Rorty,
"Habermas and Lyotard," p. 172.

    6. Bacon, *Advancement of Learning*, in *Works*, 3:422. For a similar contrast

in Aristotle, see *De sophisticis elenchis* 34.183b36–184a6. See also Quintilian, *Institutes* 5.10. These are traditional rhetorical attempts to distinguish rhetoric from sophistic, or, in my terms, prudence from heuristic opportunism. For an account of how commonplaces function persuasively and politically in a promptuary art, see also M. A. Screech, "Commonplaces of Law, Proverbial Wisdom, and Philosophy," p. 128: "Commonplaces are, by definition, passages of general application, a leading text cited in argument, used precisely because it will be recognized as generally authoritative."

7. For an explicit recognition of the importance of promptuary for a politics of style, see Pocock, "'The Onely Politician,'" p. 286: "Felix Raab's initial premiss about Machiavelli is the same as Bacon's: he described things as they were, not as they ought to be. He was therefore bound to offend Tudor Englishmen, who lived in a universe heavily furnished with means of legitimation and sanctification and were at the same time so keenly aware of the world's insecurity that they put these means to constant and incessant use."

8. Struever, "Machiavelli and the Available Language of Morality," p. 16. See also p. 19: "Both the prince and the counsellor fill roles equally lacking in ritualistic, ceremonial, unproblematic constraints." For the different ways in which both the traditional ruler and Machiavelli's new prince act in self-fulfilling manners, see Chapter 4, below.

9. Greene, *The Light in Troy*, p. 38.

10. Marx, the paradigm case of a metahistorian, talks with great sophistication in the *Eighteenth Brumaire* about the legitimating function of the past as a matter of style, but he claims that the proletarian revolution, unlike earlier revolutions, will not be able to clothe its actions in the glorifying garments of the past. Struever, in a remark that we shall return to, says, "If *The Prince* expresses a strategy of legitimation, it legitimises not politics, but theorising about politics" ("Machiavelli and the Available Language of Morality," p. 13).

11. For Aristotle on tautologies in definitions, see *Topics* 6.3.129b1. For the way Machiavelli locates a new field for prudence, see Greene, "The End of Discourse," p. 60: "Machiavelli's effort to clear a conceptual space resembles the prince's effort to clear a politico-geographical space on which to impose his will and his order. The metaphor commonly applied to the prince's activity, the imposition of form on matter, can equally be applied to the writer's activity."

12. Quentin Skinner, *The Foundations of Modern Political Thought*, 1:131.

13. Stanley Fish, *Is There a Text in This Class?* p. 182, talks about "what Roland Barthes calls variously 'classical language,' the ideology of the reference, and, most suggestively, the language of 'bad faith.' The faith is bad because it is a faith in the innocence and transparency of the mind and its ability to process and elucidate a meaning of which it is independent."

14. Above I claimed that the hereditary monarch relies on what Greene calls sacramental imitation. If Machiavelli cannot move beyond his discovery that anything can be a model, example, and precedent for anything, then he is left in Greene's second form of imitation, eclectic or exploitative. Greene's account describes what I have been calling heuristics: "A second type of imitation appears in any number of Petrarch's Latin and vernacular poems alike, where quite simply allusions, echoes,

phrases, and images jostle each other indifferently. . . . We might call this type *eclectic* or *exploitative,* since it essentially treats all traditions as stockpiles to be drawn upon ostensibly at random. History becomes a vast container whose contents can be disarranged endlessly without suffering damage." Greene, *The Light in Troy,* p. 39.

15. J. H. Hexter, "*Il Principe* and *lo stato,*" in *The Vision of Politics on the Eve of the Reformation* (New York: Basic Books, 1972), quoted with approval by Pocock in *The Machiavellian Moment,* pp. 175–76. Hexter and others think that the only alternative to automatic security, security as rest, is instability, because they do not see how Machiavelli defines security in a fashion more consonant with the new prince's activities.

16. The shift from military affairs, where there is something to learn, to handling one's subjects, where the invention of arguments is called for, parallels the shift within Aristotle's treatment of deliberative rhetoric from *Rhetoric* 1.4, where the subjects on which the orator advises are listed and he is told to acquire political knowledge, to 1.5–7, which offer the materials of argument, matter for rhetoric and not knowledge. For the idea of becoming the heir to history, see Pocock, *Politics, Language, and Time,* pp. 225–26: "The past consists of many recorded actions and images of authority, of which the greater part must be acceptable to the conservative as well as to [the radical]; these may be selected and re-arranged so as to provide a new image of the past and the sort of authority it exercises upon the present, counter-interpretations may be put forward and their rival claims may be discussed. Since the discussion of alternative versions of the past and their relation to the present is what we mean by historiography, we may risk the hypothesis that the beginnings of historiography are to be found when, in a literate tradition, an attempt is made to alter not so much the received facts of the past as the kind of authority which they exercise over the present." See also Paul Veyne, *Comment on ecrit l'histoire,* p. 6: "The citing of sources, scholarly annotation, we might even say all 'scientific' history, if we judge science by its method, came from religious or juridical controversy (the latter when the historians of two rival princes quoted authentic acts which established the rights of their master of some province). Scholarly annotation had its origin in polemic quibbling; people beat each other over the head with proofs before sharing them with the other members of the 'scientific community.'"

17. Machiavelli "implies that military situations are relatively simple two-sided affairs in which contestants fight to solve problems they cannot otherwise avoid. Political situations, on the other hand, require the discourse of the agora or forum and politics is but one alternative to a variety of options open to a man of action. Politics is not war and society is not a *battleground.*" I. Hannaford, "Machiavelli's Concept of *Virtù,*" p. 188. See also Nancy Struever, "The Study of Language," p. 406: Machiavelli used a "formally-coded perception of choice that deals . . . with the choices of the public world and the public language, rather than with those of a domain of erudition." For complications introduced by erudition in the *Discourses on Livy,* see my last two chapters.

18. Struever, "Topics in History," pp. 69–70. See also Jack D'Amico, *Knowledge and Power in the Renaissance,* p. 58: "Active success here and now requires thor-

ough understanding of the qualities customarily called virtues and vices. . . . Since [new princes] must know how to manipulate men and are concerned about glory, they must understand the terms by which men value others. They must be imaginative enough to become the embodiment of what those terms mean, while standing apart from them enough to manipulate and perhaps shape belief in a new way." Maintaining the proper connection and proper distance from the conventional virtues and conventional models for imitation is Machiavelli's equivalent of the last two kinds of imitation in Greene's classification, the types that surpass the initial pair, his ceremonial and eclectic, my algorithmic and heuristic: "The technique of eclectic imitation . . . could reconcile within its own frame momentary conflicts of heterogeneous motifs; it could tolerate the counterpoint of the voices it brought together; but it could not find out the drama of that counterpoint at a deeper pitch of conflict. When that conflict is sounded, we are already dealing with another type of imitation, . . . which could be termed *heuristic.* Heuristic imitations come to us advertising their derivation from the subtexts they carry with them, but having done that, they proceed to *distance themselves* from the subtexts and force us to recognize the poetic distance traversed. . . . Heuristic imitation shades off into a fourth and last type, which is not altogether distinct from it. . . . This type could be said to grow out of heuristic imitation in such a way as to respond to the radical incompleteness just analyzed. . . . The fourth imitative strategy . . . had to expose the vulnerability of the subtext while exposing itself to the subtext's potential aggression. It had to prove its historical courage and artistic good faith by leaving room for a two-way current of mutual criticism between authors and between eras. . . . This fourth type of imitation might be called dialectical." Greene, *The Light in Troy,* pp. 40, 43, 45.

19. In my first chapter I showed the way Machiavelli used topics to organize his argument, but did not say much about what topics were, or what their use committed Machiavelli to or allowed him to do. Earlier in this chapter, I contrasted two uses of topics, for invention and as ready-made resources available to the memory and to promptuary arts. Values function in argument in both those ways. For a useful exposition that offers good reason for calling topics "values" and for distinguishing topical or inventive from promptuary values see John Dewey, "Logic of Judgments of Practice," pp. 519–20: "As given, they are *not* determinate values. They are not *objects* of valuation; they are *data for* a valuation. . . . Were they already definite values, they would not be estimated; they would be stimuli to direct response. If a man had already decided that cheapness constituted value, he would simply take the cheapest suit offered. . . . A value, in short, means a *consideration,* and a consideration does not mean an existence merely, but an existence having a claim upon judgment. Value judged is not existential quality noted, but is the influence attached by judgment to a given existential quality in determining judgment."

20. I explore this point for Aristotle in considerable detail in "Aristotle's Genealogy of Morals." For a different approach to Aristotle on incommensurable ultimate goods, see David Wiggins, "Weakness of Will."

21. The parallel with Aristotle remains. See the discussion of liberality in *Ethics* 4.1, where the usual type of prodigal man (οἱ πολλοὶ τῶν ἀσώτων, 1121a30) gives

and takes excessively, i.e., inconsiderately and from any source and to any object (b1–3), and so the prodigal takes a good, helping others, and takes it as unqualified. In the same way, the vice of injustice, *pleonexia*, also makes a good unqualified, as cowardice elevates saving one's own life to an unqualified good and rashness makes saving a comrade an unqualified good.

22. Kenneth Burke, "Interaction: Dramatism," p. 449: "Mechanical models might best be analyzed, not as downright antidramatistic, but as fragments of the dramatistic. For whatever humanist critics might say about the 'dehumanizing' effects of the machine, it is a characteristically *human* invention, conceived by the perfecting of some human aptitudes and the elimination of others (thus in effect being not inhuman, but man's powerful 'caricature' of himself—a kind of mighty homunculus)." See also John Keegan, *The Face of Battle*, p. 296: "There is an important psychological trick to be played before a breakthrough can occur—and which . . . has to be pulled off in *both* armies, the attacking and the defending: that of getting their soldiers to stand. . . . Easy victories, between equals, almost never stick. Battle, therefore, is essentially a moral conflict. It requires, if it is to take place, a mutual and sustained act of will by two contending parties and, if it is to result in a decision, the moral collapse of one of them." And again (p. 335): "'Decision' . . . is a concept which military historians use in an ambiguous fashion. By 'decisive battle' they can mean simply a battle which has a result, which ends in a clear-cut victory of one side over the other; but by it also a battle whose results cause some real shift in the direction of human affairs far away from the battlefield."

23. Mazzeo, "Hell vs. Hell: From Dante to Machiavelli," in *Renaissance and Seventeenth-Century Studies*, p. 107. This essay is also a good source for some of the history and some observations about the richness of the details in Machiavelli's revision of this myth. Fraud in Machiavelli is a specifically human bestial method. Analogously, there is a set of specifically human bestial motives: the perverse desires explored by Aristotle under intemperance, and especially the tyrannically infinite desires he refers to in *Politics* 2.

24. McCanles, "Machiavelli's 'Principe,'" p. 8. See also p. 3: *Il Principe* "is finally not a referential text. Though it initially gestures toward validating itself by evoking its foundations in a world of transtextual 'real events,' these gestures are often empty, referring to nothing other than the discourses in which men have projected, carried out and interpreted their own enterprises and those of others, which the discourse of *Il Principe* replicates within itself mimetically." If McCanles's reading is pushed to an extreme, then rhetoric is indeed reduced to sophistic, unless these "often empty" gestures are subject to some sort of control. See p. ooo above for the way McCanles himself responds to this difficulty.

25. Colish, "Cicero's *De officiis* and Machiavelli's *Prince*," p. 87.

26. Struever, "Historical Rhetoric," p. 12.

27. Nancy Struever, "Renaissance Ethics: The Invention of an Edifying Past," p. 18: "After he treats Borgia's raw political capacity in chapter 7, Machiavelli contrasts in chapter 8 of *The Prince* the goals of glory and power in his narrative of the tyrant Agathocles. Agathocles gained pure power and lost glory; the brilliance, effulgence of glory represents a proper goal, while raw power is unworthy; efful-

gent glory denotes through and by history true princeliness." See also Pitkin, *Fortune Is a Woman*, p. 122: "It is in principle better to act even if no favorable consequences are to be expected, because there is more at stake than the consequences of any particular action — namely, an active, autonomous stance toward life."

28. Maurice Merleau-Ponty, *Signs*, pp. 211–12: "While men are trying not to be afraid, they begin to make themselves feared by others; and they transfer to others the aggression that they push back from themselves, as if it were absolutely necessary to offend or be offended," quoted by O'Neill, *Sociology as a Skin Trade* (p. 108), who comments: "Human aggression is not simply a conflict of animal or physical forces, but a polarity within a dialectic of intersubjective recognition or alienation. Political power never rests upon naked force but always presumes a ground of opinion and consensus within a margin of potential conflict and violence that is crossed only when this common sense is outraged."

29. McCanles, "Machiavelli's 'Principe,'" p. 9.

4. Paradigms and Princes

1. Kahn historicizes this double effect of rhetoric that I distinguish into Socrates' inquiry and his followers' merely destructive practices; she claims that initially, rhetoric liberated inquiry and action from traditional authorities, but later turned on itself and destroyed the prospect of effective action. For example: "The 'crisis' in medieval thought, which Eugenio Garin and others have described, involved a breakdown of traditional social, political, and religious authorities that at first led to a more flexible sense of human potentiality and a more positive sense of the human realm of contingency in which persuasion and action could take place. (Pico's *Oration on the Dignity of Man* is emblematic of this new sense of possibility.) But while this crisis created the conditions that were favorable to the renewed interest in classical attitudes towards rhetoric, it also contained the seeds of the eventual decline of this classical ideal. . . . The humanists' pragmatic critique of medieval notions of authority undermined the authority of their own pragmatism." Kahn, *Rhetoric, Prudence, and Skepticism*, p. 48. Pitkin, on the other hand, locates such restraint primarily in circumstances, rather than in the methods and practices themselves. "In a context of general virtue and public spirit, the unmasking of a deceit is salutary; but if suspicion becomes so widespread that there is no more trust, men are rendered incapable of citizenship and real manhood." *Fortune Is a Woman*, p. 101.

2. Stephen A. Dinan, "The Particularity of Moral Knowledge," pp. 69–70: "Some universals are instantiated in the same way in all particulars which exemplify them. The nature of these universals is not dependent upon the particular case, but is the same in all cases. While the adequacy of our understanding of what is common to a number of particulars may depend upon the adequacy of our experience of them, it makes no difference for our understanding *which* particulars we experience so long as they exemplify the same universal.

"[But] what makes one action just, brave or kind is not the same as what makes another action just, brave or kind; the form of moral universals *changes* from case to case. Moral universals, therefore, are not univocal. Knowledge of such universals depends very much on which individual case is used to exemplify them for the knower, because the meaning of the universal itself differs somewhat from case to case. . . . Moreover, unlike the accidental differences which mark instances of univocal universals, the differences between cases which exemplify moral universals are morally significant. For it is not justice in general that must be done, for example, but that particular form of action which can be called just in the concrete situation."

See also Clifford Geertz, *The Interpretation of Cultures,* pp. 25–26: "Theoretical formulations hover so low over the interpretations they govern that they don't make much sense or hold much interest apart from them. This is so, not because they are not general (if they are not general, they are not theoretical), but because, stated independently of their applications, they seem either commonplace or vacant. One can, and this is in fact how the field progresses conceptually, take a line of theoretical attack developed in connection with one exercise in ethnographic interpretation and employ it in another, pushing it forward to greater precision and broader relevance; but one cannot write a 'General Theory of Cultural Interpretation.' Or, rather, one can, but there seems to be little profit in it, because the essential task of theory building here is not to codify abstract regularities but to make thick description possible; not to generalize across cases but to generalize within them."

3. Bruce A. Ackerman, "The Storrs Lectures," points to the way the *Federalist Papers* are similarly concerned with a problem of representation. See especially p. 1028: "Rather than trying for phony realism by supposing that Congress (or any other institution) *is* the People, the Federalist Constitution's first objective is to paint a picture of government which vigorously asserts that Congress is merely a 'representation' of the People, not the thing itself.

"The brilliant, but paradoxical way that Publius makes this point is by proliferating the modes of representation governing normal politics. In Publian hands, the separation of powers operates as a complex machine which encourages each official to question the extent to which other constitutional officials are successfully representing the People's true political wishes. Thus, while each officeholder will predictably insist that *he* speaks with the authentic accents of the People themselves, representatives in other institutions will typically find it in their interest to deny that their rivals have indeed represented the People in a fully satisfactory way."

Ackerman distinguishes two kinds of representation, "semiotic" and "mimetic," and finds the Federalists using the former, a self-conscious relation between text and reality. In the same way, Machiavelli draws attention to, rather than suppresses, the representative character of the relation between individual political actors and kinds of politics. Machiavelli supplies an important corrective here, since his texts are self-consciously representational in this sense, without in any way being concerned with the quite different concept of representative government.

4. Richard Bernstein, *Restructuring,* p. 208: "The most perspicuous way of stating Kuhn's central insight concerning 'paradigm-switches,' or the decision among competing theoretical orientations, is that while this involves rational processes — and is not a matter of whim, arbitrary fiat, or irrational decision — our standard theories of rationality are not rich enough to illuminate these processes adequately.

Notes to Chapter 4, Page 97

Even though Kuhn stresses the importance of 'persuasive techniques' and 'conversion', it is perfectly clear that he wants to distinguish between rational means of persuasion and nonrational or irrational means."

5. My claim that it is wrong to think that paradigms are either automatically comparable or not, but rather that they must be made commensurable, is echoed in Williams' distinction between real and notional confrontations. See, e.g., *Ethics and the Limits of Philosophy*, p. 160: "We should distinguish between *real* and *notional* confrontations. A real confrontation between two divergent outlooks occurs at a given time if there is a group of people for whom each of the outlooks is a real option. A notional confrontation, by contrast, occurs when some people know about two divergent outlooks, but at least one of those outlooks does not present a real option. The idea of a 'real option' is largely, but not entirely, a social notion. An outlook is a real option for a group either if it already is their outlook or if they could go over to it; and they could go over to it if they could live inside their actual historical circumstances and retain their hold on reality, not engage in extensive self-deception, and so on."

P. K. Feyerabend, *Against Method*, p. 274, similarly notes ways in which questions of commensurability can be dissolved by ignoring their practical dimension. "Using an 'instrumentalistic' interpretation of the theories which sees in them no more than instruments for the classification of certain 'facts' one gets the impression that there is some common subject matter. Using a 'realistic' interpretation that tries to understand the theory in its own terms such a subject matter seems to disappear although there is a definite feeling (unconscious instrumentalism) that it must exist."

For further awareness of the tactical dimensions of commensuration, see Ernest Gellner, "An Ethic of Cognition," pp. 168–70, who argues that ideologies or belief systems "are all bilingual. Though they speak a language which is closed and generates a full-circle world, they must invariably — if only for the purposes of proselytizing, defence, and so forth — also entertain diplomatic-conceptual relations with other worlds, and meet on more or [less] neutral ground, or at any rate ground not wholly controlled by either side. . . . One way of looking at empiricism is as an attempt to codify and make general, absolute, the conventions of Neutral-speak. Hence that need to define 'experience', i.e. what counts as a legitimate card which can be dealt in the course of the game. But leaving aside the technical difficulties of properly codifying empiricism, by adequately defining its terms, what are the reasons for holding it valid? It says, on this interpretation, that Neutral-speak is good-speak, the best speak; not just an interim lingua franca for use in buffer zones; and that all Closed-speaks are bad speaks, and should be eschewed even when the power and diplomatic situation does not actually compel us to do so. We should give up Closed-speak even when we can get away with not doing so."

See, finally, Richard Rorty, *Mirror of Nature*, p. 316: "By 'commensurable' I mean able to be brought under a set of rules which will tell us how rational agreement can be reached on what would settle the issue on every point where statements seem to conflict. These rules tells us how to construct an ideal situation, in which all residual disagreements will be seen to be 'noncognitive' or merely verbal, or else merely temporary — capable of being resolved by doing something further.

What matters is that there should be agreement about what would have to be done if a resolution *were* to be achieved."

6. N. R. Hanson shows the way Copernicus and Galileo make Ptolemaic astronomy into a systematic astronomy for the first time in its history in order to make it comparable to the new world system, and therefore liable to comparison and refutation; see *Constellations and Conjectures*, esp. p. 196. Pierre Bourdieu recognizes the practical, circumstantial character of this act of making something explicit: "The adherence expressed in the doxic relation to the social world is the absolute form of recognition of legitimacy through misrecognition of arbitrariness, since it is unaware of the very question of legitimacy, which arises from competition for legitimacy, and hence from conflict between groups claiming to possess it." *Outlines*, p. 168. The relevance of reflections such as Bourdieu's for interparadigmatic comparison is brought out by Ernest Gellner, "The Savage and the Modern Mind," p. 175: "An individual or society already capable of distinguishing clearly between the inner circle of the testable, and the outer circle of untestable accretions to it, is already more than nine-tenths of the way towards the acceptance of the empiricist ideal. . . . A society which is truly immersed in the transcendent does not see or recognize such orderly lines of demarcation. Quite the contrary." And again, on p. 178: "There is a systematic difference in the distribution of the entrenched clauses of the sacred . . . as between savages and modern thought-systems. In a traditional thought-system, the sacred or the crucial is more extensive, more untidily dispersed, and much more pervasive. In a modern thought-system, it is tidier, narrower, as it were economical, based on some intelligible principle, and tends not to be diffused among the detailed aspects of life. Fewer hostages are given to fortune; or, looking at it from the other end, much less of the fabric of life and society benefits from reinforcement from the sacred and entrenched convictions."

In this sense, the brash, usurping new prince represents a return to the barbaric condition before institutions acquired their own stability and life history apart from individual rulers, and traditional politics, with its more developed system of protocols and deference, embodies a hierarchy without which civilization is impossible. For the relevant scientific analogy, see H. R. Post, "Correspondence," p. 238: "It is true that the interpretation of theoretic terms changes as a consequence of a revolution. The constitutional character of many an office of state changes when a monarchy is overthrown and a republic replaces it. But the function of that office may well remain almost the same as it was under the monarchy. Again, in government the nominally higher functionaries may play a lesser, mainly representative role. There is a certain loss of content as we climb higher and higher in a theory to increasingly abstract, more general laws. The higher levels usually are uninterpreted to an increasing extent. Many of the most general laws at present are of a rather formal character. . . . In countries with unstable governments there may yet be a stable Civil Service carrying on the machinery of government at lower levels. Similarly, I claim that even the most radical revolutions in science have saved not only the phenomena, the population of facts, but a good deal of the lower parts of the old theory as well."

7. Roger Scruton, *The Meaning of Conservatism*, pp. 11, 20. Cf. Bernard Crick,

In Defence of Politics, p. 117: "The conservative wants to appear as the well-bred product of a landed aristocracy. Property is then thought of as outside politics, something which should never be touched by political enactments. . . . The attempt to put property above politics merely provokes the attempt to take away property without politics." And again, p. 127: "The conservative contributes to politics like anyone else by trying to gain or maintain his interests – but his claim to be non-political only invites the suspicion that he does not always act in a political manner. He likes to be thought above politics. He prefers to settle public matters privately.

8. Lawrence Stone, "Education and Modernization," esp. p. 225, which includes a quotation from C. M. Cipolla, *Guns and Sails* (London, 1965), pp. 120–21: Stone talks about the attitude "of the Chinese when first faced with Western superiority in military technology and astronomy in the early seventeenth century. The intense cultural pride of the classically trained Chinese mandarin class prevented any assimilation. 'Military defeat was the technical reason why Western knowledge should be acquired, but it was also the psychological reason why it should not be.' The Chinese preferred admitting military defeat to the psychological shock of facing up to the inferiority of their national literary culture when challenged by Western science and engineering."

9. Alasdair MacIntyre, "Epistemological Crises," p. 459: "One of the signs that a tradition is in crisis is that its accustomed ways for relating *seems* and *is* begins to break down. Thus the pressures of scepticism become more urgent and attempts to do the impossible, to refute scepticism once and for all, become projects of central importance to the culture and not mere private academic enterprises. Just this happens in the late middle ages and the sixteenth century. Inherited modes of ordering experience reveal too many possibilities of interpretation. . . . Instrumentalism, like attempts to refute scepticism, is characteristically a sign of a tradition in crisis." For one formulation of the rhetorical, as opposed to algorithmic, relation between the implicit and the explicit, see Bourdieu, *Outlines*, p. 168: "The critique which brings the undiscussed into discussion, the unformulated into formulation, has as the condition of its possibility objective crisis, which, in breaking the immediate fit between the subjective structures, destroys self-evidence practically. It is when the social world loses its character as a natural phenomenon that the question of the natural or conventional (*phusei* or *nomo*) character of social facts can be raised." Renford Bambrough captures the military metaphors in "Conflict and the Scope of Reason" (p. 81) when he says: "A battlefield is a piece of common ground. I cannot fight unless I can find you and catch up with you. We cannot be in conflict without being in contact. Even in literal cases of fighting there is talk about being in contact with the enemy." See also Keegan, *The Face of Battle*, p. 16: "In Europe's wars of decolonization, the object of 'the other side' has, of course, been to avoid facing a decision at any given time or place, rightly presuming the likelihood of its defeat in such circumstances."

10. Richard Vernon's "Politics as Metaphor" explores some of the confusing ambiguities of "revolution" in Kuhn: "Kuhn . . . weakens his case by effectively conflating two pictures of revolution, and in treating the evidence for revolution in one sense as evidence for revolution in quite a difference sense. In the style of

John Locke, he envisages a 'political society' of science which survives change, and hence he regards revolution as at bottom an episode of (metaphorical) violence; yet, in the style of Karl Marx, he also envisages revolution as epochal change, as a rift in the continuity of society itself and not merely as an alteration of its (metaphorically) 'governing' apparatus."

11. Cf. Bourdieu's discussion of the difference between "overt (physical or economic) violence [and] symbolic violence — *censored, euphemized*, i.e. unrecognizable, socially recognized violence." *Outlines*, p. 191. See also his discussion of "officializing strategies," designed to "transmute 'egoistic', private, particular interests . . . into disinterested, collective, publicly avowable, legitimate interests" (and here we can say that such officializing strategies exist only within an established political paradigm): "Strategies aimed at producing 'regular' practices are one category, among others, of officializing strategies, the object of which is to transmute 'egoistic', private, particular interests (notions definable only within the relationship between a social unity and the encompassing social unit at a higher level) into disinterested, collective, publicly avowable, legitimate interests. In the absence of political institutions endowed with an effective monopoly of legitimate violence, political action proper can only be exercised by the effect of officialization and thus presupposes the *competence* (in the sense of a capacity socially recognized in a public authority) required in order to manipulate the collective definition of the situation in such a way as to bring it closer to the official definition of the situation and thereby to win the means of mobilizing the largest possible group, the opposite strategy tending to reduce the same situation to a merely private affair. To possess the capital of authority necessary to impose a definition of the situation, especially in the moments of crisis when the collective judgment falters, is to be able to mobilize the group by solemnizing, officializing, and thus universalizing a private incident." Ibid., p. 40. In this way political conservatives think that property should be "above politics," not treated as a political commodity or a form of force, and intellectuals see reason as an alternative to force, while others see reason just as a different form of force, one to which they lack access.

12. Vernon usefully points out the way that the fact that a revolutionary situation is a "state of war" does not mean that all arguments during the revolution are irrational: in talking about Locke's theory of consent, he shows that "we cannot put to any *institutional* basis for legitimacy other than consent; but that does not mean that there is no *standard* higher than consent, a view which belongs to quite a different notion of change, within which it would be impossible to make sense of either politics or science, for reality would be reduced to a sort of emanation of will." "Politics as Metaphor," p. 533.

13. R.G.A. Dolby, "The Transmission of Science," p. 22, discusses the "geological controversy in Edinburgh at the beginning of the nineteenth century. The reasoning of each side seemed circular to the other as it depended on so many assumptions supposed only by naive faith." Michael Bradie and Mark Gromko's essay "The Status of the Principle of Natural Selection" contains a list of alternative candidates, each with their champions, for the status of natural selection: tautology, empirical hypothesis, and metaphysical (heuristic) hypothesis. See N. R. Hanson's detailed discussion of the status of Newton's second law in *Patterns of Discovery*

for the way a principle can be regarded as possessing both formal necessity and empirical content. Bourdieu, *Outlines*, p. 164, offers a sociological explanation for the necessity, and emptiness, of tautologous first principles: "Schemes of thought and perception can produce the objectivity that they do only by producing mis-recognition of the limits of cognition that they make possible, thereby founding immediate adherence, in the doxic mode, to the world of tradition experienced as a 'natural world' and taken for granted. The instruments of knowledge of the so-cial world are in this case (objectively) political instruments which contribute to the reproduction of the social world by producing immediate adherence to the world, seen as self-evident and undisputed, of which they are the product and of which they reproduce the structures in a transformed form."

14. Crick, *In Defence of Politics*, p. 174.

15. Isaiah Berlin, "The Originality of Machiavelli," p. 65. In his comments on Berlin's essay, Williams makes it clear why problems of incommensurability and conflicts of values are practical rather than logical problems: "Value-conflict is not necessarily pathological at all, but something necessarily involved in human values, and to be taken as central by an adequate understanding of them. I also think, though Berlin may not, that where conflict needs to be overcome, this 'need' is not of a purely logical character, not a requirement of pure rationality, but rather a kind of social or personal need, the pressure of which will be felt in some his-torical circumstances rather than others." Williams, *Moral Luck*, p. 72. See also Pitkin, *Fortune Is a Woman*, p. 5: "Machiavelli nowhere says that politics is or should be different from the rest of human life, or that political action is governed by different principles than personal conduct."

16. Cf. Pocock, *Machiavellian Moment*, p. 225. "If we are to evaluate constitu-tions solely by their results, we shall presumably use the same set of values as cri-teria in all cases; but it is perfectly well known that different forms of government give priority to different values, so that we cannot proceed pragmatically unless we standardize our values in advance." The rhetorical equivalent of this lack of standards is expressed by Cicero in the *De oratore* 9.36–37, where Cicero main-tains that since different audiences have different ideas of what is best, the orator must adapt himself to those differences. There is no best orator as such.

17. The difference between the logical possibilities of segregation and of con-flict, and the equivalent practical possibilities, is noted within the literature on com-mensurability. See, e.g., Larry Briskman's useful distinction between "conflicting" and "competing" theories: "While two theories may conflict simply in virtue of their logical relations, they can only compete relative to an explanatory problem-situation." "Historicist Relativism," p. 252.

18. MacIntyre, "Epistemological Crises," p. 461: "A tradition not only embodies the narrative of an argument, but is only to be recovered by an argumentative re-telling of the narrative which will itself be in conflict with other argumentative retellings. Every tradition is therefore always in danger of lapsing into incoherence and when a tradition does so lapse it sometimes can only be recovered by a revo-lutionary reconstitution."

19. See Williams, *Moral Luck*, p. 20, quoted above, Introduction, n. 4. See also John Cooper, "Aristotle on the Goods of Fortune."

20. Berlin, "Originality of Machiavelli," p. 64. To take one of many examples of Machiavelli's rejecting a compromise between these two kinds of ultimate value, see the *Discourses on Livy* 1.26: "Men generally decide upon a middle course, which is most hazardous; for they know neither to be entirely good or entirely bad." See also 1.30 and 2.23. Similarly, these are the grounds many thinkers use to reject the ideal of a mixed government, with its "checks and balances."

21. Berlin, "Originality of Machiavelli," p. 79.

22. Pitkin (*Fortune Is a Woman*, p. 50) derives from Arendt (citing p. 120 of Arendt's *Between Past and Future*) a way of giving a political characterization to this demand for exclusivity: "It was not just any founding that the Romans considered sacred, as the Greeks had founded new *poleis* here and there. For Rome, what mattered was the one, unique, unrepeatable founding, the special beginning of the sacred tradition 'and the equally un-Greek experience of the sanctity of house and hearth . . . form the deeply political content of Roman religion. In contrast to Greece, where piety depended on the immediately revealed presence of the gods, here religion literally meant re-ligare: to be tied back, obligated to the enormous, almost superhuman and hence always legendary effort to lay the foundations, to build the cornerstone, to found for eternity. To be religious meant to be tied to the past.' The concept of authority originates in that Roman context, from the Latin verb *augere*, to augment. What is augmented by those in authority is the original, sacred foundation; one becomes an authority by merging with and furthering that traditional authority. An authority is someone who is the author of other men's deeds and is himself authored by still earlier forefathers."

23. See Crick, *In Defence and Politics*, p. 140: "The man who treats everything as a matter of principle cannot be happy with politics. . . . Whoever says 'we must never compromise our ideals' is either dooming himself to frustration or pledging himself to authoritarianism. Ideals are valuable as ideals and not as plans for a new order of immediate things. . . . The man who speaks the language of absolute demands — say a 'guaranteed living wage' or 'the right of property' (or of compensation for property taken) — should at least be expected to realize that these things are gainable or relinquishable in a multitude of different forms. They are, in a word, negotiable — political not total commitments. To entertain politics at all is inevitably to enter into a world of morality in which one is aware of sacrifice as much as of aspirations . . . and in which one is aware of public responsibility as well as of private conscience."

24. As I mentioned in the Introduction, the relevant classical allegory here is Proteus, who is thought to be the embodiment either of prudent adaptability to shifting fortune, or of opportunistic amorality and loss of one's character as a way of staying in tune with fortune. For an example of a Renaissance use of the figure of Proteus see Boyle, *Rhetoric and Reform*, quoted above, Introduction, n. 5. For this threat in Machiavelli, see Pitkin, *Fortune Is a Woman*, p. 41: "But now the costs of the human capacity for self-fashioning are more in evidence. The mistrustful self, it seems, stands in danger of losing its self altogether. Uncertain of its own identity, it profoundly needs external confirmation from its friends, yet it can never securely define anyone as friend. And it is powerfully tempted to identify precisely with its most impressive enemies. 'The best remedy that can be used against a de-

sign of the enemy is to do willingly what he intends you shall do by force.' (*Art of War* bk. 4 [G656])."

25. Berlin, "Originality of Machiavelli," pp. 69–70. See also Greene, "The End of Discourse," p. 68, who sees this radical choice as a destruction of the entire teaching of *The Prince:* "The lonely ruler, shifting his balance and his policy, remaking his own character as he remakes his style, listening for each whisper of change in the times, will nonetheless falter in the end from a tragic insufficiency of pliancy.

"This failure of the prince betokens the failure of the analyst whose admission of circumstances has caused his conceptual space definitively to implode. Stage by stage, he has withdrawn from dogmatism to qualification to contradiction to a surrender before pure contingency."

Recall, too, the quotations from Sextus Empiricus and Cicero in my Introduction, exemplifying the common traditional accusation that rhetoric and prudence fail because they require an "admission of circumstances" which prevents their reduction to method.

26. Williams, *Moral Luck*, p. 20.

27. For another variation on this theme, especially apposite here, see Charles Mercier, *A New Logic*, whose distinction between the logic of consistency and the logic of empirical reasoning is parallel to my distinction between algorithmics and prudential reasoning. See esp. pp. 194–95: "In the logic of consistency, the proposition is the grist that is put into the inferential mill; and the sole function of inference is to grind it up, and present it in a new form. Until it is furnished with a proposition, and a complete proposition, inference cannot begin. But in most of the reasonings of actual life, the material presented to the reasoning process is not a complete, but an incomplete proposition; and the main task of reasoning, the sole task of empirical reasoning, is the completion of the incomplete propositions that are continually confronting us. In short, the task of inference is the extraction of the implications of propositions; the task of Empirical Reasoning is the solving of problems. The aim of Inference is the maintenance of Consistency; the aim of Empirical Reasoning is the discovery of Truth."

28. Keegan, *The Face of Battle*, p. 296: "There is an important psychological trick to be played before a breakthrough can occur—and which . . . has to be pulled off in *both* armies, the attacking and the defending: that of getting their soldiers to stand. . . . Easy victories, between equals, almost never stick. Battle, therefore, is essentially a moral conflict. It requires, if it is to take place, a mutual and sustained act of will by two contending parties and, if it is to result in a decision, the moral collapse of one of them." And again, p. 335: "'Decision' . . . is a concept which military historians use in an ambiguous fashion. By 'decisive battle' they can mean simply a battle which has result, which ends in a clear-cut victory of one side over the other; but by it also a battle whose results cause some real shift in the direction of human affairs far away from the battlefield." This difference in meaning reflects the two meanings of revolution Vernon finds in "Politics as Metaphor." See also Imre Lakatos, "The Role of Crucial Experiments in Science."

29. Greene, "The End of Discourse," p. 69, says that chapter 26 "radically alters the rhetorical mode from deliberation to apocalypse."

30. Mazzeo, *Renaissance and Seventeenth-Century Studies*, p. 93: "The whole

problem of politics can be summed up in one platitude: the best advice and the most exact implementation of it cannot always succeed. Therefore all attempts at rational prediction must take account of what we might call an irreducible element of chaos, fatality, necessity or ignorance, a realm of darkness whose boundary, however, can never be clearly defined. It may appear as chance or fate, only apparently opposites, and it can only be discovered in action itself. When action succeeds we have experienced freedom and created order, when it fails we have experienced fate or malevolent chance. Historical experience teaches us, according to Machiavelli, that it is possible for will to overcome fate or chance about half of the time, and, unlike many fatalists in the Renaissance who toyed with similar ideas, Machiavelli strikes a new note in giving man a fifty-fifty chance against the malice of the inanimate as well as against the malice and irrationality of the animate."

31. Thomas Kuhn, *Essential Tension*, p. 332.

32. Greene, "The End of Discourse," p. 69: "If in fact he had established with calm logic the prescriptive science his book had seemed to promise, there would be no need for miracles and messiahs." See also Pitkin, *Fortune Is a Woman*, p. 104. "The Founder, one might say, is a fantasy of the impotent; and to the extent that the situation looks utterly hopeless, Machiavelli himself is drawn into the Founder image and yearns for rescue. The attraction of magic is proportional to the apparent hopelessness of action."

33. Pitkin, *Fortune Is a Woman*, p. 54. "The Founder, then, is an unmoved mover, a source of change, not the product of earlier changes, a break in the causal chain of history. He stands out almost like a god among men. He is pure source, not product, one who 'give[s] laws and do[es] not take them from other men.'"

5. The *Discourses on Livy*

1. LaCapra, *Rethinking Intellectual History*, p. 26: "One of the more challenging aspects of recent inquiries into textuality has been the investigation of why textual processes cannot be confined within the bindings of the book. The context or the 'real world' is itself 'textualized' in a variety of ways, and even if one believes that the point of criticism is to change the world, not merely to interpret it, the process and results of change themselves raise textual problems. Social and individual life may fruitfully be seen on the analogy of the text and as involved in textual processes that are often more complicated than the historical imagination is willing to allow."

2. These three—dramatism, constitutionalism, and dialogue—are not an exhaustive set of ways of confronting plural ultimate ends. To mention one more, Mill attempts a different mode of attack in *Utilitarianism*; his apparently direct argument on the choice of ultimate value turns on the notorious ambiguities of the desirable, what can be desired and what ought, by some measure, to be desired. There ought to be still more ways of confronting rather than evading the problem.

3. Pocock points out that the matter on which the mythical founders of republics work has less character of its own than that of the new prince: "Not only is

the legislator's *virtù* related to *fortuna* in a way utterly different from that of the new prince; he is performing an innovation of a different order. He finds his *materia* — the people he is to mold — in a condition so anomic that his *virtù* needs only a sword to impose form upon it; very little is said of the previous structure of accustomed behavior which other innovators displace. Moreover, in imposing form upon matter he is the founder of a political order: Cyrus, Theseus and Romulus founded kingdoms, Lycurgus a polity and Moses a nation in covenant with God. The *stato* — normally employed by Machiavelli and Guicciardini to mean ' rule by some others' — does not appear to denote what the legislator brings into being, a highly viable political community, stabilized by his *virtù* and (at least if it is a republic) the *virtù* of its citizens; a kingdom is stabilized by use and inheritance. By contrast, the new prince does not find matter lacking all form; he takes possession of a society already stabilized by customs of its own." Pocock, *Machiavellian Moment*, p. 175. My contrast, though, is between the matter on which the prince works in comparison with the relatively more determinate matter on which republican *citizens* work. This comparison is analogous to the one Pocock draws between "second causes encroaching upon the figure of *fortuna*" (p. 212), "the concept of corruption tending to replace that of the mere randomness of *fortuna*" (p. 211).

4. The passage continues: "If you are well informed as to what is good or bad among these wares, it will be safe for you to buy doctrines from Protagoras or from anyone else you please: but if not, take care, my dear fellow, that you do not risk your greatest treasure on a toss of the dice. For I tell you there is far more serious risk in the purchase of doctrines than in that of eatables. When you buy victuals and liquors you can carry them off from the dealer or merchant in separate vessels, and before you take them into your body by drinking or eating you can lay them by in your house and take the advice of an expert whom you can call in, as to what is fit to eat or drink and what is not . . . so that in this purchase the risk is not serious. But you cannot carry away doctrines in a separate vessel: you are compelled, when you have handed over the price, to take the doctrine in your very soul by learning it, and so to depart either an injured or a benefited man."

5. Aristotle's point is that people do not dispute over what can be securely known, regardless of whether it is an object of human action, and so the distinction between the realm of choice and the rest is not equivalent to a distinction between nature and convention: "There is no room for deliberation about matters fully ascertained and completely formulated as sciences; such for instance as orthography, for we have no uncertainty as to how a word ought to be spelt" (*Ethics* 3.3.1112b1–3).

6. Aristotle recognizes, of course, that actions that are their own end, including virtuous ones, can be done for the sake of something beyond themselves. An act of justice can be undertaken for the sake of the security of the state. What the idea of an action that is its own end bars, though, is its employment for the sake of *any* end at all, in the way medicine can kill or cure. The two sides of that dilemma allowed Socrates to confront Polus with the claim that rhetors and tyrants do not do what they want, but only what they think best (*Gorgias* 466e). Socrates'

line of questioning depends on the distinction between an activity and its object (467c–468c), which is just the distinction needed here.

7. In another context, Gerald Bruns notes that the skepticism so often connected to rhetoric, in effect, falls in the same uncomfortable middle territory between arts, which do not engage one's character, and prudence, which does: "This doubt is methodical, not personal or ethical; it does not touch the whole man, as does Pyrronism, because it does not stipulate a mode of conduct (for example, withdrawal into silence)." Bruns, *Inventions*, p. 77. While such doubt has its appeal, it also seems to be a technique acquired and employed too easily and casually. It is appropriate to express the same ambivalence about Machiavellian prudence.

8. Of course this "turning to" does not represent an actual act by the historical Machiavelli, finishing *The Prince* and beginning to write the *Discourses*. The evidence about the historical relation between the two texts is complex and, I think, incomplete. That evidence does not bear directly, though, on the career of the character Machiavelli and his role in the history of prudence.

9. See also *Discourses* 1.20: "If . . . two successive good and valorous princes are sufficient to conquer the world, as was the case with Philip of Macedon and Alexander the Great, a republic should be able to do still more, having the power to elect not only two successions, but an infinite number of most competent and virtuous rulers one after the other." Recall, too, Sidney's distinction between nature, which can produce one Cyrus, and art, which can produce many Cyruses. Those attractive features of categorical *virtù* have their less appealing side as well. *Discourses* 2.2: "The hardest of all servitudes is to be subject to a republic, and this for these reasons: first, because it is more enduring, and there is no hope of escaping from it; and secondly, because republics aim to enervate and weaken all other states so as to increase their own power."

10. Pitkin, *Fortune Is a Woman*, p. 81: "Although the Citizen is, like the fox and the Founder, an image of manhood, it embodies *virtù* in a fundamentally different way. For both fox and Founder have *virtù* through their personal, individual autonomy, understood as needing no others, having ties to no others, acting without being acted upon. For the Citizen, by contrast, *virtù* is sharing in a collective autonomy, a collective freedom and glory, yet without loss of individuality. *Virtù* is systemic or relational. Thus it not merely is compatible with, but logically requires, interaction in mutuality with others like oneself. It lies not in isolation from or domination over others, but in shared taking charge of one's objective connections with them. 'Each Man by Himself is Weak,' as a chapter title in the *Discourses* announces, but 'The Populace United is Strong.' When individuals realize this, they act together to pursue the shared public good and thereby sustain it. When they perceive as (if they were) isolated individuals, their actions become both selfish and cowardly, for 'as soon as each man gets to thinking about his personal danger, he becomes worthless and weak,' his *virtù* vanishes; his actions begin to undermine the community and produce his isolation. Citizen *virtù* is thus a matter both of objective activity and of outlook or attitude, each affecting the other. And in both respects, such individual *virtù* is available only in a republic; it presupposes an ethos and an institutional framework. Individuals can achieve only 'such

excellence [*perfezione*]' as the 'way of life (*modo del vivere*)' of their community 'permits.'" Pocock, *Machiavellian Moment*, p. 185, makes a similar point briefly: "Whereas the prince whose *virtù* failed lost his *stato*, the citizens whose republic failed lost their virtue, in the sense of their citizenship." See also ibid., p. 165: "When men are used to obeying a ruler, they do not have to alter their natures in order to obey someone else; but the experience of citizenship . . . sets an indelible mark upon their natures, so that they must indeed become new men if they are to learn willing obedience to a prince."

11. Pocock, *Machiavellian Moment*, pp. 349–50; italics mine. See also 492: "Machiavelli, defining civic values as ultimately incompatible with Christian, had employed the concept of arms to express both the citizen's total devotion to his republic and the notion of a world too harsh in its treatment of noncitizens to profess any universal humanity." See, finally, p. 178: "Each simple virtue must degenerate precisely because it was simple and particular. The problem of the particular was its finitude, its mortality, its instability in time, and once a virtue (itself universal) was embodied in a particular form of government it partook of this general instability."

12. The argumentative advance from skill to virtue is one Socrates frequently employs in confronting the Sophists. His principal question to them has to do with character and identity, not craft. He tells Chaerephon at the beginning of the *Gorgias* to ask Gorgias who he is (447d), and he asks Hippocrates who he will become if he studies with Protagoras. Hippocrates' ensuing embarrassment is symptomatic, because he wants to learn from the Sophists without becoming one himself. That prospect would not be a paradox, or something to be ashamed of, if he were just learning a craft.

13. Aristotle develops the difference between virtue and the arts and sciences, considered as capacities for action, especially in *Metaphysics* 9.2.1046b15–24 and 5.1047b35–1048b35, and in *De anima* 2.5.417b19–26. That the arts serve ends outside themselves while the virtues do not is also noted at the beginning of his treatment of justice: "It is not the same with dispositions ["Εξεις] as with sciences and faculties. It seems that the same faculty or science deals with opposite things; but a disposition or condition which produces a certain result does not also produce the opposite results" (*Ethics* 5.1.1129a12–16).

14. Aristotle shows the way the arts and virtue differ as relations of form to matter not only in the passages cited above, but more explicitly in *De generatione et corruptione* 1.7.324a5–11. One straightforward exposition of Aristotle's point is found in George von Wright, *Varieties of Goodness*, p. 52: "Organs resemble instruments or tools in that they have both morphological and functional characteristics. Faculties again have no morphological features proper to them; in this and other respects they resemble abilities and skills."

15. Aristotle develops these contrasts between the virtues and the arts in the distinction between rational and irrational abilities in the *Metaphysics* and in the section on justice in the *Ethics* (book 5; see esp. 5.1.1129a12–16). Justice is the virtue of character in which the distinction between artistic, or algorithmic, and prudent inferences becomes most urgent because it is the most "productive" of the virtues, since it issues in distributions of goods, and those distributions can be

evaluated independently of the decisions that brought them about. Therefore justice is the one place in Aristotle's discussion of character in which a conflict between an ethics of principles and one of consequences emerges.

16. Pitkin, *Fortune Is a Woman*, p. 68: "Republics, above all, . . . produce human greatness, for the competition of outstanding men may threaten a monarch, but it can only benefit a republic. Therefore, 'excellent men come in larger numbers from republics than from kingdoms, since republics usually honor human wisdom and bravery [*virtù*]; kingdoms fear them.'" As Pitkin puts it, "Republican authority must be exercised in a way that further politicizes the people rather than rendering them quiescent. Its function is precisely to keep a political movement or action that the people have initiated . . . from disintegrating into riot, apathy, or privatization."

17. Pocock, *Machiavellian Moment*, p. 164. See also p. 188: "The *Discorsi* have throughout the focus on those situations in which, because the legislator was imperfect or non-existent, the citizens have been called upon to reform their own *ordini* and themselves — those in which the matter has had to shape itself into form." The idea of "matter shaping itself into form" makes no sense under a technical conception of the relation of matter of form, and, under a physical interpretation, sounds like spontaneous generation. In the context of literary criticism, R. S. Crane, thus, points out: "'Conventional' denotes any characteristic of the matter or technique of a poem the reason for the presence of which cannot be inferred from the necessities of the form envisaged but must be sought in the historical circumstances of its composition. . . . In relation to the nature and inherent necessities of any kind of poetry a convention is thus an accidental attribute, however long-lived or influential it may be." Crane, *Languages of Criticism*, p. 198, n. 62. For a consideration of some of the interrelations between literary and practical conventions in the Renaissance, see Manley, *Convention*.

18. For an ancient version of this *topos*, see Tacitus' *Dialogue on Oratory*. Thucydides applies the topic in the opposite way (1.10): future generations would judge Sparta to be insignificant, because there were no technical achievements and monuments to survive, but practical achievements survive to human memory.

19. Greene, "The End of Discourse," p. 60: The language of *The Prince* "betrays the traces of an academic *disputatio*: 'If you advance this objection, then I reply thus. . . .' "*Disputero come questi principati si possino governare*" (7)['I shall debate how these principalities can be governed" (33)]; the verb adumbrates an adversarial relationship. To extend the circumscribed area of truth requires a felt effort, a courage, a risk, as well as a violence upon convention and morality. Given the resistances, it becomes hard to believe that the extensions outward will come to control all the delimiting space. One suspects that something will always remain to be appropriated. Closure at best, it seems, will fence in a finite territory against the uncharted space always lying outside."

20. Apposite here is Collingwood's contrast, in *The New Leviathan*, of eristic debates pitting false abstractions against each other with dialectical arguments between actually held views, ideas that are practical in the sense developed here: "It is between fictitious entities like this that 'eristic' discussion most loves to get up a dog-fight. The best kind of dog-fight; one in which the combatants, being

fictitious, can never be killed and, being tied together by a dialectical bond, can never run away. [That dialectical bond is the sense in which the old and new politics need each other.] A fight of this kind is the best example of those make-believe discussions which are called 'academic discussions.'" R. G. Collingwood, *The New Leviathan*, p. 193. And about academic discussions, what I have referred to as the set pieces of a textbook, Collingwood says: "Men teach their offspring to use their tongues in a kind of puppy-play where all speech has to be as insignificant as a doll's teacup is empty or a boy's sword harmless; where the talk is only pretence talk or what is called *academic discussions* and the problems talked about only pretence problems or what are called *academic problems*." For another example of the difference between live and "academic," or real and notional, debates, see Ian Hacking, "Proof and Eternal Truths," pp. 178–79: "The concept of formal proof was created in the time of Leibniz to overcome quite specific breakdowns in traditional ontology. The Cartesian concept of anti-proof has the same origin. These concepts were derived, almost unwittingly, to fill a vacuum. We still employ those concepts but live in a vacuum that those concepts cannot fill. Consider the sterility of modern philosophy of mathematics, . . . our conflicting theories of mathematical truth, mathematical knowledge and mathematical objects. The most striking single feature of work on this subject in this century is that it is very largely banal. This is despite the ample fertilization from the great programmes and discoveries in the foundations of mathematics. The standard textbook presentations of 'Platonism', constructivism, logicism, finitism and the like re-enact conceptual moves that were determined by an ancient and alien problem situation, the disintegration of the concept of *scientia* and the invention of the concept of evidence culminating in the new philosophy of the seventeenth century. We have forgotten those events, but they are responsible for the concepts in which we perform our pantomine philosophy." For the way in which essentially contested concepts permit only *ad hoc* and not permanent resolutions of debate, see my "Rhetoric and Essentially Contested Arguments."

21. Williams, *Ethics and the Limits of Philosophy*, p. 160. "If we are going to accommodate the relativist's concerns, we must not simply draw a line between ourselves and others. We must not draw a line at all, but recognize that others are at varying distances from us. We must also see that our reactions and relations to other groups are themselves part of our ethical life, and we should understand these reactions more realistically in terms of the practices and sentiments that help to shape our life."

22. One source of data for how Machiavelli distances himself from the texts he is commenting on consists in those instances in which he explicitly disagrees with Livy. For one crucial instance, that bears on the conception of the republic as virtù universalized, see 1.58. The title of the chapter, "The People Are Wiser and More Constant than Princes," is explicitly at variance with Livy's teaching that "nothing is more uncertain and inconstant than the multitude."

23. Struever, "Historical Rhetoric," p. 26. See also Pocock, "On the Non-Revolutionary Character of Paradigms," in *Politics, Language, and Time*, p. 274: "Historical awareness was, first, begotten by the sense of instability upon the sense

of traditional continuity, and second, heightened by measuring the distance separating European society from its written and unwritten, classical and customary paradigms."

24. Cave notes the connection between this sort of experimental method and reading texts as performances: "In so far as the two words [*performance* and *enactment*] have a special sense, they refer to a 'practice' (*exercitatio*) which is close to theory, which often carries fragments of theory in its folds, and which is thus a kind of demonstration. They also suggest the exuberance of a discourse in action, exploring its own liberties." *The Cornucopian Text*, p. xx.

25. Williams, *Ethics and the Limits of Philosophy*, p. 161: "It is important that options may be asymmetrically related. Some version of modern technological life has become a real option for members of surviving traditional societies, but their life is not a real option for us, despite the passionate nostalgia of many. The theories we have about the nature of such asymmetries, and how far they extend, affect our views about the possibilities of radical social and political action."

Greene, "The End of Discourse," p. 59: "The author's goal is to clear away a conceptual space uncluttered by prejudice or ethics or loyalty or myth, a space where the pure intelligence can operate freely to discover the laws of political behavior and precepts for political success.

"The faculty engaged in clearing this space is elsewhere termed *discorso* by Machiavelli (*Discourses*, 1, Proemio, 73), a term which might be glossed as the power of rational analysis."

26. One apposite strategy for effecting such an intellectual reversal is suggested by Kahn, *Rhetoric, Prudence, and Skepticism*, p. 34: "Whereas the classical orator was trained to argue *in utramque partem*, i.e., on both sides of a question, in any particular case he argued on one side or the other. But when the Renaissance humanist adopted the Aristotelian and Ciceronian rhetorical skills, he was not constrained by the same immediate concerns as is the orator in the forum or the lawcourt. As a result he could actually present both cases, and in so doing, persuade the reader not to any specific action, but to exercise the prudential judgment that is required for all actions." This strategy makes sense here, given my claim that one difference between *The Prince* and the *Discourses* is that the latter work is concerned with the conditions of effective political action, rather than with any particular actions.

27. Crick, *In Defence of Politics*, p. 32: "A political doctrine is only doctrinaire [or, in the sense I have been using the term, ideological], firstly, if it refuses to recognise the power and existence of other forces and ideas within an established political order; or, secondly—and more obviously—when it seeks to argue that some of these groups must be eliminated, urgently, illegally and unpolitically if other great benefits are to follow." Again, p. 33: "Politics is a process of discussion. . . . For discussion to be genuine and fruitful when something is maintained, the opposite or some contrary case must be considered or—better—maintained by someone who believes it." And, p. 151: "One is not acting politically if one pursues as part of a policy devices intended to ensure for certain that [the policy] can never be overthrown. This condition embraces both the well-meaning but fu-

tile attempts of constitution makers to put something permanently above politics (though it may be part of politics to make the gesture), and the autocratic attempt to forbid or destroy opposition."

6. Civic Virtue and the New Rhetorical Virtues

1. Machiavelli, *Florentine Histories* 3.1 (Gilbert ed.).

2. Pitkin, *Fortune Is a Woman*, p. 301. See also Boyle, *Rhetoric and Reform*, p. 22, describing the way Erasmus isolates essentially contested arguments and distinguishes civil disputes from polemical, and schismatic, ones: "He does not condemn those who inquire into them in moderate disputation but rather those who clash swords seditiously in mortal combat."

3. *Fortune Is a Woman*, p. 92: "The genuine appeal to justice and the sense of mutuality and limits even within serious conflict are further correlated with this other requirement: the conflict must be open rather than clandestine and invidious. True *virtù* requires the open staking of a claim on the basis of right and justice, along with the effort to defend it through organizing power; destructive factionalism, by contrast, relies on evasion, private cabals, and secret intrigues." Pitkin goes on to note, though, that the rhetorical virtue of openness cannot exist without the proper circumstances: "To 'make war openly' is the 'more honorable' way, though it is not available to the weak. (*Discourses on Livy*, 3:2)."

4. Pitkin, *Fortune Is a Woman*, p. 313. See also ibid., pp. 300–301: "This political struggle involves both power and principle, each side mustering what power it can, yet also appealing to the other in terms of law, right, justice, and the common good. Indeed, in the *vivere civile* might and right are interrelated, for law and justice are themselves partly resources of power; and conversely, a purely abstract 'right' that serves no community needs and can muster no community support is politically ineffectual and wrong. Because we are simultaneously both distinct and connected, politics always simultaneously concerns both the distribution of costs and benefits among competitors, and the nature and direction of their shared community, both 'who gets what, when, and why,' and 'who we are.' Every law or policy allocates, advantaging some and disadvantaging others; but every law or policy also affects their shared common life and the principles for which they stand."

5. James B. White, "Law as Language," p. 443, n. 54: "When power is given to an actor and at the same time circumscribed, the limitation is made not merely out of distrust of the actor, but in order to create an institutional and social context in which that power may be wisely and firmly exercised—in which it can be a more genuine *power*. The case and controversy requirement for judicial review, for example, is a way not only of keeping a rein on the judges, but of creating circumstances in which they can do best what they do."

6. I think that this rhetorical scheme for understanding corruption sheds better light on the phenomenon than the true and important dictum of Pocock's: "Corruption, a term among whose many meanings perhaps the salient one is the replacement by private relationships of those public relationships among citizens by which the republic should be governed." *Machiavellian Moment*, p. 93. The issue

turns on whether corruption is the intrusion of an inappropriate principle of action, as when private motives drive out public ones, or whether it is a failure at doing what should be done, as in my analysis. Pocock himself makes a related point later in the book (p. 405): "We are about to enter upon a period in which the terms virtue, *virtus*, and *virtù* are of great significance in their Roman and Renaissance connotations, but their antithesis is no longer circumstantial *fortuna* so much as historical corruption. . . . The material and moral conditions necessary to the commonwealth in which virtue was possible had been established in a series of increasingly acceptable paradigms; the problem now seemed to be legislative and political—could these conditions be established, and if so could they be maintained?—and to admit of answers in material and moral, rather than voluntaristic or charismatic, terms."

7. See Pitkin, *Fortune Is a Woman*, p. 298: "The political counterpart of what Nietzsche called *ressentiment* Machiavelli called corruption. Corrupt people are obsessed with past injustice, desiring vengeance more than any direct gratification. The reward they desire from victory is not . . . glory' but rather the 'satisfaction of having conquered the others.' Thus when they come to power they kill or exile their enemies, making laws 'not for the common profit but altogether in favor of the conquerer.' Their real desire being to undo the past, which is impossible, they cannot let the past go or look rationally toward the future. They would rather 'go back over past things' endlessly than 'provide for future ones' in ways designed to 'reunite, not to divide the city.' So they launch escalating feuds or even ally themselves with their own state's enemies abroad. No law is 'more dangerous for a republic,' says Machiavelli, 'than one that looks back for a long time.'

"But a different sort of 'looking back for a long time,' one that renews contact with origins and founders and recovers the self, is also Machiavelli's cure for such factional resentment. Only, as already argued, this curative looking back can be understood in either of two ways: the one misogynistic and ultimately crippling, the other genuinely liberating."

8. Ezio Raimondi, "Machiavelli and the Rhetoric of the Warrior," p. 6: "If on the one hand military activity must be absorbed in political activity, because a soldier who is nothing but a soldier is a menace to all other social activities, on the other hand it is a matter of deepening the concept of armed *virtù*, so as to transform the question of the participation of the many in citizenship and to found on the identity of soldier and citizen a democratic logic of consensus, of the organic and active nexus between the man of government and popular groups." In this instance I think Pocock obliterates some important distinctions, in *Machiavellian Moment*, p. 499: "The citizen who allowed another to be paid to fight for him parted with a vital element of his *virtus*, in every sense of that word; and the priest, the lawyer, and the rentier have been grouped with the soldier as paradigmatic instances of individuals whose specialization made them the servants of others who became servants to them in turn. Specialization, in short, was a prime cause of corruption; only the citizen as amateur, propertied, independent, and willing to perform in his own person all functions essential to the polis, could be said to practice virtue or live in a city where justice was truly distributed. There was no *aretē* that he must not be willing to make his own. But if the arts proved to

have been built up through a process of specialization, then culture itself was in contradiction with the ethos of the *zoon politikon;* and if it were further argued – as it clearly could be – that only specialization, commerce, and culture set men free enough to attend to the goods of others as well as their own, then it would follow that the polis was built up by the very forces that must destroy it. Once land and commerce were placed in historical sequence, civic man found himself existing in a historical contradiction."

9. Not only does Machiavelli think that Christianity is a religion founded on statements that need interpretation, as opposed to rituals and ceremonies, but he also believes that even the religion of the Roman republic was so grounded: "The religion of the Gentiles had for its foundation the responses of the oracles, and the tenets of the augurs and auspices; upon these alone depended all their ceremonies, rites, and sacrifices" (*Discourses* 1.12).

The three kinds of material correspond not only to the three kinds of rhetoric but also to Vico's three kinds of language, which are variously articulate: "The first [kind of language] was a divine mental language by mute religious acts or divine ceremonies, from which there survived in Roman civil law the *actus legitimi* which accompanied all their civil transactions. This language belongs to religions by the eternal property that it concerns them more to be reverenced than to be reasoned, and it was necessary in the earliest times when men did not yet possess articulate speech.

"The second was by heroic blazonings, with which arms are made to speak; this kind of speech survived in military discipline.

"The third is by articulate speech, which is used by all nations today." Giambattista Vico, *The New Science*, p. 340.

10. Pocock, *Machiavellian Moment*, p. 248: "If *virtù* was not ascriptive, but had to be acquired, displayed and recognized, there must be a certain openness about the political system founded upon it." One of the consequences of such openness is the ambivalence of moral response to Machiavelli's teachings.

11. Ibid., p. 250. Pocock notes the contrast between these ties and the relation between man and citizen in Aristotle (p. 68): "Aristotle did not think that the individual as citizen, engaged in the universal activity of pursuing and distributing the common good, should be considered out of relation with the same individual engaged in the particular activity of pursuing and enjoying the particular goods he preferred. Since it was the definition of the citizen that he both ruled and was ruled, the activity of ruling must be coupled with the activity in respect of which he was ruled. (*Pol.* III.x.1281a, xii.1282b–1283, xiii.1283a–1284b.) Universal and particular met in the same man, and if a citizen assumed a particular social personality as a result of pursuing, enjoying, and excelling in the attainment of the particular values he preferred, this must modify his capacity to engage in the universal activity of making decisions aimed at distributing the common good."

12. Ibid., pp. 262–63. See also p. 402: "The civic humanists of the Renaissance had faced the almost insoluble problem of constituting the republic as both a universal community of value and a phenomenon in the world of particularity; their theory had consequently presented it as a device for mobilizing all rationality and

all value, and remaining stable as a totality of virtue. This set of problems remained fundamental for post-Renaissance and Enlightenment minds; but in the intellectual lineage running through Bruni, Machiavelli, and Harrington, theories of mixed government, arms, and finally of property had provided — at least for those able to overlook Machiavelli's underlying pessimism — a set of norms for the attainment of stability which reduced the totality of virtue to concrete and manageable terms."

13. Ibid., p. 160. See also p. 219: "Unlike the writings of Machiavelli, those of Guicciardini are always specifically related to the context of Florentine politics and lack the older man's theoretical and speculative freedom. This is an index not only to Guicciardini's greater concern with the actual and the practicable, but also to his aristocratic conservatism. The specific and particular world, almost by definition, could be known and controlled only with a considerable admixture of experience."

14. For the opposite use of the same topic, see, first, Guicciardini, *Ricordi*, p. 155: "It is said that anyone who does not know all the details well cannot judge well. And yet I have often seen it happen that someone of poor judgment will judge better if he knows only generalities than if he is shown the details. For on the general level, a proper conclusion will often present itself to him; but as soon as he hears all the details, he becomes confused." More generally, the relation between the ability to make specific and general judgments is a topic that generates such diverse arguments as Hume's in "On the Standard of Taste" and Vico's in *The New Science*. First, here is Hume: "The sentiments of men often differ with regard to beauty and deformity of all kinds, even while their general discourse is the same. There are certain terms in every language, which import blame, and others praise; and all men, who use the same tongue, must agree in their application of them. Every voice is united in applauding elegance, propriety, simplicity, spirit in writing; and in blaming affectation, coldness, and a false brilliancy. But when critics come to particulars, this seeming unanimity vanishes; and it is found that they had affixed a very different meaning to their expressions. In all matters of opinion and science the case is opposite. The difference among men is oftener found to lie in generals than in particulars and be less in reality than in appearance. An explanation of the terms commonly ends the controversy, and the disputants are surprised to find, that they had been quarreling, while at bottom they agreed in their judgment." Hume's argument is especially rich in the light of the topical distinction Machiavelli appeals to at the beginning of book 2 of the *Discourses* between aesthetic and practical judgment.

For still further complications, see Vico's *New Science*. After giving "civil equity" a sense that corresponds to *prudence* as I have been using it — an acquired ability to adapt principles to circumstances — he draws the following contrast between modes of legal judgment: "The certain in the laws is an obscurity of judgment backed only by authority, so that we find them harsh in application, yet are obliged to apply them just because they are certain. In good Latin *certum* means particularized, or, as the schools say, individuated; so that, in overelegant Latin, *certum* and *commune*, the certain and the common, are opposed to each other" (p. 93).

And he continues: "The quickest way of opening the eyes of the people is to find the means of making them descend to particulars, seeing that to look at things only in a general way deceives them."

15. Machiavelli therefore makes us reject easy claims for the practicality of his own and our own enterprise. For example, Crick, *In Defence of Politics*, makes things too easy when he maintains (p. 193) that "political theory is, in practice, an essential part of any political system. There are no cases of political systems which have not contained a tradition of political speculation. Such a tradition explains rationally why power always exists in the form of authority. . . . Political theory is itself political." In contrast, Pitkin seems to me to get the matter right: "On the whole, Machiavelli refused to permit himself the dissociated so-called detachment of the intellectual, but insisted that abstract ideals like autonomy be tied to the reality of body and feeling. His was to be a theory self-consciously relevant to the harsh practicalities of political life; and the practicalities of his time precluded any simple division of the world into 'good guys' and 'bad guys'" (*Fortune Is a Woman*, pp. 18–19). She also notes that there are times when the proper practical role of thought is precisely that critique of ideology leading to a clear view of reality that I have claimed Machiavelli eschews: "The political theorist is not merely an observer but also a teacher, a bridge builder offering a new vision of the familiar world and trying to make it accessible to people through and despite their own ways of seeing. But how does one teach in such times of dislocation in judgment and action? Confronted by such conditions, a theorist may feel that the most urgent task is to destroy the remaining pretensions of existing ideals and unmask those who exploit them. Moved by a yearning for truthfulness, a rage at the prevailing hypocrisy, he may speak in the cynical mode, teaching that ideals are fraudulent devices, not merely conventional but foisted by the powerful on the credulous. He may, that is, equate truth-telling with the systematic description of current, exploitive, and hypocritical practice" (p. 308).

16. Williams, *Ethics and the Limits of Philosophy*, p. 148.

17. Vico, *the New Science*, p. 428. For a similar conception of the relation between speaking well and acting well, see Montaigne, *De la vanite des paroles*, in *Essais* (Paris, 1958), pp. 342–43 (trans. in Fumaroli, "Rhetoric, Politics, and Society"): "[Rhetoric] is a tool used only in sick states, like medicine, in those where the vulgar and ignorant were in power. . . . Eloquence flourished best in Rome when affairs were in their worst state and when the storm of civil wars agitated them: as a free and indomitable field bears the most vigorous weeds. From that it seems that the policies that depend on a monarchy need it less than the others: for the stupidity and facility that is found in the common people and which make them subject to be led and twisted by the sweet sound of that harmony without coming to weigh and know the truth of things by force of reason, this facility, I say, is not so easily found in a single man, and it is easier to keep him safe, by good education and advice, from the effect of this poison." See also Kahn, *Rhetoric, Prudence, and Skepticism*, p. 7: "In early humanism, dialogue and other instances of deliberative rhetoric are encomia of the will: the very fact of written debate is taken to be evidence of the reader's ability to respond, and thus of the existence of free will and the genuine possibility of rhetorical persuasion. In later

humanist-influenced works, dialogue turns in on itself and the encomium of the will becomes paradoxical." One way Machiavelli refuses to allow the achievement of rhetorical persuasion to be so easily performative is to question such freedom of the will not by offering scholastic counterarguments to its assertion but by showing how its assertion is itself an instance of detachment from circumstances as readers — princes and citizens — purchase such freedom in the coin of ineffectuality. Far from being self-confirming, assertions of freedom become self-refuting. See, finally, Pitkin, who notes an analogous comment of Machiavelli's: "Letters come after arms, and . . . generals are born earlier than philosophers. Because after good and well-disciplined armies have brought forth victory, and their victories quiet, the virtue of military courage cannot be corrupted with a more honorable laziness than that of letters; nor with a greater and more dangerous deception can this laziness enter into well-regulated cities" (*Florentine Histories* 5.1, Gilbert ed. p. 1232). On this Pitkin comments: "Machiavelli ranks theorizing, philosophy, and thought relatively low in comparison with effective action in the world. In the ranks of famous men whose fame is well deserved, as we noted, 'men of letters' come only fourth, after the Founders and fighters. In the *Florentine Histories*, even more strikingly, 'letters' and 'philosophy' are disparaged as a sign of degeneration from 'ability *virtù*' into corruption" (*Fortune Is a Woman*, p. 103).

18. Williams, *Ethics and the Limits of Philosophy*, p. 102. See also p. 200: "The ideal of transparency and the desire that our ethical practice should be able to stand up to reflection do not demand total explicitness, or a reflection that aims to lay everything bare at once. Those demands are based on a misunderstanding of rationality, both personal and political. We must reject any model of personal practical thought according to which all my projects, purposes, and needs should be made, discursively and at once, considerations *for* me. I must deliberate *from* what I am. Truthfulness requires trust in that as well, and not the obsessional and doomed drive to eliminate it." In the terms of our discussion, Williams ends by showing how prudence depends on philia.

19. Recall the way that the stylistic embellishments and disguises that were excluded in book 1 of Aristotle's *Rhetoric* once again become relevant in book 3. See also Fumaroli, "Rhetoric, Politics, and Society," p. 259, who makes the useful contrast between "deliberative 'candor'" and "epideictic 'flattery.'" It is beyond my scope here to elaborate the changes in the meanings of *sincerity, honesty, authenticity*, etc., as they function in the three kinds of rhetoric.

20. Sabina Lovibond, *Realism and Imagination in Ethics*, pp. 122–23.

21. Ibid., p. 158.

22. Stanley Cavell, "Wittgenstein's Later Philosophy," pp. 166–67n: "The reason why methods which make us look at what we say, and bring the forms of language (and hence our forms of life) to consciousness, can present themselves to one person as confining and to another as liberating is understandable in this way: recognizing what we way, in the way that is relevant in philosophizing, is like recognizing our present commitments and their implications; to one person a sense of freedom will demand an escape from them, to another it will require their more total acceptance."

23. Sidney, *Apologie*, ed. Sheperd, p. 22.

24. Pitkin, *Fortune Is a Woman*, p. 52 (quoting ch. 6 of *The Prince*).

25. Similarly Socrates' refutation of Polemarchus, which shows the consequences of erecting the two sorts of duties, or praxis versus poesis, into separate realms. My distinction between the ideological conception of action as execution and of the ideological conception of practical reason as embodied in the practical syllogism, as against the richer conception of practice and practical reason encountered in prudence, is also reflected in Kant's distinction between wide and narrow duties. Cf. Onora Nell, *Acting on Principle*, p. 46: "Wide duties are expressed in maxims of ends; narrow duties in maxims of actions. Wide duties are duties to have policies; narrow duties are duties to do certain acts."

BIBLIOGRAPHY

Ackerman, Bruce A. "The Storrs Lectures: Discovering the Constitution." *Yale Law Journal* 93 (1984): 1013–72.

Arendt, Hannah. *Between Past and Future.* New York: Viking Press, 1961.

Aristotle. *The "Art" of Rhetoric.* Trans. John Henry Freese. London: William Heinemann; New York: G. P. Putnam's Sons, 1926.

Aristotle. *The Nicomachean Ethics.* Trans. H. Rackham. Rev. ed. 1934. Reprint. Cambridge: Harvard University Press; London: William Heinemann, 1982.

Aristotle. *On Sophistical Refutations.* Trans. E. S. Forster. Cambridge: Harvard University Press; London: William Heinemann, 1955.

Aristotle. *Politics.* Trans. H. Rackham. 1932. Reprint. Cambridge: Harvard University Press; London: William Heinemann, 1950.

Aristotle. *Topica.* Trans. E. S. Forster. Cambridge: Harvard University Press; London: William Heinemann, 1966.

Bacon, Francis. *The Advancement of Learning.* In *Works.* Ed. James Spedding. London: Longmans, 1857–74.

Bambrough, Renford. "Conflict and the Scope of Reason." *Ratio* 20 (1978): 77–91.

Baron, Hans. *The Crisis of the Italian Renaissance.* Princeton: Princeton University Press, 1966.

Berki, R. N. "Machiavellianism: A Philosophical Defense." *Ethics* 81 (1971): 107–27.

Berlin, Isaiah. "The Originality of Machiavelli." In Isaiah Berlin, *Against the Current: Essays in the History of Ideas,* pp. 25–79. New York: Penguin, 1980.

Bernstein, Richard. *Beyond Objectivism and Relativism.* Philadelphia: University of Pennsylvania Press, 1983.

Bernstein, Richard. *Philosophical Profiles.* Philadelphia: University of Pennsylvania Press, 1986.

Bernstein, Richard. *Praxis and Action.* Philadelphia: University of Pennsylvania Press, 1971.

Bernstein, Richard. *The Restructuring of Social and Political Theory.* Philadelphia: University of Pennsylvania Press, 1976.

Bondanella, Peter E. *Machiavelli and the Art of Renaissance History.* Detroit: Wayne State University Press, 1973.

Bourdieu, Pierre. *Outlines of a Theory of Practice.* Cambridge: Cambridge University Press, 1977.

Boyle, Marjorie O'Rourke. *Rhetoric and Reform: Erasmus' Civil Dispute with Luther.* Cambridge: Harvard University Press, 1983.

Bradie, Michael, and Mark Gromko. "The Status of the Principle of Natural Selection." *Nature and System* 3 (1981): 3–12.

Briskman, Larry. "Historicist Relativism and Bootstrap Rationality." *Monist* 60 (1977): 509–39.

Bibliography

Bruns, Gerald. *Inventions.* New Haven: Yale University Press, 1982.

Burke, Kenneth. "Interaction: Dramatism." In David Sills, ed. *International Encyclopedia of the Social Sciences,* 7:445–52. New York: Macmillan, 1968.

Burke, Kenneth. *Rhetoric of Motives.* New York: Prentice-Hall, 1950.

Burke, Richard J. "Politics as Rhetoric." *Ethics* 93 (1982): 45–55.

Cantimori, D. "Rhetoric and Politics in Italian Humanism." *Journal of the Warburg Institute* 1 (1937): 83–102.

Cave, Terence. *The Cornucopian Text: Problems of Writing in the French Renaissance.* New York: Oxford University Press, 1979.

Cavell, Stanley. "The Availability of Wittgenstein's Later Philosophy." In George Pitcher, ed., *Wittgenstein: The Philosophical Investigations.* Englewood Cliffs, N.J.: Prentice-Hall, 1966.

Cicero. *De Inventione.* Trans. H. M. Hubbell. Cambridge: Harvard University Press; London: William Heinemann, 1976.

Cicero. *De Oratore.* Trans. E. W. Sutton and H. Rackham. Cambridge: Harvard University Press; London: William Heinemann, 1967.

Cioffari, Vincenzo. "The Function of Fortune in Dante, Boccaccio, and Machiavelli." *Italica* 24 (1947): 1–13.

Cochrane, Eric. "Machiavelli: 1940–60." *Journal of Modern History* 33 (1961): 113–36.

Colie, Rosalie. *The Resources of Kind.* Berkeley and Los Angeles: University of California Press, 1973.

Colish, Marcia L. "Cicero's *De Officiis* and Machiavelli's *Prince.*" *Sixteenth-Century Journal* 9 (1978): 443–49.

Collingwood, R. G. *The New Leviathan.* New York: Oxford University Press, 1942.

Condren, Donald. "Authorities, Emblems, and Sources: Reflections on the Role of a Rhetorical Strategy in the History of History." *Philosophy and Rhetoric* 15 (1982): 170–86.

Cooper, John. "Aristotle on the Goods of Fortune." *Philosophical Review* 94 (1985): 173–96.

Crane, R. S. *The Languages of Criticism and the Structure of Poetry.* Toronto: University of Toronto Press, 1953.

Crick, Bernard. *In Defence of Politics.* 2d ed. Chicago: University of Chicago Press, 1972.

Crick, Bernard. "On Theory and Practice." In Bernard Crick, *Political Theory and Practice.* New York: Basic Books, 1973.

D'Amico, Jack. *Knowledge and Power in the Renaissance.* Washington, D.C.: University Press of America, 1977.

Descartes, Rene. *The Philosophical Writings.* Ed. and trans. John Cottingham, Robert Stoothoff, and Dugald Murdoch. Vol. 1. Cambridge: Cambridge University Press, 1985.

Devons, Ely, and Max Gluckman. *Closed Systems and Open Minds.* Chicago: Aldine, 1964.

Dewey, John. "Logic of Judgments of Practice." *Journal of Philosophy* 12 (1915): 505–23, 533–54.

Dinan, Stephen A. "The Particularity of Moral Knowledge." *Proceedings of the American Catholic Philosophical Association* 58 (1984): 65–72.
Dolby, R.G.A. "The Transmission of Science." *History of Science* 15 (1977): 1–43.
Donagan, Alan. *The Theory of Morality.* Chicago: University of Chicago Press, 1977.
Douglas, Mary. *In the Active Voice.* London: Routledge and Kegan Paul, 1982.
Dowdall, H. D. "The Word 'State.'" *Law Quarterly Review* 39 (1923): 98–125.
Emmet, Dorothy. *Rules, Roles, and Relations.* Boston: Beacon Press, 1975.
Feyerabend, P. K. *Against Method.* London: New Left Books, 1975.
Fish, Stanley E. *Is There a Text in This Class? The Authority of Interpretive Communities.* Cambridge: Harvard University Press, 1980.
Fumaroli, Marc. "Rhetoric, Politics, and Society: From Italian Ciceronianism to French Classicism." In Murphy, *Renaissance Eloquence*, pp. 253–73.
Garin, Eugenio. *L'educazione in Europe, 1400–1600.* Bari: Laterza, 1966.
Garin, Eugenio. *Italian Humanism, Philosophy, and Civic Life in the Renaissance.* New York: Harper and Row, 1965.
Garver, Eugene. "Aristotle's Genealogy of Morals." *Philosophy and Phenomenological Research* 48 (1984): 471–92.
Garver, Eugene. "Machiavelli's *The Prince:* A Neglected Rhetorical Classic." *Philosophy and Rhetoric* 13 (1980): 99–120.
Garver, Eugene. "Rhetoric and Essentially Contested Arguments." *Philosophy and Rhetoric* 11 (1978): 156–72.
Geerken, John. "Pocock and Machiavelli: Structuralist Explanation in History." *Journal of the History of Philosophy* 17 (1979): 309–18.
Geertz, Clifford, *The Interpretation of Cultures.* New York: Basic Books, 1977.
Geertz, Clifford. "Thinking as a Moral Act." *Antioch Review* 28 (1968): 139–58.
Gellner, Ernest. "An Ethic of Cognition." In R. S. Cohen, P. K. Feyerabend, and Marx W. Wartofsky, eds., *Essays in Memory of Imre Lakatos.* Dordrecht: Reidel, 1976.
Gellner, Ernest. "The Savage and the Modern Mind." In Robin Horton and Ruth Finnegan, eds., *Modes of Thought*, pp. 162–81. London: Faber, 1972.
Gilbert, Allan H. *Machiavelli's "Prince" and Its Forerunners.* Durham: Duke University Press, 1938.
Gilbert, Felix. "The Humanist Concept of the Prince and *The Prince* of Machiavelli." *Journal of Modern History* 11 (1939): 449–83.
Gilmore, Myron. "The Renaissance Conception of the Lessons of History." In W. Werkmeister, ed., *Facets of the Renaissance.* Los Angeles: University of Southern California Press, 1959.
Goedecke, Robert. "On the Use of Crucial Terms in Jurisprudence." *Philosophy and Phenomenological Research* 30 (1970): 576–89.
Gramsci, Antonio. *The Modern Prince and Other Writings.* New York: International Publishers, 1957.
Grassi, Ernesto. "Can Rhetoric Provide a New Basis for Philosophizing? The Humanist Tradition." *Philosophy and Rhetoric* 11 (1978), pt. 1, 1–18; pt. 2, 75–97.

Bibliography

Gray, Hannah Holborn. "Renaissance Humanism: The Pursuit of Eloquence," *Journal of the History of Ideas* 24 (1963): 497–514.

Greene, Thomas. "The End of Discourse in Machiavelli's *Prince.*" *Yale French Studies* 67 (1984): 57–71.

Greene, Thomas. *The Light in Troy: Imitation and Discovery in Renaissance Poetry.* New Haven: Yale University Press, 1982.

Guicciardini, Francesco. *Ricordi.* New York: Harper and Row, 1965.

Hacking, Ian. "Proof and Eternal Truths: Descartes and Leibniz." In Stephen Gaukroger, ed., *Descartes: Philosophy, Mathematics, and Physics.* New York: Barnes and Noble, 1980.

Hall, R. A. "Linguistic Theory in the Renaissance." *Language* 13 (1963): 96–107.

Hannaford, I. "Machiavelli's Concept of *Virtù* in *The Prince* and *The Discourses* Reconsidered." *Political Studies* 20 (1972): 185–189.

Hanson, N. R. *Constellations and Conjectures.* Dordrecht: Reidel, 1973.

Hanson, N. R. *Patterns of Discovery.* Cambridge: Cambridge University Press, 1965.

Harvey, F. D. "Two Kinds of Equality." *Classica et Mediaevalia* 26 (1965): 101–46.

Hegel, G. W. F. *Vorlesungen über die Philosophie der Geschichte.* Frankfurt am Main, 1970.

Heidegger, Martin. "The Age of the World Picture." In *The Question Concerning Technology and Other Essays,* trans. William Lovitt. New York: Garland, 1977.

Hexter, J. H. Review essay on *The Machiavellian Moment,* by J. G. A. Pocock. *History and Theory* 16 (1977): 306–36.

Hirsch, E. D. *The Aims of Interpretation.* Chicago: University of Chicago Press, 1976.

Hulliung, Mark. *Citizen Machiavelli.* Princeton: Princeton University Press, 1983.

Jameson, Frederic. "The Symbolic Inference; or, Kenneth Burke and Ideological Analysis." *Critical Inquiry* 4 (1978): 507–24.

Javitch, Daniel. *Poetry and Courtliness in Renaissance England.* Princeton: Princeton University Press, 1978.

Johnstone, Henry. *Philosophy and Argument.* University Park: Pennsylvania State University Press, 1959.

Kahn, Victoria. *Rhetoric, Prudence, and Skepticism in the Renaissance.* Ithaca: Cornell University Press, 1985.

Kant, Immanuel. *Fundamental Principles of the Metaphysics of Morals.* Trans. Thomas K. Abbot. Indianapolis: Bobbs-Merrill, 1949.

Kariel, H. S. "Expanding the Political Present." *American Political Science Review* 43 (1969): 768–76.

Kariel, H. S. *Open Systems: Arenas for Political Action.* Itasca, Ill.: F. E. Peacock, 1969.

Keegan, John. *The Face of Battle.* New York: Viking, 1976.

Kuhn, Thomas. *The Essential Tension.* Chicago: University of Chicago Press, 1977.

LaCapra, Dominick. *Rethinking Intellectual History: Texts, Contexts, Language.* Ithaca: Cornell University Press, 1982.

Lakatos, Imre. "Infinite Regress and Foundations of Mathematics." In Imre Lakatos,

Mathematics, Science, and Epistomology: Philosophical Papers, ed. John Worrall and Gregory Currie, 2:3–23. Cambridge: Cambridge University Press, 1978.

Lakatos, Imre. "The Role of Crucial Experiments in Science." *Studies in the History and Philosophy of Science* 4 (1974): 309–25.

Lanham, Richard. *Motives of Eloquence*. New Haven: Yale University Press, 1976.

LaRusso, Dominic. "Rhetoric in Italian Humanism." In Murphy, *Renaissance Eloquence*, pp. 37–55.

Lechner, Marie. *Renaissance Concepts of the Commonplaces*. New York: Pageant Press, 1962.

Lefort, Claude. *Le Travail de l'oeuvre Machiavel*. Paris: Gallimard, 1972.

Lovibond, Sabina. *Realism and Imagination in Ethics*. Minneapolis: University of Minnesota Press, 1983.

McCanles, Michael. *The Discourse of "Il Principe."* Malibu: Undena Publications, 1983.

McCanles, Michael. "Machiavelli's *Principe* and the Textualization of History." *Modern Language Notes* 97 (1982): 1–18.

Machiavelli, Niccolo. *The Chief Works and Others*. Trans. Allan Gilbert. 3 vols. Durham: Duke University Press, 1965.

Machiavelli, Niccolo. *Machiavelli's "The Prince."* Trans. and ed. Mark Musa. New York: St. Martin's, 1964.

Machiavelli, Niccolo. *Opere*. 8 vols. Milan: Feltrinelli, 1960.

Machiavelli, Niccolo. *The Prince and the Discourses*. Trans. Luigi Ricci and Christian E. Detmold. New York: Modern Library, 1940.

McIntosh, Donald. "The Modernity of Machiavelli." *Political Theory* 12 (1984): 184–203.

MacIntyre, Alasdair. "Epistemological Crises, Dramatic Narrative, and the Philosophy of Science." *Monist* 60 (1977): 453–72.

MacIntyre, Alasdair. "How Virtues Become Vices: Values, Medicine, and Social Context." In H. T. Engelhardt, Jr., and S. F. Spicker, eds., *Evaluation and Explanation in the Biomedical Sciences*, pp. 97–111. Dordrecht: Reidel, 1975.

MacIntyre, Alasdair. "Objectivity in Morality and Objectivity in Science." In H. T. Engelhardt, Jr., and Daniel Callahan, eds., *Morals, Science, and Society*. New York: Plenum, 1978.

Manley, Lawrence. *Convention: 1500–1750*. Cambridge: Harvard University Press, 1980.

Mazzeo, Joseph Anthony. *Renaissance and Seventeenth-Century Studies*. New York: Columbia University Press, 1964.

Mercier, Charles. *A New Logic*. London: William Heinemann, 1912.

Murphy, James J., ed. *Renaissance Eloquence: Studies in the Theory and Practice of Renaissance Rhetoric*. Berkeley and Los Angeles: University of California Press, 1983.

Nell, Onora. *Acting on Principle: An Essay on Kantian Ethics*. New York: Columbia University Press, 1975.

Newman, John Henry. *An Essay in Aim of a Grammar of Assent*. Garden City, N.Y.: Doubleday, 1955.

Bibliography

O'Neill, John. *Sociology as a Skin Trade: Essays towards a Reflexive Sociology.* New York: Harper and Row, 1972.
O'Neill, Onora. "The Power of Example." *Philosophy* 61 (1986): 5–29.
Parkinson, G.H.R. "Ethics and Politics in Machiavelli." *Philosophical Quarterly* 5 (1955): 37–44.
Peirce, C. S. *Collected Papers.* Ed. Charles Hartshorne and Paul Weiss. Cambridge: Harvard University Press, 1931–60.
Perkins, David N. "Reasoning as Imagination." *Interchange* 16 (1985): 14–26.
Pitkin, Hannah Fenichel. *Fortune Is a Woman: Gender and Politics in the Thought of Niccolo Machiavelli.* Berkeley and Los Angeles: University of California Press, 1984.
Plato. *Protagoras.* Trans. W.R.M. Lamb. Cambridge: Harvard University Press; London: William Heinemann, 1957.
Pocock, J.G.A. "Custom and Grace, Form and Matter: An Approach to Machiavelli's Concept of Innovation." In Martin Fleisher, ed., *Machiavelli and the Nature of Political Thought,* pp. 153–72. New York: Antheneum, 1972.
Pocock, J.G.A. *The Machiavellian Moment: Florentine Political Thought and the Atlantic Republican Tradition.* Princeton: Princeton University Press, 1975.
Pocock, J.G.A. "*The Machiavellian Moment* Revisited: A Study in History and Ideology." *Journal of Modern History* 53 (1981): 50–72.
Pocock, J.G.A. "Machiavelli in the Liberal Cosmos." *Political Theory* 13 (1985): 559–74.
Pocock, J.G.A. "'The Onely Politician': Machiavelli, Harrington, and Felix Raab." *Historical Studies: Australia and New Zealand* 12 (1965): 265–95.
Pocock J.G.A. *Politics, Language, and Time.* New York: Atheneum, 1971.
Pocock, J.G.A. "Prophet and Inquisitor; or, A Church Built upon Bayonets Cannot Stand: A Comment on Mansfield's 'Strauss's Machiavelli.'" *Political Theory* 3 (1975): 385–401.
Pocock, J.G.A. "Review of Skinner." *Canadian Journal of Political and Social Theory* 3 (1979): 95–113.
Polka, Brayton. "Machiavelli's Concept of Innovation: Commentary." In Martin Fleischer, ed., *Machiavelli and the Nature of Political Thought.* New York: Antheneum, 1972.
Post, H. R. "Correspondence, Invariance, and Heuristics." *Studies in the History and Philosophy of Science* 2 (1971): 213–55.
Quintilian. *Institutio Oratoria.* Trans. H. E. Butler. Cambridge: Harvard University Press; London: William Heinemann, 1958.
Raab, Felix. *The English Face of Machiavelli.* London: Routledge and Kegan Paul, 1964.
Raimondi, Ezio. "Machiavelli and the Rhetoric of the Warrior." *Modern Language Notes* 92 (1977): 1–16.
Rawls, John. *A Theory of Justice.* Cambridge: Harvard University Press, 1971.
Reiss, Timothy J. *The Discourse of Modernism.* Ithaca: Cornell University Press, 1982.
Renucci, Paul. "Machiavel et la volonte de puissance." *Revue des Etudes Italiennes* 24 (1978): 146–63.

Rice, Eugene F. *The Renaissance Idea of Wisdom.* Cambridge: Harvard University Press, 1958.

Richetti, John Journal. *Philosophical Writing: Locke, Berkeley, Hume.* Cambridge: Harvard University Press, 1983.

Rorty, Richard. "Habermas and Lyotard on Postmodernity." In Richard Bernstein, ed., *Habermas and Modernity,* pp. 161–76. Cambridge: MIT Press, 1985.

Rorty, Richard. *Philosophy and the Mirror of Nature.* Princeton: Princeton University Press, 1979.

Ryan, John K. "Two Instances of the Tripartite Method in Machiavelli." In John K. Ryan, ed., *Studies in Philosophy and History of Philosophy,* 2 (1963) 249–56.

Sasso, Gennaro. *Niccolo Machiavelli: Storia del suo pensiero politico.* Bologna: Societa editrice il Mulino, 1980.

Schneewind, J. B. "The Divine Corporation and the History of Ethics." In Richard Rorty, J. B. Schneewind, and Quentin Skinner, eds., *Philosophy in History.* Cambridge: Cambridge University Press, 1984.

Screech, M. A. "Commonplaces of Law, Proverbial Wisdom, and Philosophy." In R. R. Bolgar, ed., *Classical Influences on European Culture, A.D. 1500–1700,* pp. 127–34. Cambridge: Cambridge University Press, 1976.

Scruton, Roger. *The Meaning of Conservatism.* Totowa, N.J.: Barnes and Noble, 1980.

Scruton, Roger. "The Significance of Common Culture." *Philosophy* 54 (1979): 51–70.

Seigel, Jerrold. "Civil Humanism or Ciceronian Rhetoric?" *Past and Present* 34 (1966): 3–48.

Seigel, Jerrold. *Rhetoric and Philosophy in Renaissance Humanism.* Princeton: Princeton University Press, 1968.

Seigel, Jerrold. "Virtù in and since the Renaissance." In Philip P. Wiener, ed., *Dictionary of the History of Ideas,* 4:476–86. New York: Scribner's, 1968.

Sidney, Philip. *An Apologie for Poetrie.* Ed. Geoffrey Sheperd. New York: Barnes and Noble, 1973.

Skinner, Quentin. "Conventions and the Understanding of Speech Acts." *Philosophical Quarterly* 20 (1970): 118–38.

Skinner, Quentin. *The Foundations of Modern Political Thought.* 2 vols. Cambridge: Cambridge University Press, 1978.

Skinner, Quentin. *Machiavelli.* New York: Hill and Wang, 1981.

Skinner, Quentin. "Meaning and Understanding in the History of Ideas." *History and Theory* 8 (1969): 1–53.

Skinner, Quentin. "Motives, Intentions, and the Interpretation of Texts." *New Literary History* 3 (1972): 393–408.

Skinner, Quentin. "Some Problems in the Analysis of Political Thought and Action." *Political Theory* 2 (1974): 277–303.

Stierle, Karlheinz. "L'Histoire comme exemple, l'exemple comme histoire." *Poetique* 10 (1972): 197–98.

Stone, Lawrence. "Education and Modernization in Japan and England." *Comparative Studies in Society and History* 9 (1966–67): 208–32.

Bibliography

Strong, Roy. *Splendour At Court: Renaissance Spectacle and the Theatre of Power.* Boston: Houghton Mifflin, 1973.

Struever, Nancy. "Historical Rhetoric." Unpublished paper, Humanities Center, Johns Hopkins University.

Struever, Nancy. "Historiography and Linguistics." In George G. Iggers and Harold T. Parker, eds., *International Handbook of Historical Studies,* pp. 127–50. Westport, Conn.: Greenwood Press, 1979.

Struever, Nancy. "Lorenzo Valla's Humanist Rhetoric and the Critique of Classical Languages of Morality." In Murphy, *Renaissance Eloquence,* pp. 191–206.

Struever, Nancy. "Machiavelli and the Critique of the Available Languages of Morality in the Renaissance." Unpublished paper, Humanities Center, Johns Hopkins University.

Struever, Nancy. "Renaissance Ethics: The Invention of an Edifying Past." Unpublished paper, Humanities Center, Johns Hopkins University.

Struever, Nancy. Review of *Rhetoric and Philosophy in Renaissance Humanism,* by Jerrold E. Seigel. *History and Theory* 11 (1972): 63–72.

Struever, Nancy. "The Study of Language and the Study of History." *Journal of Interdisciplinary History* 4 (1974): 401–15.

Struever, Nancy. "Topics in History." *History and Theory* 19 (1980): 66–79.

Tarcov, Nathan. "Quentin Skinner's Method and Machiavelli's *Prince.*" *Ethics* 92 (1982): 692–709.

Taylor, Charles. "Growth, Legitimacy, and the Modern Identity." *Praxis International* 1 (1981): 111–25.

Tetel, Marcel. "Montaigne and Machiavelli: Ethics, Politics, and Humanism." *Rivista di Litteratura Moderne e Comparate* 29 (1976): 165–81.

Trinkaus, Charles. "The Question of Truth in Renaissance Rhetoric and Anthropology." in Murphy, *Renaissance Eloquence,* pp. 207–20.

Trousdale, Marion. "A Possible Renaissance View of Form." *ELH* 40 (1973): 179–204.

Uphaus, Robert W. *The Impossible Observer: Reason and the Reader in Eighteenth-Century Prose.* Lexington: University Press of Kentucky, 1979.

Vernon, Richard. "Politics as Metaphor: Cardinal Newman and Professor Kuhn." *Review of Politics* 41 (1979): 513–35.

Veyne, Paul. *Comment on ecrit l'histoire.* Paris: Editions du Seuil, 1971.

Vico, Giambattista. *The New Science.* Trans. Thomas Bergin and Max Fish. Ithaca: Cornell University Press, 1984.

von Wright, George Henrik. *The Varieties of Goodness.* London: Routledge and Kegan Paul, 1963.

Wallace, John. "Examples Are Best Precepts: Readers and Meanings in Seventeenth-Century Poetry." *Critical Inquiry* 1 (1974): 273–90.

Ward, John O. "Rhetoric and the Writing of History in Medieval and Renaissance Culture." In Frank MacGregor and Nicholas Wright, eds., *European History and Its Historians.* Adelaide: Adelaide University Press, 1979.

Whigham, Frank. "Interpretation at Court: Courtesy and the Performer-Audience Dialectic." *New Literary History* 14 (1983): 623–39.

White, Hayden. "The Politics of Contemporary Philosophy of History." *Clio* 3 (1973): 35–54.

White, Hayden. "The Question of Narrative in Contemporary Historical Theory." *History and Theory* 23 (1984): 1–33.

White, James B. "The Ethics of Argument." *University of Chicago Law Review* 50 (1983): 849–95.

White, James B. "Law as Language: Reading Law and Reading Literature." *Texas Law Review* 60 (1982). (Reprinted in *Heracles' Bow*, pp. 77–106. Madison: University of Wisconsin Press, 1985.)

Wieruszowski, Helene. "Rhetoric and the Classics in Italian Education of the Thirteenth Century." *Studia Gratiana* 11 (1967): 169–208.

Wiggins, David. "Weakness of Will, Commensurability, and the Objects of Deliberation and Desire." In Amelie Rorty, ed., *Essays on Aristotle's Ethics*, pp. 241–65. Berkeley and Los Angeles: University of California Press, 1981.

Wilcox, Donald. *The Development of Florentine Humanist Historiography in the Fifteenth Century*. Cambridge: Harvard University Press, 1969.

Williams, Bernard. *Descartes: The Project of Pure Enquiry*. New York: Humanities Press, 1978.

Williams, Bernard. *Ethics and the Limits of Philosophy*. Cambridge: Harvard University Press, 1985.

Williams Bernard. *Moral Luck*. Cambridge: Cambridge University Press, 1981.

Wood, Neal. "Machiavelli's Humanism of Action." In Anthony Parel, ed., *The Political Calculus: Essays on Machiavelli's Philosophy*, pp. 46–47. Toronto: University of Toronto Press, 1972.

INDEX

Ackerman, Bruce, 203n3
Algorithmic methods, 13, 16–20, 27, 39,
  53, 54, 57, 65, 71, 76, 92, 95–96, 111,
  114–15, 127, 143, 175–76n15, 206n9,
  210n27
Arendt, Hannah, 209n22
Aristotle, 17, 38–39, 65, 82–84, 126,
  128–29, 149, 164–65, 173n7, 175n14,
  177–78n18, 180n27, 183n8, 186n22,
  189n28, 194n12, 198n11, 200n20,
  214nn13, 14, 214–15n15; de Sophisticis
  Elenchus, 22, 189n29; Nicomachean
  Ethics, 11, 20–21, 85, 91, 94–95, 117–
  18, 121, 174n9, 181n31, 200–201n21,
  212n5, 212–13n6; Poetics, 29; Politics,
  22, 58, 99, 147, 149–50, 201n23,
  220n11; Rhetoric, 41, 48, 52, 116, 121,
  141, 149–50, 179n24, 187n25, 192n5,
  199n16, 223n19
Atechnical proofs, 70, 77, 117, 143, 152
Atechnoi. See Atechnical proofs

Bacon, Francis, 28–29, 49, 69, 82, 86,
  171n1, 182–83n8, 189n29, 192n5, 197–
  98n6, 198n7
Bambrough, Renford, 206n9
Berki, R. N., 177n17
Berlin, Isaiah, 102, 107, 110–12, 208n15,
  209nn20, 21, 210n25
Bernstein, Richard, 173n7, 195n13, 203–
  4n4
Bondanella, Peter, 185n16
Borgia, Cesare, 32, 184n15, 185n16
Bourdieu, Pierre, 204–5n5, 206n9, 207n11,
  207n13
Boyle, Marjorie, 173n5, 183n10, 209n24,
  218n2
Bradie, Michael, 207–8n13
Briskman, Larry, 208n17
Bruns, Gerald, 13–14, 172n4, 178nn20, 21,
  197n5, 213n7
Burke, Kenneth, 82, 201n22
Burke, Richard, 175n12, 180n26

Cave, Terence, 181n1, 193n8, 194n9,
  217n24
Cavell, Stanley, 223n22
Character, 21, 61, 94–95, 109, 110–12,
  119–21, 126, 185n16
Cicero, 67, 89, 133, 175n13, 177n18,
  179n25, 183nn10, 11, 190–91n33,
  201n25, 208n16
Colie, Rosalie, 29, 183n9
Colish, Marcia, 89, 177n18, 201n25
Collingwood, R. G., 215–16n20
Commensurability. See Incommensura-
  bility
Consensus gentium, 19, 67–68, 71, 80
Cooper, John, 208n19
Crane, R. S., 215n17
Crick, Bernard, 102, 187–88n26, 205–6n7,
  208n14, 209n23, 217n27, 222n15
Custom. See Tradition

D'Amico, Jack, 199–200n18
Deliberation, 133, 135, 137, 140, 142–43,
  147, 149, 194n11, 210n29, 223n19
Descartes, 3–5, 13–14, 19, 48, 54, 86, 92,
  122, 171n1, 180n28, 196n3
Devons, Ely, 196n3
Dewey, John, 200n19
Dinan, Stephen, 202–3n2, 203n3
Dolby, R. G. A., 207–8n13
Donagan, Alan, 175n12

Emmet, Dorothy, 196n3
Epideixis, 38, 52, 82, 134, 194n11, 223n19
Essentially contested concepts, 54, 133–35,
  138–40, 143, 148, 149, 154, 166,
  179n25, 215n20
Ethics: of consequences, 12, 16–20, 32, 77,
  94, 176–77n17; of principles, 12, 16–20,
  32, 72–73, 78, 114–16, 161, 175n12,
  176–77n17
Examples, reasoning from, 32, 35, 47, 49,
  57, 65, 69, 84, 92, 96–97, 142, 181n30,
  182n7, 192n5

Factions, 127, 142–48, 153, 160–61
Fallacy, 161; circularity, 101; connected to
    heuristics, 14
Feyerabend, Paul, 204–5n5
Fish, Stanley, 198n13
Flexibility, 10, 23, 106–7, 111, 114–15,
    126, 142–43, 153, 156, 173n5, 209n24
Fortuna, 44, 61, 105–11, 158, 161, 173n5,
    184n15, 185–86n17, 186–87n23, 190n32,
    196n16, 212n4
Fumaroli, Marc, 188n27, 194n11, 222–
    23n17, 223n19

Garin, Eugenio, 181n1, 202n1
Geertz, Clifford, 203n3
Gellner, Ernest, 204–5n5, 206n5
Gilbert, Allan, 181n4
Glory, 42, 90–91, 100, 119, 152, 153, 162,
    219n7
Gluckman, Max, 196n3
Grassi, Ernesto, 181n1
Gray, Hannah, 181n1, 191n2
Greene, Thomas, 70, 191–92n4, 195n14,
    198n9, 198n11, 198–99n14, 199–200n18,
    210nn25, 29, 211n32, 211–12n3,
    217nn19, 25
Gromko, Mark, 208n13
Guicciardini, Francesco, 107, 153–55, 180–
    81n29, 187–88n26, 221nn13, 14

Hacking, Ian, 215–16n20
Hannaford, I., 199n17
Hanson, N. R., 205n6, 207–8n13
Hegel, 192n6
Heidegger, Martin, 175–76n15
Heuristics, 13, 16–20, 40, 54, 64, 65–66,
    74, 77, 79, 88, 95, 103, 108, 114, 127–
    28, 175–76n15
Hexter, J. H., 187n24, 199n15
Hirsch, E. D., 176n15
History, 4, 66, 136–37, 153–54, 165,
    194n10, 197n5, 199n16; reasoning from,
    79, 89–90, 134, 143–44, 151–58, 192n5,
    194n10, 198–99n14
Hobbes, Thomas, 53, 171n1, 182n7
Hulliung, Mark, 176n17

Ideology, 39–40, 53, 57–58, 59, 62, 73–74,
    92–93, 107, 109, 136, 152, 159, 187–
    88n26, 217–18n27

Imitation, 4, 23, 28, 45, 46–47, 49–50, 55,
    60, 62, 65–66, 69, 70, 74, 89, 96–97,
    119, 133, 143, 151, 165, 182n7, 191nn2,
    3, 191–92n4, 198–99n14, 199–200n18
Inartificial proofs. *See* Atechnical proofs
Incommensurability, 95–96, 100, 101–2,
    104–6, 109–11, 203–4n4, 204–5n5,
    208n17
Incommensurable values, 118–19, 122–23,
    125–26, 127, 129, 130–31, 132, 136
Innovation, 27, 30, 38, 42, 44, 104, 136,
    155, 174n8, 183n11, 186n21, 186–87n23,
    187–88n26
Invention, rhetorical, 24, 27, 43–44, 65,
    69, 74, 77, 79–81, 85–86, 95, 104, 133,
    141–42, 154, 190n32. *See also*
    Innovation.

Javitch, Daniel, 182n7
Johnstone, Henry, 179n25
Judgment, rhetorical, 133, 136–37, 145,
    155–57

Kahn, Victoria, 178n22, 197n5, 202n1,
    217n26, 222–23n17
Kant, Immanuel, 130, 163, 180n27,
    224n25
Keegan, John, 201n22, 206n9, 210n28
Kuhn, Thomas, 99, 114, 203–4n4, 206–
    7n10, 211n31

LaCapra, Dominick, 193n8, 9, 194n11,
    211n1
Lakatos, Imre, 176n15, 179n25, 210n28
Lanham, Richard, 193n8
Lovibond, Sabina, 159–60, 223n20, 21
Loyalty. *See Philia*

McCanles, 187n25, 189n30, 196n18,
    201n24, 202n29
MacIntyre, Alasdair, 171–72n2, 174n10,
    206n9, 208n18
Mandeville, Bernard, 53
Manley, Lawrence, 182n7, 188–89n27,
    192n5, 215n17
Mazzeo, Joseph, 91, 177n17, 184n11, 189–
    90n30, 201n23, 210–11n30
Mercier, Charles, 210n27

Military affairs, contrasted to politics, 37–38, 60, 72, 75–76, 79–81, 87, 90, 121, 145, 150, 199nn16, 17
Moderation, 61, 107, 148–49, 162, 163, 209n20, 222n15
Montaigne, 222–23n17

Nell, Onora, 181n30, 224n25
Newman, J. H., 178n20

O'Neill, John, 180n27, 202n28

Paradigms. *See* Incommensurability
Peirce, C. S., 179n26
Perkins, David, 178nn19, 20
Philia, 152–54, 280, 223n18
Pitkin, Hannah, 59, 145, 163, 185n16, 185–86n17, 188–89n27, 190n32, 193–94n9, 195nn12, 15, 196n16, 201–2n27, 202n1, 208n15, 209n22, 209–10n24, 211nn32, 33, 212–13n10, 215n16, 218nn2, 3, 4, 219n7, 222nn15, 17, 224n24
Plato, 11, 17, 19, 22, 65, 109, 172n4; *Gorgias*, 36, 212–13n6, 214n13; *Protagoras*, 7, 47, 120–21, 161, 212n4, 214n13; *Republic*, 107, 120, 125, 165, 174–75n11, 224n25. *See also* Socrates
Pocock, J. G. A., 27, 31–32, 46, 81–82, 117, 125–26, 130, 153–54, 155, 172n3, 173n5, 174n8, 181–82n5, 182n6, 184nn12, 13, 14, 184–85n15, 186n19, 186–87n23, 187n24, 189n30, 188n27, 190n31, 194n12, 198n7, 199nn15, 16, 208n16, 212n4, 213n10, 214n11, 215n17, 216n23, 218–19n6, 219n7, 220nn10, 11, 220–21n12, 221n13
Politics, 24, 64–65, 68, 87–88, 94–97, 98–99, 99–101, 102–3, 107, 113, 123–24, 133, 138, 141, 151, 161–62, 171n1
Polka, Brayton, 181–82n5
Post, H. R., 204–5n5
Prudence, 64, 83, 89, 93–95, 97, 101–2, 111–12, 113–14, 117–18, 122–24, 127, 132, 142, 153–57, 162–63, 165, 178n22, 182n7, 187–88n26, 195n13, 221–22n14; contrasted with aesthetic judgment, 46, 49–50, 89–90, 118, 132; contrasted with science, 20, 91, 93, 113–15, 121, 140, 141, 161, 165; contrasted with skill and

art, 11, 20–21, 117, 120–22, 127–30, 142, 149, 154, 224n25; history of, 3–4, 150, 164–67, 171n1, 174n8; reading and writing as problems of, 9–10, 194nn10, 11, 194–95n12, 195–96n15

Quintilian, 178n22, 179n25, 196n3

Raab, Felix, 171n1, 186n19, 198n7
Raimondi, Ezio, 219n7
Ramus, Peter, 14
Rawls, John, 15, 179n23
Religion, 142, 147–48, 220n9
Renucci, Paul, 174n8, 186n18
Responsiveness to circumstances. *See* Flexibility
Rhetoric, 21, 22–23, 26, 37, 48, 51–52, 54–56, 63–64, 68, 79–80, 84–85, 90, 92–93, 96, 98–100, 104, 113–14, 130, 133, 135, 137, 140, 159, 163, 175nn12, 13, 181n2, 181–82n5, 197n5, 202n1, 215n19, 217n26; Machiavelli's use of, 26–28, 34, 54–56, 63, 74–75, 80, 98–99, 118–19, 130, 133–34, 136–37; relation of speaker and hearer, 52, 66; traditional kinds of, 40–41, 54, 135, 142–43, 146, 220n9
Richetti, 193n8
Rorty, Richard, 171n1, 197n5, 204–5n5
Rules, reasoning from, 11–22, 92, 171–72n2

Schneewind, J. B., 171n1
Screech, M. A., 198n6
Scruton, Roger, 97, 205n7
Security. *See* Stability
Sextus Empiricus, 175n13
Sidney, Philip, 29, 161, 183n9, 213n9, 223n23
Siegel, Jerrold, 181nn1, 2, 185n16, 186n18
Skinner, Quentin, 184n15, 191n3, 198n12
Socrates, 6–8, 15–16, 37, 81, 85, 92, 99, 111, 120–21, 124, 125–26, 157–62, 164, 172–73n4, 173n5, 197n5. *See also* Plato
Sophistic, 7, 22, 92, 128, 163, 180n27, 214n13
Stability, 8, 23, 28, 29–31, 33–38, 42–43, 44, 51, 71, 76–78, 83, 88, 95, 101, 103, 111, 114, 126, 129, 141–42, 156, 186nn19, 21
Stierle, Kalheinz, 182n7, 192n5

Stone, Lawrence, 206n8
Struever, Nancy, 80–81, 181n2, 191n4,
   194n10, 196nn4, 18, 197n5, 198nn8, 10,
   199–200n18, 201nn25, 27, 216–17n23
Style, 26–27, 49, 70, 82, 90–91, 92, 181n2,
   193n8, 198nn7, 10
Success, 37, 92, 96, 125, 185n16, 200n18

Tacitus, 215n18
Thoreau, H. D., 181n31
Topics, 29, 39–41, 68–69, 74, 78, 80–81,
   81–83, 131, 132, 149, 154–57, 164–65,
   181n3, 183n10, 190n32, 197–98n6,
   200n19
Tradition, 44, 103–4. *See also* History
Trousdale, Marion, 182n7

Vernon, Richard, 206–7n10, 207n12,
   210n28
Veyne, 199n16
Vico, 158, 220n9, 221n14, 222–23n17

Virtù, 31–32, 33–36, 44, 47, 51, 71, 81,
   129, 150, 153–54, 174n8, 183n11,
   185nn15, 16, 185–86n17, 186n18, 186–
   87n23, 212n4, 213n10, 219–20n6; connection to civic virtue, 25, 145, 214n11,
   218n3; connection to traditional virtues,
   39, 84, 148–49, 153, 220n11; connection
   to virtuosity, 23, 48, 162
von Wright, George, 214n14

Wallace, John, 182n7
Ward, John, 66, 196n1
White, Hayden, 67–69, 71, 72, 80, 81,
   196n2, 196n4
White, James, 218n5
Wilcox, Donald, 181n2
Williams, Bernard, 15, 111, 158–59, 171–
   72n2, 172–73n4, 175n14, 176n15,
   179n25, 180n28, 204–5n5, 208n15,
   375n19, 379n26, 216n21, 217n25,
   222n16, 223n18

COMPOSED BY METRICOMP, GRUNDY CENTER, IOWA
MANUFACTURED BY EDWARDS BROTHERS, INC., ANN ARBOR, MICHIGAN
TEXT AND DISPLAY LINES ARE SET IN PALATINO

Library of Congress Cataloging-in-Publication Data
Garver, Eugene.
Machiavelli and the history of prudence.
(Rhetoric of the human sciences)
Bibliography: pp. 225–233.
Includes index.
1. Machiavelli, Niccolò, 1469–1527. Principe.
2. Prudence—History.   3. Rhetoric—History.
I. Title.   II. Series.
JC143.M3946G37   1987   320.1'092'4   86-40454
ISBN 0-299-11080-X